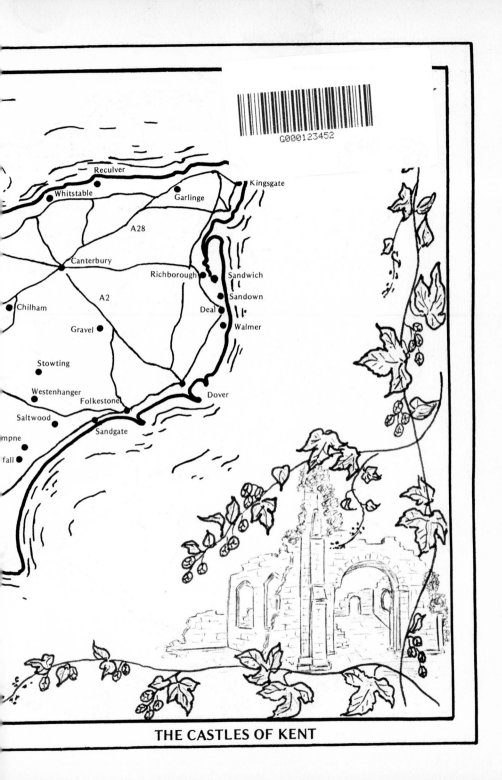

Reculver

Whitstable

Garlinge

Kingsgate

A28

Canterbury

Richborough

Sandwich

Sandown

A2

Deal

Chilham

Walmer

Gravel

Stowting

Westenhanger

Folkestone

Dover

Saltwood

mpne

Sandgate

fall

THE CASTLES OF KENT

KENT CASTLES

KENT CASTLES

JOHN GUY

Plans and line drawings by Colin Guy.

A comprehensive guide to sixty castles and castle sites for both the visitor and the historian

MERESBOROUGH BOOKS
1980

Published by Meresborough Books, 7 Station Road, Rainham,
Gillingham, Kent. ME8 7RS. Medway 371591.

Printed and bound by Tonbridge Printers Ltd., Tonbridge, Kent.

CONTENTS

	Page
Acknowledgements	6
Introduction	7
Chronological Table	10
Glossary of Terms	11

Part One: A History of Castle Building in Relation to the
Castles of Kent 15
Pre-Norman Fortifications 15
The First Norman Castles 21
The Development of the Norman Castle 26
Plantagenet Castles 31
The Internal Arrangements of Castles 49
The Flowering of the Medieval Castle 57
The Years of Decline 65
The Tudors' Contribution 68
The Fighting Finish 71
The Memory Lives On 74

Part Two: Gazetteer of Castles and Castle Sites in Kent 77
Miscellaneous Earthworks 251

Bibliography 257
Index 259

ACKNOWLEDGEMENTS

It is difficult to know where to begin in acknowledging the help received in writing a book such as this, but I should like to express my thanks to the following:

Colin Guy for the excellent series of plans and line drawings; my sister, Susan Hidson for typing the manuscript; the owners and administrators of all the castles visited by me, particularly those not normally open to the public; Mrs. Harris of Leybourne Castle; Christopher Knight of Cooling Castle; Mr. and Mrs. Clark of Saltwood Castle; Kent Messenger Newspaper Group for the photograph of Upnor Castle and the aerial photograph of Deal Castle; The Chatham News for the photograph of Starkey Castle; Cliff Hansford for the loan of the print, and his help in compiling the gazetteer entry, for Queenborough Castle; Aylesford Galleries for the loan of all other prints; the staff of the Public Record Office, the Department of the Environment, the Royal Commission on Historic Monuments, Greenwich Museum, the British Museum, Kent Archives Office and numerous libraries in Kent, particularly at Gillingham; the staff of Medway Litho; Leonard Hill Ltd., for their photographic services; Joyce Phillips of Solo Typesetting; my parents and family for their continued encouragement, and finally to my publisher, Hamish Mackay-Miller.

To anyone not included here, but who should have been, I offer my apologies and also give my thanks.

J.N.G.

A NOTE ON THE ILLUSTRATIONS

All the photographs in this book were taken by myself, except where otherwise stated. The line drawings and plans are all originals, mostly based upon my own measurements and from old drawings. The plans depicting castle earthworks employ the use of hachures to show the direction of the slopes and gradients of the banks. Hachures are the tadpole like lines on the plans, their thick ends representing the top of an embankment, the thin ends representing the lower part of the slopes. The closer the lines are together, the steeper the slope.

6

INTRODUCTION

I have divided the text of this book into two distinct sections. In the first part I have attempted to give a detailed history of castle building in Britain, but illustrated (both verbally and pictorially) with specific reference to the castles of Kent. The second part of the book takes the form of a gazetteer in which I have listed all the castles in Kent known to me. Regrettably, a few sites have had to be omitted because of the lack of authoritative information on them.

Kent, because of its close proximity to the Continent, has often presented the first obstacle to any intending invader of these islands. In consequence it has acquired a large and very varied collection of castles dating from almost every period of castellar construction, making it an ideal county in which to study the history of fortification generally.

The word 'castle' is itself a most confusing term. It is now generally agreed to refer to the private, fortified residences of feudal lords in the Middle Ages and was a type of fortress introduced into Saxon England by the Norman Conquerors. Strictly speaking, the term 'castle' should only be applied to those fortifications erected between 1066 and the end of the 15th century, but a number of structures that deserve the title of castle certainly existed in England prior to the Conquest.

While fortifications were known in Saxon England they are generally held to be communal defences for the protection of an entire community — eg. burghs. Similarly, the fortifications erected from Tudor times onwards were built for national defence and were really military forts (as also were Roman fortifications) not designed for domestic habitation. This then brings us to the singularly most distinctive feature of a castle, for it alone amongst the many types of fortification known to us was the private residence of a lord, or landowner, and although each in effect formed part of the country's national defence system, it was first and foremost a fortified house.

Such a definition is, of course, restrictive and by no means does it apply to all of the buildings that bear the name 'castle', or similarly, to those that do not but which are in fact castles. It is, however, a good general rule providing it is not applied too rigorously. Many earlier and later types of fortification often, somewhat confusingly, bear the name 'castle'.

Maiden Castle in Dorset is really an Iron Age hillfort and Richborough Castle in Kent is a Roman fort built for coastal defence. Other types of building that do not fit into this general rule of thumb, are the 'mock' or 'sham' castles. These were erected mostly during the 18th and 19th centuries as romantic attempts at reviving the 'glorious age of chivalry'. Sometimes wealthy gentlemen simply added the word 'castle' to the name of their house as a symbol of prestige, often the houses themselves not bearing any resemblance to a castle at all.

The history of castle building has often been depicted as following a smooth graphical curve of events, displaying the various aspects of fortification in a neat, chronological sequence. A popularly held misconception is that all castles began as simple earth and timber castles of the Normans which developed into mighty stone keeps surrounded by curtain walls and square towers. Next followed the development from square to round towers, the construction of immense gate-houses and finally the use of concentric lines of curtain walls, with the advent of guns sounding the death knell of the castle.

A few castles can be traced so as to display this pattern, but they are indeed a rarity. In reality, a number of castles were built in stone from the start, round towers were familiar to builders in Roman times, concentric lines of defence had been used in Iron Age hillforts and square towers were still being built at the end of the Middle Ages. In truth there never was a neat chronological development of castle design.

Each individual castle developed according to its own pattern, but its design and development were dictated by its site and the defensive requirements or wealth of its owner. Most castles display a medley of styles and designs from all periods and few, if any, are datable to one period only. What we see today at each castle is a highly individual development from simple beginnings, culminating in the best type of fortification for each particular site. Medieval builders did not continually up-date their castles to meet the latest requirements of defence. At most, modifications might be made, but that is all. New forms of attack necessarily entailed changes in defence, but each castle did not embody all the latest defence techniques.

Up to now most books on castles have fallen into one of two distinct categories — tourist guide or academic study. What is needed, I believe, and what I hope I have gone a little way to achieve, is a blend of the two approaches, providing a book that will be of interest to both the general reader and the avid historian alike. I hope in so doing also to give a little understanding of the society that first raised these wonderful structures.

An aspect often omitted from books on castles, of whatever type, is a detailed description of the castle sites today and the roles and recreational functions they now fulfil. The history of a castle does not end at the last battle fought from behind its walls or the evacuation of its last owner, it carries on. Their role as tourist attractions today is but the latest in a long line of uses and must not be separated from the histories of the buildings.

Similarly, castles should not be divorced from their surroundings. The countryside and rambling gardens that surround many of our castles are as important as the buildings themselves, or the historical events that have been enacted behind their walls. Because of this, in the gazetteer section, I have tried to place each castle within the context of its surroundings by making notes and observations whilst actually visiting each of the sites described. I hope also, in so doing, to have added a small personal touch to the narrative.

It is often assumed that castles were instruments of war and were armed to the teeth at all times in readiness for a seige. In reality they were rarely, if ever, maintained in a state of readiness. Castles, by their very nature, are passive, not aggressive. They were built for the protection of their owners against aggressors and are not themselves instruments of attack. Whilst the sometimes violent political events of the time may have necessitated their construction (initially to hold down a newly conquered land, but afterwards to protect it from subsequent invasion) they were built for defence. Too much emphasis is placed upon the military role of castles and virtually none on its other, yet far more important role of acting in an administrative capacity.

It is important to keep things in perspective when studying history, for often what may have begun as a Victorian impression of the past, can soon become generally accepted as fact, frequently with no substantiating evidence whatever.

While it is important not to look at the past through rose-tinted spectacles, it is just as important not to raise our own society above all others, as is the modern trend. Though we may have advanced enormously in fields such as electronics, it has not been without sacrifice.

We should never underestimate a society merely because it is different to our own, but learn to see it in relation to the times in which it existed. I feel sure that as you wander among the ruins of the castles listed in this book, you will feel, as I do, that perhaps the people who built them could teach our technology a thing or two.

CHRONOLOGICAL TABLE

STONE AGE:	c.1800 BC.
BRONZE AGE:	c.1800 BC — c.600 BC
IRON AGE:	c.600 BC — 55 BC
ROMAN OCCUPATION:	55 BC — 410 AD
SAXON PERIOD:	410 — 1066

William I	1066 — 1087	Mary I	1553 — 1558
William II	1087 — 1100	Elizabeth I	1558 — 1603
Henry I	1100 — 1135	James I	1603 — 1625
Stephen	1135 — 1154	Charles I	1625 — 1649
Henry II	1154 — 1189	Interregnum	1649 — 1660
Richard I	1189 — 1199	Charles II	1660 — 1685
John	1199 — 1216	James II	1685 — 1688
Henry III	1216 — 1272	William III	1689 — 1702
Edward I	1272 — 1307	and Mary II	1689 — 1694
Edward II	1307 — 1327	Anne	1702 — 1714
Edward III	1327 — 1377	George I	1714 — 1727
Richard II	1377 — 1399	George II	1727 — 1760
Henry IV	1399 — 1413	George III	1760 — 1820
Henry V	1413 — 1422	George IV	1820 — 1830
Henry VI	1422 — 1461	William IV	1830 — 1837
Edward IV	1461 — 1483	Victoria	1837 — 1901
Edward V	1483	Edward VII	1901 — 1910
Richard III	1483 — 1485	George V	1910 — 1936
Henry VII	1485 — 1509	Edward VIII	1936
Henry VIII	1509 — 1547	George VI	1936 — 1952
Edward VI	1547 — 1553	Elizabeth II	1952 —

GLOSSARY OF TERMS

ADULTERINE	Castles built without royal permission.
AISLE	Space between an arcade and outer wall.
ALLURE	Wall-walk on top of curtain wall, behind parapet.
ARCADE	A row of arches, called 'blind arcade' if immediately in front of wall.
ASHLAR	Finely dressed and squared facing stones.
AUMBREY	Mural cupboard in thickness of wall.
BAILEY	Defended courtyard of a castle.
BALLISTA	Powerful siege engine discharging heavy bolts.
BARBICAN	Outer fortified extension to a gate.
BARREL-VAULT	Vault with semi-circular or semi-eliptical arches.
BARTIZAN	Overhanging turret supported on corbels.
BASTION	Projection of wall for additional defence, usually semi-circular or pointed.
BATTER	Splayed wall base giving wider and stronger foundation.
BELFRY	Tall wooden siege tower used to gain access to wall top.
BERM	Flat space between wall and inner edge of ditch.
BIVALLATE	Type of hillfort, protected by two concentric lines of ditches.
BLOCKHOUSE	Small artillery fort usually of 16th century.
BOWER	Apartment in castle reserved for ladies.
BUTTERY	Room at lower end of medieval hall to store wine and ale.
BUTTRESS	Solid projection from wall face for added strength.
CAPONIERE	Covered passageway to defend base of ditch.
CASTELLAN	Officer in charge of a castle.
CATAPULT	Large siege engine discharging stones or heavy arrows.
COPINGS	Protective, often pointed stones on wall top or battlements.
CORBEL	Projecting stone from wall face to support floor joists or overhanging parapet.
COUNTER SCARP	Outer slope of defensive ditch.
CRENEL	Notches cut into parapet wall — battlements.
CROSS-WALL	Wall built across bailey, or in keep as room divider and support for floor joists.
DAIS	Raised platform at upper end of medieval hall.
DECORATED	English Gothic architectural style. Approx 1250-1350.
DORMER	Window formed partly out of roof-space, projecting upwards from it.
DRUM TOWER	Circular tower in line of wall, often backless.

EARLY ENGLISH	First English Gothic architectural style. Approx 1135-1250.
EMBRASURE	Splayed internal recess of window opening, loop or parapets.
ENCEINTE	Total enclosure within walls of fortification.
FOREBUILDINGS	Entrance tower built against side of keep.
FOSSE	Defensive ditch.
FREESTONE	Stone of a very high quality.
GARDEROBE	Latrine.
GARTH	Open courtyard of castle.
HERRINGBONE	Courses of brick or stone layed diagonally in alternating layers.
HILLFORT	A Bronze or Iron Age enclosure protected by earthen ramparts.
HOARDING	Covered wooden gallery, attached to and overhanging wall top.
JAMB	Side member of door or window opening.
KEEP	Largest and strongest of castle's towers containing lord's apartments.
LANCET	Long, narrow window with pointed, arched head (Early English Style).
LIST	Cleared space surrounding castles.
LOOP	Narrow openings in walls or parapet to observe field, admit light or to fire through — arrow-loops, gun-loops.
MACHICOLATION	Overhanging parapet supported on corbels.
MANGONEL	Powerful stone throwing siege engine.
MANTLE	Plain curtain wall with no towers.
MERLON	Raised portion of parapet, between crenellations.
MOTTE	Large earthen mound of early castles, often articifical.
MULTIVALLATE	Type of hillfort protected by three or more concentric lines of ditches.
NEWEL COLUMN	Central column of circular staircase.
NORMAN	English architectural style. Approx 1066-1135.
OILETTE	Round opening at base of loop, giving key-hole shape.
ORIEL	Projecting window, originally a kind of porch.
OUBLIETTE	Dungeon entered from floor of room above.

12

PARADOS	Projecting wall extending from inner face of wall-walk.
PARAPET	Projecting wall extending from outer face of wall-walk.
PERPENDICULAR	English Gothic Architectural style. Approx 1350-1485.
PILASTER	Flat buttress to support wide expanse of wall.
PORTCULLIS	Iron covered timber grille, lowered into gate passage.
POSTERN	Small, inconspicuous gate in castle wall; back door.
QUOIN	Dressed stone at angle of building or around door and window arches.
RAMPART	Originally earthen embankments, later applied to castle walls.
RAVELIN	Detached, angled earthwork occupying ground in front of fort.
REVETMENT	Retaining wall, either of stone or earth.
RIB	Raised, moulded arches of a vault.
ROMANESQUE	Architectural style embodying Saxon and Norman work.
SCARP	Inner slope of a defensive ditch.
SHELL KEEP	Not really a keep — stone wall replacing palisade round top of motte.
SLIGHTING	Deliberate destruction of a castle's defences.
SOLAR	Lord's withdrawing room at upper end of medieval hall.
SQUINT	Observation hole in wall between rooms.
TRACERY	Intersecting rib-work in upper stages of windows.
TREBUCHET	Powerful siege engine, similar to a giant sling.
VAULT	Arched ceiling, usually of stone or brick.
VICE	Spiral, or newel Stair.
VOUSSOIR	Wedge shaped stone in centre of arch.
WARD	Courtyard or bailey.
WEEPERS	Channels for carrying away rainwater from wall-walk.
WING-WALL	Wall built down slope of motte connecting shell keep to curtain.
YETT	Iron grilled gate, similar to portcullis, but hung.

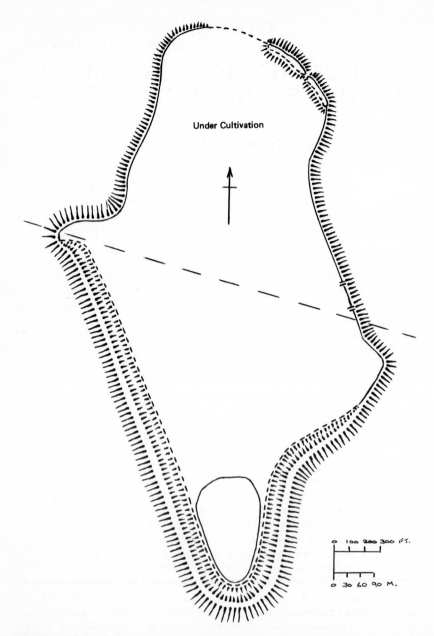

Under Cultivation

0 100 200 300 FT.

0 30 60 90 M.

Oldbury Hillfort, the largest Iron-Age enclosure in Kent. About half the fort has been
destroyed by cultivation.

PART ONE

A HISTORY OF CASTLE BUILDING IN RELATION TO THE CASTLES OF KENT

Pre-Norman Fortifications

To trace the origins of fortifications in Britain it is necessary to reach back to the Iron Age, and beyond, though it is with some reservation that I do so. The first structures which we are able to identify as being fortified are loosely termed hillforts and date from the late Bronze Age and the early Iron Age, though often traces of even earlier structures can be detected.

They usually crown the tops of hills so as to command the surrounding area and consist of a levelled enclosure, or plateau, on the hill top itself, encircled by one or more rows of defensive ditches cut into the hillside. The earth from the ditches was heaped up to form ramparts at their outer and inner edges, called scarps, the inner rampart in turn carrying a stout timber palisade (as the post holes reveal on excavation) or stone walls. Where traces of stone walling survive they are usually found to be of a very high standard of construction.

There are approximately 2500 known hillforts in Britain, most of which have been located on Ordnance Survey maps and plans drawn of their defences. Of these about 1400 or so are south of a line roughly corresponding to Hadrian's Wall. Most of these are to be found in the south-west and west, with very few examples in the east. The remaining 1100 lie north of the line and fully one third of these are in the area immediately north of Hadrian's Wall, with again, very few examples in Scotland. Only a handful of them are to be found in Kent and those which do survive are mostly in a mutilated condition. We must turn to the west of England for the finest examples.

Most hillforts are small, only about the size of a fortified homestead. Most of the larger examples are to be found in the south. Maiden Castle in Dorset covers over 120 acres, that at Llanymynech Hill, Powis, 138 acres. Oldbury Hill in Kent covers about 125 acres, Hengistbury Head in Hampshire about 173 acres and Binden Hill in Dorset covers an incredible 270 acres.

Hillforts, if indeed that is what they are, were designed it would seem for the protection of a whole community. A great many of them, however, reveal no trace of habitation at all, not even a well. Where such remains do exist they are usually confined to one small area of the enclosure only, indicating perhaps that they were built for some other purpose but taken over for habitation or defence some time during the Iron Age. There are seldom any signs of continued usage, except in the years immediately preceding the Roman occupation.

A further curiosity of hillforts is that, even allowing for the subsequent erosion of their surfaces by about 3000 years of exposure to the elements, their fortifications were not, on the whole, very substantial. The impressive examples to be seen at Maiden Castle and Old Sarum (Wiltshire) are really an exception. Whatever their original purpose may have been many were occupied during the later years of the Iron Age and defended against the Romans, their ramparts protecting quite a large populace at times, as excavations reveal.

Because of the comparative absence of hillforts in Kent I shall not dwell too long upon their discussion. Such comments as I feel necessary I have contained within brief notes at the end of the gazetteer section.

By about the 1st century AD most of the hillforts were out of use. The Romans established their own bases and centres of habitation away from the old areas of occupation and succeeded in weening the British away from the hillforts. Occasionally the Romans rendered a hillfort useless by slighting it, and sometimes constructed a fort of their own within the Iron Age ramparts (eg Hod Hill in Dorset). For the most part, however, hillforts could not offer a stout enough resistance to the full weight of the Roman military machine, so they tended to be simply ignored.

Once established, the Romans lost no time in building their own towns and forts. These invariably took the form of rectangular enclosures usually with round (or rectangular) towers projecting from the corners and along the wall faces, as at Richborough. Sometimes the corners might simply be rounded off, as at Reculver.

Roman walls and towers tended to be of an encircling capacity only, being built solid in most cases up to the wall-walks. Any buildings were free-standing

The ruined south-west bastion and wall, Richborough Castle.

16

within the circuit of walls, the walls themselves not being incorporated into the general building design. Roman towers were built not so much to provide flanking fire to protect the wall bases, but to support large siege engines, which were often mounted on revolving platforms on top of the towers.

The layout inside a fort or town was based on the grid system, the streets being laid out in regular, rectangular blocks. The whole system conformed strictly to military ideals where quick musters by the legions in times of emergency had always to take precedence. Even when the legions were on the march they erected temporary camps based on the same system — rectangular earthworks surmounted in this case by timber palisading.

The Romans tended more to choose a site that suited their building techniques, invariably level ground, rather than adapting their style of building to suit the site, as was the case in the Middle Ages. Roman buildings were always strictly regular in design. They placed towers not at strategic points along the walls of their forts, but at regular, equally spaced distances. The strength of Roman forts lay in the sheer manpower within them. They acted more as military (or civilian) bases from which assaults could be conducted rather than relying on their defensive strength.

With the threat of invasion from the Saxons, a series of signal stations and forts were constructed along the eastern and southern coasts of England, known collectively as 'Forts of the Saxon Shore'. An alternative theory has been advanced in recent years, however, as to the purpose of this chain of forts, which will be discussed in more detail in the gazetteer section under Richborough Castle. Carausius set himself up as Emperor of Britain and may have erected the forts to keep his fellow Romans, not the Saxons, out of Britain.

Stutfall Castle. The tumbled walls of the Roman Shore Fort.

The forts of the Saxon Shore were massively constructed, far stronger than was normal for Roman forts or town walls, and are perhaps unique in that not only were they built to house a military garrison, but also to withstand a siege. This could lend support to the theory that the forts were designed to withstand a mighty onslaught from the legions of Rome itself.

The finest examples of these forts are to be found at Burgh in Suffolk and Portchester in Hampshire, the latter mentioned surviving almost in its entirety. There are, however, substantial remains of three of the four built in Kent at Reculver, Lympne and Richborough, the latter being by far the most impressive. The fourth fort built in Kent was at Dover. Nothing now remains above ground, though the site has recently undergone extensive excavation.

Roman forts were only effective if fully manned, but when Roman rule in Britain came to an end (in about 410 AD) the Roman legions were summoned to the defence of Rome, leaving the British to man the forts themselves. The British it seems were unable, or unwilling to defend the forts against the invading Saxons. Similarly, once the Saxon occupation had been effected, they too declined from manning them. The result was that, although occupied in the years immediately following the departure of the Romans, the Roman forts and many of the towns gradually fell out of use for a time. The Iron Age hillforts on high ground seem to have come back into use. The hillforts were mostly occupied by the British as the Saxons gradually forced them further and further west.

The Saxons, although heralding their arrival with a series of raids on coastal towns, gradually began settling in Britain during the 5th and 6th centuries in a more peaceful fashion. Scarcely an invasion in the true sense of the word they did, however, succeed in driving the native Celts further west, at the same time taking over the governmental and administrative duties of the country. Essentially, they were urban dwellers and built extensively in wood, though they were well capable of building in stone too. One of the main reasons, though often over-looked, for few of their buildings surviving whether built of stone or timber, is quite simply that the Normans replaced them with their own structures.

Through the 'Anglo Saxon Chronicle' we know that the Saxons built a number of stone castles and fortified towns but few traces remain, often replaced by later work. A good many Saxon fortifications took the form of fortified manor houses, designed to protect their owners from local marauders or wild animals rather than an organised assault by an army. In this respect, they are not too dissimilar from castles. While the Normans may have advanced and perfected the system of private fortification, it can be seen to have its roots in the centuries preceding the Conquest. The feudal system generally was not quite so much of a new innovation to Saxon England as is generally supposed.

The predominant type of Saxon defensive works were communal fortifications. Alfred, because of the threat of invasion from the Scandinavians, stepped up the refortification programme of England. He established a number of fortified townships, known as burghs, and also a series of forts to guard important estuaries and coastal towns. On the eastern heights above Dover the Saxons established a fort, or castle, alongside the old Roman Pharos, incorporating the original Iron Age defences of the site. The fortifications on the cliff top later became the site of Dover Castle.

Alfred first instigated a system of forced labour, burh-bol, to erect his fortifications and once built, the local inhabitants were also required to man the defences on a rota basis. This system, employed by later Saxon kings (and also throughout the entire Middle Ages) came to be known as 'castle work' or 'castle guard' and was instrumental in the operation of the feudal system.

The Norman Conquest, in essence, only took advantage of the system that existed in Saxon England supplanting Saxon thanes with Norman barons and generally controlling the country's governance. The Normans did not invent either castles or the feudal system. Further evidence of this can again be found in the 'Anglo Saxon Chronicle' where we find references to private fortresses being built by Saxon thanes, but with full permission of the king, to protect themselves against Viking raiders. The system of government and castle building employed by the Normans was not new then, but was greatly accelerated by them.

William the Conqueror, like the Romans before him, only advanced forward after he had erected some sort of fortification behind him to fall back on if forced to retreat. These early fortifications were not castles in the true sense of the word, that is, a private fortress, but were more of military rallying points, again like Roman forts. They consisted most probably of earthen ramparts and timber

The Saxon church of St. Mary in Castro and Roman Pharos, Dover Castle.

palisades only. As the Conquest proceeded and more time and money became available, castles proper began to be erected in great numbers and of a more permanent nature.

Whilst there had been a filtration of Norman ideas and culture in the years immediately prior to the Conquest, and a small number of castles had also been built, the Saxon defences of England had largely fallen into disrepair. Duke William's task became considerably easier therefore, in conquering the country following the defeat of the English at Hastings in 1066. While it can be seen that the Normans borrowed certain of their ideals of government from the Saxons themselves, there can be little doubt that their conquest of England was both swift and final, displaying an incredible ability in organisation.

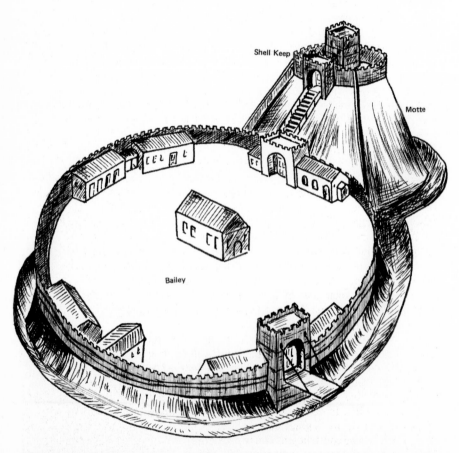

A hypothetical example of a motte and bailey castle. Few, if any, such castles conformed to this ideal layout, but the general principle can be observed here.

The First Norman Castles

The first castles to be built in this country following the arrival of the Normans were not the grand, stone-built and often stately structures we see today, but were very much humbler affairs. They were built not of stone and mortar but of earth and timber in most cases, though some, like the Tower of London, were built in stone from the start.

Following his victory at Hastings the Conqueror quickly set about holding the country down with his castles. When building these early castles first, a large mound of earth was made, either by constructing an entirely artificial one or by adapting an earlier mound or natural feature. Around the perimeter of the top of the mound a timber palisade was erected and a timber tower set within it. A ditch was then dug around the base of the mound.

Adjoining the mound a large compound, known as a bailey, was then marked out and a ditch dug round its perimeter, joining up with the ditch surrounding the mound and so forming a continuous figure of eight shaped ditch, or moat. The earth taken from the digging of the ditch was then used to construct ramparts on either side of the ditch, with a further timber palisade erected on the inner-most rampart so as to completely encircle the compound. Walls, also of timber, were constructed up the slopes of the mound so as to connect the palisades of the bailey and mound together. A defensive bridge and staircase were built within the bailey giving acesss to the top of the mound.

These earth and timber structures are known as motte and bailey, or mound and bailey castles. They were cheap and quick to erect and were surprisingly strong, despite their obvious weaknesses. Timber buildings were erected within the safety of the bailey palisades and gradually, as time and money allowed, they came to be replaced by the mighty stone castles with which we are more familiar. The first castle to be built at Rochester was of the motte and bailey type. Although none of the timber defences have survived the centuries, many castle sites still clearly show the often impressive earthworks of the original motte and bailey castles, particularly where the later stonework has also disappeared. Kent can boast many examples of such castles, including fine remains at Thurnham, Binbury, Stockbury and Tonge, but perhaps the most impressive examples are to be found at Tonbridge and Folkestone.

It used to be supposed that the Normans chose the sites for their castles and began the earthworks from scratch, unless advantage could be made of an existing natural feature. Recent evidence, however, has led me to the conclusion that perhaps they utilised already existing mounds of earlier, often prehistoric date, wherever possible to provide the nucleus of their own earthworks, to which they attached a bailey. It would certainly account for the Normans erecting so many castles so quickly for a great deal of time would indeed be saved if the mounds did not have to be constructed. The construction of earthworks was a monumental task and it does not seem unlikely for the shrewd Normans to have taken advantage of any existing feature, particularly when there are estimated to be upwards of 40,000 mounds of prehistoric date in England alone. Perhaps it would be worthwhile to expand this thesis a little here, for while it does nothing to undermine the ingenuity of the Normans, it may lead to a better understanding of the origins of our castle sites.

Many of the mounds which are thought to be deserted castle sites, but for which there is no historical evidence, may simply be prehistoric mounds which were not adapted for castle earthworks. Castle mounds are exactly similar to known prehistoric mounds, many of which contain burials. When excavated, some castle mounds are also found to contain pre-Norman burials or other remains. In folklore, mounds are steeped in legends relating to their prehistoric use, which may or may not originally have been that of burial, and many such ancient legends still attach themselves, somewhat confusedly to modern historians, to the castles which later came to occupy the sites. Mounds are also almost always found on excavation to be older than their attached earthworks.

The reusing of prehistoric earthworks was a common practice. For quite different reasons, when the Christian Church was re-establishing itself in Britain in the 6th and 7th centuries, it quite deliberately made use of the sacred sites of the ancient British. In a famous letter from Pope Gregory to Abbot Mellitus, dated 601, it is clear that a programme of 'Christianising' pagan sites was thought preferable to destroying them.

Instead of trying to woo the people away from their sacred sites, the Church allowed them to remain but Christianised them, embodying the essence of the Old Religion into the New. The practice was continued throughout the Middle Ages and practically all churches built up until the Reformation occupy the sites of ancient sacred places.

The huge mound of Tonbridge Castle. It dates from prehistoric times and formed the nucleus of the original motte and bailey castle.

Almost every medieval church still displays some sign of the ancient origins of its site. Sometimes these take the form of megalithic structures which once stood there (as can be clearly seen at Upchurch, Cobham and Challock churches and at Rochester Cathedral — to quote but a few examples) or in the shapes of circular churchyard walls, which on inspection are found to follow the outline of the stone circles once occupying the sites. But by far the most common form of prehistoric site utilised by the church are the mounds upon which many of our churches stand.

Builders throughout the medieval period freely utilised ancient earthworks for their own purposes, even though they may well have been ignorant of the original uses of the sites. The Normans often superimposed their castles on mounds which were, I feel, never intended for defensive purposes originally, but their potential for such uses was quickly recognised. As the Normans advanced across Europe they doubtless also built many entirely new earthworks, but the origins of a vast majority of early Norman castles are to be found in prehistory — perhaps even their inspiration.

On the occasions when castle mounds have been excavated, a number of important discoveries have been made. Apart from revealing finds of an earlier period to the Normans, the mounds themselves are often found to be carefully constructed of alternating layers of materials (eg earth, chalk, turf, gravel). They were not hurriedly thrown up from the earth excavated from the encompassing ditches, as is popularly supposed. This method of construction is frequently discovered in the excavation of known prehistoric mounds, as at Silbury Hill, in Wiltshire. I decline, however, at this stage to offer an explanation for the original purpose of such mounds.

Remains of the megalithic stone monument that once crowned Boley Hill, site of the original motte and bailey castle at Rochester.

Just as the Church threw down the existing ancient structures when building its churches, tangible evidence can also be seen at a number of castle sites of the structures which once stood on the mounds. At Rochester Castle the original motte and bailey castle stood to the south of the present structure — outside the Roman city walls — on a site known as Boley Hill. The hill was reduced in height after a siege in 1215, but from the Esplanade below, the original mound can still be clearly seen. Lying near to the bottom of the slope are three large, ancient megalithic stones, which probably originally stood on top of the mound but were tumbled down the hill by the Normans when they erected their castle on the site.

Many castles have an earlier mound name than the castle name. At Hereford Castle is a mound known as Hogg's Mount, and Exeter Castle stands on a mound long known as the Red Mount but which was later 'Normanised' to Rougemont. The word 'camp' often seen on maps against earthworks did not originally have a military meaning, but was a word attached to mounds — eg at Folkestone, the confusingly named Caesar's Camp is really an ancient mound that later became the site of a motte and bailey castle.

The Tower of London is popularly credited as attaining its prefix of 'white' because it was painted white in the Middle Ages. Painting the exteriors of castles was in fact quite a common practice, and it seems the name has far older origins. A White Mount in London is referred to many times in folklore and epic poems as being the seat of national justice. The 6th century poet Taliesin refers to a White Mount in London, as do later writers. The head of the ancient British king, Bendigeid Vran, is reputed to be buried in the mound, being placed there at his own request after receiving mortal injuries whilst fighting in Wales. The Norman castle later to occupy the site appears to have adopted the name 'White' from the name of the ancient mound, long before it was ever painted white.

Further evidence of the more ancient origins of castle sites, if not the actual castles themselves, can be found on excavation. At Caerlon in Monmouthshire, a mound with the remains of a Norman castle built on it was found, on excavation, to have Roman remains buried inside it. Similarly, at Worcester Castle, the mound was found to contain both Roman and, at ground level, Bronze Age relics. The castle has long since been demolished and these finds were made while levelling the mound. They strongly indicate an earlier date of erection than the Norman period, as do the Saxon remains discovered beneath the mound of the now destroyed castle at Duffield. Many castles have legends of hidden treasure being buried within their mounds and, where they exist, such legends often predate the castles themselves, as at Longtown Castle for example.

Excavation usually reveals the earthworks of the bailey at most castle sites to be of a later date than the mounds, which remained entirely separate and free-standing in most cases, as at Tonbridge. At Lewes, in Sussex, there were two mounds. The word Lewes meant 'grave hill' in Saxon times and a grave of some kind is known to exist beneath one of the mounds, known as Brack Mount. In 1086 William de Warenne built his castle on this same mound.

Often, local names for castle mounds differ from their later names as is pointed out by W. Johnson in his 'Byways in British Archaeology'. He notes that a mound at Pirton (Herts) is called a Norman motte on old maps, but has long been known locally as Toot hill, the word toot being a very old word meaning look-out hill. Johnson also quotes examples of supposedly Norman earthworks yielding pre-Norman remains on excavation, as at Hallaton in Leicestershire, where the motte and bailey castle there proved to occupy a site previously settled in turn by the British, Romans and Saxons.

All this is not to belittle the achievements of the Normans in erecting their earthworks, but merely to illustrate how ancient sites have successfully been adapted for different uses through the ages. The extensive earthworks which the Normans attached to mounds were themselves both considerable and impressive, many still surviving beneath later work.

There has been some doubt cast upon the real origin of the word 'castle', once simply thought to have been derived from the Roman word 'castrum' — a fort. It often appears on old maps against sites where no castle is recorded and there is also no trace whatever of one ever having existed. There is strong evidence to suggest that the word originally meant quite simply, an earthwork or moated mound, which because of their later use by the Normans as fortified sites, came also to refer to the structures built upon them ie castles.

Further evidence to support this view can be found in tracing the origins of 'castle farms' frequently marked on Ordnance Survey maps. Very often no evidence of a castle can be traced at such sites, but the farmhouses do very often stand on obvious mounds surrounded by moats, or remnants of moats. Such sites, as with the countless numbers of 'moats' also marked on the maps and which are of a similar design, appear in most cases never to have been strongly fortified. The word 'castle' may here harken back to its original meaning of being simply an early earthwork. These earthworks may not originally have been defensible, but fortified residences of the type we now identify as castles may have grown out of them, as at Hever, while all, rather confusingly, retain the name 'castle' or 'moat'.

Prehistoric mounds and other structures are often found in groups, which may explain why churches and castles frequently stand together. At times they stand ridiculously close to one another, as at Stockbury. Here, the castle earthworks and church mound actually touch, indicating that both of these medieval institutions (church and state) occupy sites predetermined by their prehistoric origins and not by the commonly held, but unsubstantiated belief, that the two were built together as joint symbols of medieval power. In reality, the two institutions were often in opposition and seldom did a state of harmony exist between them, certainly not so that a feudal lord would want the church literally on his doorstep. Most castles contained their own chapels within their precincts anyway. The castle and church at Leybourne are similarly sited alongside one another and here, traces of re-used megalithic stones can still be seen incorporated into the castle stonework.

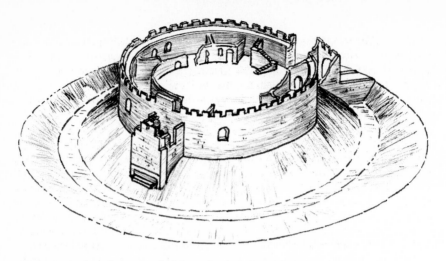

A typical, stone shell keep that later came to crown the motte.

The Development of the Norman Castle

When erecting their castles, whether in timber or in stone, the Normans employed the forced labour of the Saxon population. Even in more settled times in the years following the Conquest, the old system of castle work (burh-bol) was employed by the Norman overlords. Everyone was required to assist in the construction of castles, both in supplying materials and labour. In the early years of the Norman occupation this system was necessarily intensified, but as the Middle Ages went on it was possible to commute the services to monetary payments. Payment of a fixed sum of money excused those who could afford it of their castle service. Work on the construction of castles, particularly with the early Norman castles, was continued throughout the winter months and also at night, working by light of rushes and candles. As late as the 1360's we find references in the Calendar Rolls of candles being transported to Queenborough so that work on the new royal castle there could continue by night.

The first priority was to erect the main structure of a castle and, as time and money allowed, so more elaborate and decorative features could be added. The Normans always preferred to build in stone if the prevailing conditions allowed, and where timber was employed for many of the first castles, the replacement of key parts in stone was always a priority. Apart from the obvious advantages from a defensive point of view, building in stone also allowed much grander suites of residential rooms to be built. The Normans employed similar building techniques to the Romans constructing massively thick walls and making great use of round arches and vaults. The walls invariably had a rubble core (a solid mass of irregular stones held together by thick mortar) and were then faced with either randomly placed dressed stones or finely worked ashlar. The walls were bonded with layers of brick or timber for added strength.

Where timber had first been used a programme of replacement in stone was carried out. This would not be executed all at once, but carried out in stages, according to priority. Invariably the first part to be rebuilt in stone would be the gatehouse, closely followed by the palisade surrounding the top of the mound, in the case of a motte and bailey castle, or the main strong tower where a mound had not been included in the defences.

Where a wall was built surrounding the top of the mound it became known as a shell keep, though strictly speaking the term is both incorrect and confusing. The wall completely enclosed the area on top of the mound, sometimes standing on top of it, sometimes revetting a part of it so as to make the level inside higher than that outside. To carry any substantial building a mound had to be sufficiently settled, so a stone wall could not be added too soon after the erection of the mound. It should be remembered that even where an already existing mound or natural feature had been utilised by the Normans, it was invariably made higher and its slopes steepened before being considered suitable for defensive purposes.

Within the outer wall constructed on top of the mound would be added an inner one running concentric to it, which then left a small circular, or ovoid courtyard in the middle. The space between these two walls would then be subdivided to form the living rooms. An alternative arrangement to this was to build only an outer wall on top of the mound and then construct lean-to buildings in timber on the inside. Sometimes a central column for support of the roofs was employed, as was the case at Tonbridge.

Remains of the shell keep on top of the mound, Tonbridge Castle.

27

Exploded view of Rochester keep as it probably would have appeared in the 12th century.

Most castles which did not have mounds or shell keeps were provided with large stone towers, though this of course is an over-generalisation since there were really more than two basic types of Norman castle. These towers were called donjons originally (from where the modern but entirely different word dungeon has been derived) but are now generally known in England as keeps. Although no two keeps are alike, they fall roughly into two basic categories: hall keeps and tower keeps.

The distinction is quite simple, hall keeps having a height less than their greatest width measurement, while tower keeps are higher than they are broad. Internally the rooms are similar, but whereas in a hall keep the main apartments stand alongside one another, in a tower keep they are placed one on top of the other.

Keeps were almost always built of stone from the start even where the rest of the castle might still be of wood, or were added to castles which already had a stone curtain wall. In Kent we are fortunate in having a number of excellent examples, most in a good state of preservation. At Dover we have undisputedly the finest hall keep ever constructed in Europe, while at Rochester is a splendid example of an early tower keep, the tallest in England. The internal arrangements of keeps will be referred to under individual entries in the gazetteer section, but basically they embodied the hall and all of the lord's private chambers normally found in an ordinary manor house.

Norman keeps were very strong and combine all the essential elements of feudal life compressed into one compact unit. Their weakness lay in their vulnerability to mining and sapping operations. Also, once a defending force retreated to within the confines of the keep, not only was it almost impossible for the attackers to gain entry, but they themselves could not effect an escape. Keeps were really their own undoing by being too strong.

Once a timber built castle had replaced its gatehouse in stone and erected a strong tower or keep of some description, the next step was to replace the timber palisades of the bailey with a stone curtain wall. Once this had been accomplished the castle was virtually invulnerable to fire, the greatest single threat to a wooden castle. From behind the safety of its walls a lord could then replace all of the wooden buildings of the bailey at his leisure and add towers along the line of the wall for flanking fire and to provide extra rooms. Unlike Roman towers, the towers of medieval castles were incorporated into the main building itself, their internal rooms often being used as offices, stores or bedrooms.

An alternative system to the gradual replacement in stone of a timber castle was to rebuild the castle on a completely new site, as was done at Rochester. Bishop Gundulph built his stone castle alongside the old motte and bailey, which provided the necessary protection while the new castle was being built. He was responsible for the first stone curtain wall at Rochester, built about 1088, and at least one mural tower — though towers are rare in early castles. The magnificent keep was added half a century later by Archbishop William de Corbeil between 1127-39.

No two castles are exactly alike. Similarities certainly exist but no regular pattern was employed. The availability of time, money, materials and, most important of all, the peculiarities of each individual site, made each castle unique in design. Each developed at a different pace according to its own criteria. Once building in stone had become the norm, very few castles followed the motte and bailey design.

Castle builders only modified the designs of each castle if events made it absolutely necessary. They did not continually up-date each one to meet the latest standards of defence. The less important a castle was, the less it would have been changed, so in consequence, more of its original masonry is likely to survive today. Conversely, the more important a castle was or the longer it was lived in, the more the original fabric will have been altered and replaced.

Thus at Eynsford, where the castle was unimportant and deserted from an early date, practically all of the remains we see today are original to the building as first erected. Dover, however, was always a strategically important castle, so it has suffered drastic alterations during Tudor and Napoleonic times. Similarly at Leeds, which has a history of continuous habitation, only about half of what we see today is original. The rest is a mixture of styles from many periods, but which also add a certain charm to the building. This of course is a general rule and does not always apply. Queenborough was, in its time, a very important castle, while Stockbury was insignificant, yet both have now almost entirely disappeared except for their earthworks.

Castles were expected to return a profit and be self-supporting. In order to raise money a castle served as the administrative and judiciary centre for its surrounding community. Its tenants worked the land and were expected to give the lord the lion's share of their crops or produce, being allowed to keep a small proportion for their own consumption or for sale. The more happy and content were the people living and working on a large castle estate, the more likely they were to return a good profit.

Despite stories to the contrary, many lords were fair and often generous to their tenants, whether they worked the land or continued some other occupation on the estate. It was not in a lord's interest to be harsh or unjust to his subjects and for every story we hear of a tyrant baron, there were very many more who were fair and just.

Each manor with its attached village, regardless of whether the lord lived in a castle or simply a house, was an integral part of the feudal system. To operate properly it had not only to be a self-contained unit, but also a congenial and a functional one. The modern interpretation of the system is somewhat distorted, for the ordinary people were very much better looked after than we might imagine. A considerable amount of freedom was enjoyed by all classes and just as the villagers were responsible to their lords, so in turn were the lords answerable to the king, from whom they held their lands. Most people on an estate, in addition to working the land for the lord, also had their own piece of land which could be used as they themselves saw fit.

The efficiency of the system is reflected in the castles themselves and the finest examples are often those which returned a good profit. Those which did not, either because of inefficiency or exploitation, often fell into disrepair and eventually into ruin at an early date. An exploited populace could hardly be expected to give of their best and medieval lords were quick to recognise this.

While peace prevailed the temptation was often very strong for a lord to make his castle more comfortable at the expense of defensive requirements. Every opportunity was taken to decorate castles, both internally and externally, for they were built by the same craftsmen who erected the churches of the time. The Middle Ages, far from being a dowdy period, was a riot of colour and decoration.

The interior walls of castles were not left as bare stone as we see today, but were plastered and painted in bright colours or heraldic type designs. Unfortunately, because of the less permanent nature of interior decorations and the effects of time, few decorative details have survived. Their absence today has led many writers to incorrectly assume that such decoration never existed. It was also a common practice to plaster and paint the exterior walls of castles in bright

Rochester Castle from the north-east showing the curtain wall with drum tower far left, and one of Edward III's mural towers centre.

colours. Rochester Castle keep was painted white in the 13th century. Even the earlier wooden motte and bailey castles were painted in bright colours.

Following the initial impetus of castle building by the Normans and the gradual replacement in stone of the timber defences, it was under the dynasty of the next family of English kings that castle building reached its climax — the Plantagenets.

Plantagenet Castles

The Plantagenets were avid castle builders, introducing many revolutionary ideas into castle building and in designing new siege engines. Henry II was known for his ability to successfully take any castle by siege, no matter how impregnable it might appear. As a result, castle design improved immensely. In fact, apart from Henry II's extraordinary achievements, few castles were ever taken by force. A handful of defenders could, in a well designed castle, successfully withstand the strongest of assaults. Most castles fell through capitulation, treachery from within, or simply by being starved out.

When Henry II came to the throne he immediately set about the task of restoring law and order. Under Stephen, the last of the Norman kings, the country had been placed in a state of anarchy with rival barons vying for power. Many barons then used their positions and their castles to oppress the general populace.

31

It is largely because of this comparatively brief interlude that many of the popular misconceptions of life in the Middle Ages have been brought about.

Henry destroyed nearly all of the unlicensed, or adulterine castles (taking by force those still held by rebellious barons) which had been erected without royal consent during Stephen's reign. He also removed all the castellans from the barons' castles and installed his own custodians, so bringing all castles in the land back under royal control. He did allow new castles to be built, or rebuilding pro-grammes to continue, but strictly controlled by him. If any baron showed the slightest hint of disloyalty to the crown his castle was confiscated by the king. Henry firmly believed that national defence relied heavily upon a system of strong castles under the direct control of the crown.

In addition to his policy of destroying the adulterine castles, Henry II. strengthened all of his existing castles and also built a string of new ones. At the same time he provided many towns with strong defensive walls. Castle and town thus became integral parts of the same defensive system.

A certain Maurice the Engineer was his master builder and he became regarded as one of the most expert innovators in defence techniques. It is not generally realised that medieval builders drew intricate and extremely detailed plans of each building, every bit as detailed as a modern architect's drawings. The actual designers were called Master Masons and a considerable degree of secrecy was employed by them to protect their designs (this later led to the formation of freemasonry societies).

Few of the original drawings have survived, partly due to the deliberate destruction of the plans once the buildings were complete, and partly because

For many years this stretch of Rochester city wall was hidden inside the structure of a school, demolished in 1969.

many of them were drawn onto plaster casts actually embodied in the fabric of the buildings themselves. It is wrong to think that medieval buildings were erected in a haphazard fashion with no overall plan or concept.

Henry II introduced into England the circular and polygonal shaped keeps (shapes known and employed in Roman and later times but not hitherto used for keeps) such as Pembroke and Conisborough (circular) and Chilham (polygonal) — the latter being in Kent and detailed accounts of which appear in the Pipe Rolls. This innovation departed from the rectangular designs of keeps with their inherent blind corners and angles, though he reverted to this shape in his keeps at Dover and Newcastle. There were, however, very few circular or polygonal keeps built in England, for it was at about this time (the late 12th century) that keeps were becoming an outmoded form of defence.

Henry also introduced the idea of having numerous towers placed at intervals along the curtain walls to protect the wall bases from mining or sapping operations. At Dover he also re-introduced the principle of concentric lines of defence where a higher inner bailey wall was surrounded by a lower outer wall, thus giving two rows of fire power simultaneously. Archers on the inner wall fired over the heads of those on the outer wall.

In addition to being the administrative and judiciary centres of the areas they controlled, castles also served as revenue collection points for taxes, rent, wool and the like. Henry II subsequently maintained or built castles in strategic points, often grouping two or three smallish castles together in order to put a stranglehold on all the key areas (see map on front end papers to show distribution of Kent's castles). These were not necessarily 'key areas' in the military sense, but

Palace Gate and south barbican, Dover Castle inner bailey.

33

anyone wishing to invade or take over the country had first to acquire and hold every castle to control the economy. Castles did not have to be large or particularly strong to fulfil this function, as each castle protected and was in turn protected by its near neighbours.

The Crusades have often been credited with influencing castle design. Although some totally new ideas on methods of attack and defence were introduced, the Crusades were more of a military testing ground. The best ideas were subsequently transferred back to the west. Methods of attack (stone throwing engines and mining operations in particular) had also become so advanced by this time that all dead ground in front of a castle and blind spots created by rectangular towers had to be in some way controlled by the defenders. Many innovations were built into castles on something of a trial and error basis, designers juggling with the castle's basic component parts to effect the best mode of defence for each castle.

The other Plantagenets — with the single exception of Edward II — were also proficient castle builders. They granted many licences between them for manor houses to be fortified (as at Allington, Scotney and Cooling) to defend key points in the country, especially with the continued threat of a French invasion.

Although rectangular keeps had already been outdated by the time Dover came to be erected (1180) other new innovations had been introduced into other parts of the castle there (ie wall towers, strong gatehouses and concentric lines of defence) which allowed the keep to be built in the more convenient rectangular style. At Dover, unlike other castles of its type, its strength did not lie solely in its keep.

Rectangular keeps, though weaker, were cheaper and quicker to build than circular or multiangular ones, allowing for much larger and more comfortable living accommodation within them. Henry II probably considered Dover Castle strong enough to allow him the luxury of building a large and comfortable rectangular keep with quite sophisticated domestic arrangements.

Water defences, such as moats and rivers, had long been made use of, but Henry III introduced a new form on a vast scale. It was he who first used large areas of water, lakes in effect, to any great advantage. At Kenilworth, in Warwickshire, the water defences cover over 100 acres. The main advantages were in eliminating the dangers of mining and by forcing siege engines to be placed well back from the castle walls. At Leeds Castle (Kent) a similar artificial lake was created by damming the River Len. In this case a small natural expanse of water already existed with outcrops of rock protruding into it, the islands upon which the castle is built.

The crown adopted a policy of maintaining its own castles in a state of good repair, though not necessarily embodying all the latest forms of defence. Only the wealthiest barons could thus afford to keep up with the crown in the arms race. No longer was it possible for barons to take complete control as they had done in the anarchial reign of Stephen. The crown, particularly Henry III, by spending large sums of money on its own castles successfully eliminated much of the baronial competition. But, as the process continued throughout the 13th and

34

later centuries, the number of castles, even of royal castles, maintained to the latest designs and kept in good repair steadily fell. Although a large number of castles existed and still survive today, the number of 'active' castles is considerably less than the overall total would suggest.

A great deal of the money spent on castles from the late 13th century onwards was used, not as one might expect on improving their defences, but on the interior decorations and domestic arrangements. Many of the larger royal castles — Windsor, Winchester, Nottingham, Dover and Leeds (Kent) — were really palaces contained within a fortified shell. The next most important item in a castle's budget was carrying out essential repairs and maintenance, leaving very little money to be spent on adding to the existing defences.

Very few castles of new foundation were built following the initial Norman impetus — with the exception of Edward I's mammoth castle building programme in Wales — and by the late 12th century most of the castles we see, or know of today, were already in existence. Many castles were destroyed by the Plantagenets and never rebuilt. The castles remaining by the end of the Middle Ages, particularly the royal castles, although few compared to the vast numbers erected in the early Middle Ages under the Normans, were considerably larger structures.

Many castles were forced out of existence through lack of money. The cost, not only of maintaining the fabric but also of paying the garrison was astronomical, even in those times, and was constantly rising. Although the local population would help man a castle under the 'castle guard' system, most barons found it necessary to employ a small body of regular retainers, often mercenaries,

Gatehouse block and bridge, Leeds Castle.

35

who would sell their services to the highest bidder. As a result, during peaceful times many barons (and the king to a certain extent) neglected their castles, allowing them to fall into disrepair.

The peasant classes had a general dislike for castles. This was not because of the oppression they represented (a much overrated aspect) but because castles imposed a heavy financial burden upon them. Although many villeins were able to commute their castle guard service to a monetary payment, the problem was not solved. Far from relieving them of their burden, it often imposed a heavier one, for the villeins were then required to help pay the increasingly higher wages demanded by the mercenaries hired in their place. Castles did, however, offer considerable protection to a community in return.

Other services were also required of the local inhabitants around a castle including, help with repairs and maintenance, supplying firewood and food, cleaning and other domestic chores. But no castle could survive for very long without the support of its local community (village or town). The two, villein and castle, were heavily dependent upon one another. Despite everything, there did exist a state of harmony between the two for the most part.

To protect and maintain this state of harmony siege warfare, as has already been noted, was usually averted. Attackers first laid waste the lands around a castle (much of which was agricultural and worked by the same villeins who were defending the castle) and often this was sufficient for the garrison to surrender. At other times, the attacking force might simply give up and disperse if faced with too fierce an opposition from a well defended castle. Even if the assailants resorted to starving a garrison out, the huge expense of paying and feeding his army would often defeat the baron without before the baron and his retainers within a castle were forced to surrender.

There were times, however, when sieges could not be averted, but they became increasingly a matter for experts. Once mounted, a full-scale siege assault would be devastating, the crown being the greatest exponent of its use in putting down rebellions — few that there really were — or fighting abroad. The methods of attack became increasingly powerful employing ever more sophisticated weapons to batter the walls down.

By far the majority of sieges were executed by one man — Henry II. But even he resorted to siege warfare only if compelled to do so. Few barons were strong enough to lead their own rebellion, even if they had wanted to, let alone mount a siege against their neighbours. On the occasions when they did revolt, they did so collectively and more often than not the results of their rebellions were decided not in laying siege to castles, but on the battlefield or through discussion, the latter always being more strongly favoured.

Having decided that a siege was inevitable there were a number of ways in which an attacking force could gain entry to a castle, excluding the rather lengthy process of simply starving out the garrison. Specific tasks were allocated to certain classes of individuals. Engineers, who were basically carpenters but who had skills in many forms of mechanical engineering, were the highest paid, representing a kind of eletist group. Other specialists were those who took care of the moats and ditches (both defenders and attackers) stone masons, quarrymen, men employed to destroy counter fortifications, construct hoardings, gather food and ammunition and the like. This, however, is to jumble up the whole practice of siege warfare. Let us begin by first describing the various forms of attack.

The first and most obvious, though least effective method, was direct assault upon the castle walls. From behind a wooden screen archers could fire through shuttered openings at defenders on the wall-walks. These would give covering fire to fellow attackers who were assaulting the walls, attempting to scale them by simple ladders or from the protection of a belfry. A belfry was a wooden tower that could be wheeled into position against the wall and then a drawbridge lowered from its top stage onto the wall top giving attackers direct access to the walls. Neither of these were terribly effective in the early stages of a siege for scaling ladders could be easily pushed away and belfry towers were susceptible to fire. If the castle was surrounded by a moat it had first to be filled in before a belfry could be employed.

More effective methods of attack were to use battering rams and bores to storm gates or batter away at weak points in the masonry, but all methods of direct assault were completely exposed to fire from defenders on the castle battlements. A much more effective form of attack was that of bombardment where heavy stones or missiles could be hurled against the walls by siege engines, specially designed for the purpose and positioned some distance away.

There were many different types of siege engine, most being variations on the same theme. The three main ones were the ballista, the mangonel and the trebuchet, of which the last mentioned was the most powerful, still in use long after the advent of the cannon. The ballista was, in effect, a huge crossbow. A large windlass was used to pull back the bow and then a giant iron bolt was fired. It could be used effectively on wooden gates if a lighted wad of combustible material were attached to the bolt.

The mangonel was a large stone throwing machine, akin to the catapult. A skein of rope, through which the main arm of the machine was threaded, was tightened by twisting a windlass, while cogged wheels held the arm in a lowered position. A large boulder was then placed in a cup at the end of the arm and when released, the power of the skein of rope untwisting hurled the boulder against the castle walls or gate.

The trebuchet was an incredibly powerful machine capable of inflicting enormous damage to a castle wall. It relied upon gravity for its power and took the form of a giant sling. A heavy counter-weight was used, by winding the arm downwards, to hurl large boulders on its release. It was more accurate than the mangonel and much more devastating. Although none of these siege engines have survived, drawings and descriptions in contemporary accounts allow for a reasonably accurate reconstruction to be attempted. The trebuchet could easily throw

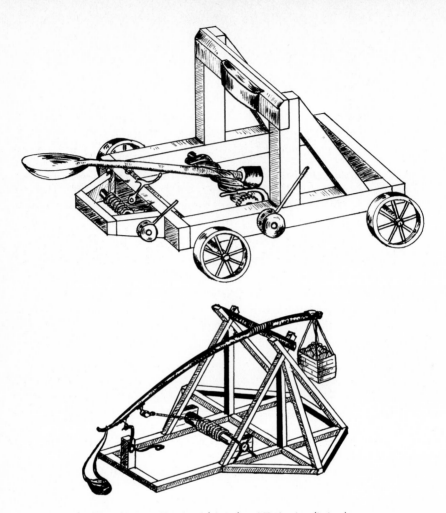

Siege Engines. Mangonel (above) and Trebuchet (below).

a 3cwt boulder a distance of some 100 yards or more and a large one could hurl a dead horse over the wall of a castle into the bailey.

Many of the larger castles were also equipped with siege engines for counter attack, sometimes housed in the bailey sometimes mounted on the top of the towers on a swivelling platform, in the Roman fashion. By the time cannons were powerful enough to inflict damage on castles, the day of the castle had already passed.

Apart from battering the walls down the next most effective form of attack was to undermine the walls, as was achieved with devastating effect at Rochester in 1215. A mine shaft would be started some distance from the castle wall, its entrance being protected by a timber screen. The mine would then be carried to

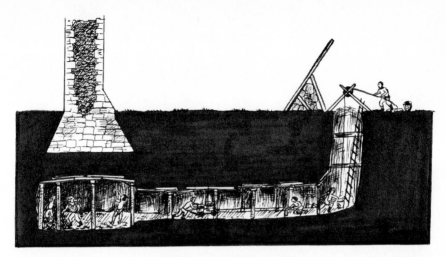

Method of undermining a wall.

the foundations of the wall or tower, where a large chamber would be hollowed out. Heavy timber supports were inserted to take the weight of the wall. Finally, the chamber was filled with combustible material, which when set on fire, brought about the collapse of the wall above, the wall's own immense weight assisting with the initial collapse.

Mining was a difficult operation. The defenders sometimes dug a counter-mine to break into the shaft of the attackers and thwart their efforts. Mine shafts still exist at some castles, as at Bungay in Suffolk and in the underground works at Dover. Once a mine was begun its inevitable consequences were often sufficient for a garrison to surrender, as the many unfinished examples testify. The use of a wide, deep moat was the most effective form of defence against mines or the construction of an extremely wide and battered foundation.

Higher and thicker walls were built in answer to these various forms of attack, but most of a castle's defences were directed upon its entrances and in the effectual manning of the walls. Even if siege engines were successful in forcing an entry through a castle's defences, the actual taking of the castle rested finally in direct assault, man to man. It was in this form of defence that castles really came into their own.

The provision of towers at intervals along the walls allowed, by arrow loops and from the battlements, for flanking fire along the wall base, forcing attackers to keep a respectable distance. One of the first uses of such flanking towers is to be found in the inner bailey of Dover Castle.

Towers were built in numerous styles — round, square, D-shaped or multiangular — and often had square bases with round or multiangular upper stages, tall pyramidal spurs adapting the towers to the bases. Some towers stand astride the wall-walk of the curtain, the wall-walk passing through the tower and thus allowing the section of curtain wall it commanded to be shut off. Sometimes the wall-walk passed round the back of the tower, making a continuous circuit. While

Cooling Castle. View of the gatehouse from within the courtyard.

this facilitated easy access by the garrison, in the event of an enemy gaining access to the wall top, they could soon over-run the entire castle by simply by-passing the towers. Examples of both these types can be seen at Saltwood Castle.

Many castles, in their outer defences, had backless towers so that even if an enemy were successful in over-running the outer defences the towers would hold no strategic advantage for the attackers. Being backless, defenders on the usually higher walls of the inner bailey could fire on any attackers gaining access to them. The towers of Dover Castle inner bailey are backless and are protected by the keep. Both the towers and gatehouse of the outer ward at Cooling Castle are backless. The battlement walks of both towers and walls were usually paved with flagstones, but sometimes they were covered in lead.

Drainage was an important aspect of the wall tops and roofs in castles. The roofs were steeply pitched and wall-walks had drainage channels cut into their surfaces, through which the excess water was removed. Many castles had quite elaborate systems employing the use of guttering and drain pipes at a very early date. Remains of the iron clasps and brackets can sometimes still be detected in the outer walls.

The wall-walks on top of the walls were protected by battlements, the charac-teristic and most easily recognisable feature of castles. They consisted of a parapet wall continuous with the outer face of the curtain wall, but rising above and in front of the wall-walk. Battlements are divided into what may be termed 'teeth' with gaps between them. The 'teeth' are known as merlons and the gaps as crenels (hence the term 'licence to crenellate' meant to fortify one's house with a battlemented wall). In times of siege wooden shutters, hinged at the top,

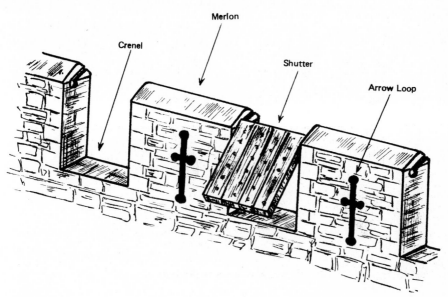

Shutters. In times of siege wooden shutters were often fitted between the merlons of the battlements.

were hung between the merlons so as to fill the crenels. Very occasionally wall-walks were roofed in, but this practice was more common on the Continent.

During a siege timber hoardes, or brattices, were attached to the parapets of castle walls. These were temporary wooden galleries built on to the outside of the walls so as to overhang and protect the wall base from sapping operations, or to fire missiles down upon attackers. The galleries were supported on timber joists which passed through square holes cut in the parapet wall just below the level of the battlements. These can still be clearly seen round the top of the keep at Rochester.

Because of the vulnerability of such timber hoardes to fire, they later came to be replaced permanently in stone, known as machicolations. They were stone extensions to the parapet carried on a series of corbels so as to overhang the wall base. They had removable floors so that missiles — not molten lead as is popularly supposed, for then as now, lead was an extremely valuable material — might be dropped through the chutes onto attackers below. They first appeared over gateways (see Hever and Leeds) and were probably intended originally to extinguish fires which attackers might build against the doors or drawbridge.

Later, in the 14th century, machicolations were provided around the gate towers as well, as at Cooling, and sometimes around the tops of intermediate towers and along the parapet of the curtain wall, as can be seen on the remaining tower at Scotney.

Machicolations, in addition to protecting the outer face of the gate, were also

41

Hoarding. Exploded view showing the method of construction.

often provided in the vaults of the entrance passage itself. The chutes in this case connected to the upper rooms of the gatehouse instead of with the battlements. Similar openings in walls came to be built in later times, particularly in fortifications employing the use of guns, and were known as meutrierrés (murder holes). There seems to be some confusion as to whether the openings in the vaults of entrance passages, because of their similarity, should be known as meutrierrés or machicolations. Because meutrierrés are more in keeping with firearms, I shall refer to such openings as machicolations, in accordance with Mr. Sidney Toy who studied them in great detail.

The finest examples of machicolations being used in an entrance passage are to be seen in the gatehouse at Tonbridge. Here they take the form of individual square holes opening out in the vault of the roof. Sometimes they took the form

42

Machicolations. An obvious development of hoarding, projecting the parapet out over the wall base.

of a continuous slot across the gate passage (as can be seen at Cooling). Machicolations are often arranged in banks, each group communicating with a different level of the gatehouse upstairs. In this way, the separate component parts of the gatehouse defences were controlled from different parts of the building.

Such a system had the advantage that, should part of the gatehouse fall to an enemy, they would not necessarily gain control of all of its defensive mechanisms. Again this arrangement can be clearly seen at Tonbridge, where each row of machicolations in the entrance passage connects with a different room upstairs. Tonbridge gatehouse is one of the finest fully developed gatehouses in the entire country.

In some castles, in the absence of the more sophisticated machicolations, a simple chute opened out above the gateway connecting with an upper chamber in the gatehouse. Its purpose was much the same as that of machicolations. At Leybourne Castle, near Maidstone, a fine example of such a chute survives intact. It is about 18 inches long and 2 inches wide externally and slopes upwards so as to emerge as a funnel-shaped recess in the sill of the window above the gateway.

43

Detail of the entrance passage, Leybourne Castle. Note the 'chute' above the gate and extra long arrow-loops in towers.

Drawbridges were the most common form of outer defence to a castle gate. Because of their timber construction, few original examples survive, though an excellent reproduction can be seen at Hever Castle and later examples can be seen at Dover Castle. There were various methods of raising a drawbridge. Some simply slid into position in the floor of the gate passage, but most were hinged in some way.

A popular method was to attach chains to the two outer corners of the drawbridge and then pass them through two holes in the wall above the gate arch. Inside the gatehouse they passed over pulleys to a winching gear. When raised, as well as creating the obvious gap immediately before the gate over the moat or ditch, they also formed an additional gate fitting snugly into a recessed alcove in the outer surface of the gateway. These recesses can often be detected today (eg Allington, Leeds, Saltwood) even though the drawbridges themselves may have long since disappeared.

The gatehouse at Allington Castle showing recess for drawbridge and machicolations above gate.

In complement to the drawbridge there was usually at least one portcullis (at Hever there were three) in the entrance passage of the gatehouse. A portcullis was an iron-shod timber grille that was lowered from the upper levels of the gatehouse so as to block the entrance passage. It ran in slots, or grooves, at either side of the passage passing through an opening in the vault, if one existed, or behind a stone screen. Although few portcullises survive (though originals can be seen at Hever Castle) the grooves in the walls of entrance passages can often be clearly seen. They were usually operated by winching gear with chains attached to the top of the portcullis. At some castles the machinery was so linked that as the drawbridge was raised it automatically lowered the portcullis, though this could have distinct disadvantages.

There were a number of reasons for the portcullis taking the form of a grille and not a solid door. Firstly it enabled the defenders to fire through it, whilst still blocking the gateway. Secondly, attackers trapped in the gate passage by a

Looking through the entrance gateway of Hever Castle, from the courtyard.

46

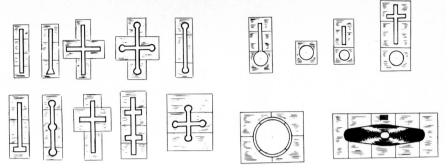

Comparative types of arrow-loops.   Comparative types of gun-loop.

portcullis at either end could be 'picked off' by the defenders through the grilles. Thirdly, any fires started by the attackers in the entrance passage could be extinguished by throwing water through the portcullis. Lastly, it allowed strangers to be interviewed at the gate before being allowed admission to the castle. In Scotland and the north of England yetts were used instead of a portcullis. These were two-leaved gates made from strips of iron fixed together in a lattice framework.

In addition to the drawbridge and portcullis, stout two-leaved doors were also closed against the gateway, often at both ends of the entrance passage. At Tonbridge Castle every door from the entrance passage into the gatehouse and from the upper levels to the wall-walks was protected by its own portcullis. The gatehouse was capable of being held separately should the rest of the castle fall, particularly important when a lord might well be employing mercenary troops.

The gate passage of a castle was further protected (as were other key points in the defences) by arrow-loops in the gate towers, enabling archers to sweep the ground immediately in front of the castle. Arrow-loops, and the later gun-loops which developed from them, are a distinctive feature to be found over all parts of a castle. Externally they took the form of a simple slit (which might take various shapes, see illustration) but internally, a small chamber was hollowed out to house an archer. The sides of this chamber, called an embrasure, were deeply splayed so that from the inside an archer had a very wide field of view whilst presenting only a long, narrow slit to the outside.

Originally designed for the use of the longbow, they soon came to be adapted for crossbows with recesses made in the sides of the embrasure to accommodate the weapon. The crossbow, although an inferior weapon, was more convenient to use in the confines of a castle. The first loops designed specifically for crossbows are to be found at Avranche's Tower at Dover and at Framlingham Castle, Suffolk. Arrow-loops can also be seen in the merlons of battlements, as at Allington and Saltwood castles. Some arrow-loops had additionally, a horizontally cut slit to view the field of fire. Later on these same embrasures were adapted for the use of hand guns and small cannons. A typical type of early gun-loop was of a key-hole shape, as can be seen in the West Gate at Canterbury and at Cooling Castle, and was made by simply cutting a circular hole at the base of an arrow-loop.

Key-hole shaped gun-loop in Canterbury City walls.

The splayed internal walls of arrow and gun-loops also allowed a fair amount of light to enter into the castle without presenting a large window area externally — rather in the manner of a camera lens. This system was used extensively in all castle openings, especially windows, so that while window openings might, for defensive reasons be comparatively small, the rooms were lighter and much more comfortable than we might assume.

Interior of Rochester Castle keep showing window embrasure on stairway.

The Internal Arrangements of Castles

Castles contained all the essential elements of a medieval house, arranged in the usual manner around a hall. The hall was the hub of a medieval house and from it a great deal of the lord's business was conducted. It was not, as was the case in smaller (and later) 'hall houses', a communal room in which everyone lived, ate and slept. It would seem that in castles and larger manor houses, the hall was mostly reserved for administrative duties and special occasions, which in medieval times were quite frequent, the festivities being enjoyed by everyone and not confined to the lord and his family.

It is a common mistake to regard castles as singular buildings when in fact they were a collection of buildings linked together and surrounded by a defensive wall. The great hall was the largest of these buildings (excluding such structures as keeps, of course, which in any case contained a hall) but there were many others.

There was frequently more than one hall and numerous suites of residential rooms. Minor lords tended to stay in residence in their castles throughout their lives, but most of the more important barons and also the king himself, were continually on the move between the various castles and manors of their estates. In addition, they often visited the castles of neighbouring barons or in turn, played host to them, so castles were provided with a number of complete suites of residential rooms for guests. Members of the household also had their own suites of rooms. Bodiam Castle had seven separate halls, of varying degrees of importance and comfort, while Rochester and Saltwood castles had three each. It has often been assumed that keeps fell out of use for residential purposes when later buildings were built in the bailey and became reserved for places of last resort in a siege only. There is, however, no reason to suppose this for why should so large a structure be maintained if it were redundant? It seems more likely that its rooms merely formed yet another suite of residential rooms for the use of guests or the garrison.

The buildings within a castle were often free-standing structures, and where they were, few have survived — a fine example of a detached hall-house still stands at Eynsford, however, though in ruins. Most of the bailey buildings which survive are those adjoining the curtain wall, using it as one of the exterior walls of the buildings themselves. At Saltwood there are two excellent examples of halls built against the curtain wall. In this respect, castles can be likened to a tortoise shell, a strong defensive covering (in this case the curtain walls and towers) completely encompassing and protecting the organism within.

It is ironic that, just as a tortoise shell survives long after the creature it protected has died, so the outer protection of castles, their walls and towers, have survived in bulk, while of the administrative, household and domestic buildings — which accounted for the greater part of a castle's life and purpose — scanty remains only are to be seen today.

The domestic buildings of castles were not only plentiful, but were gloriously

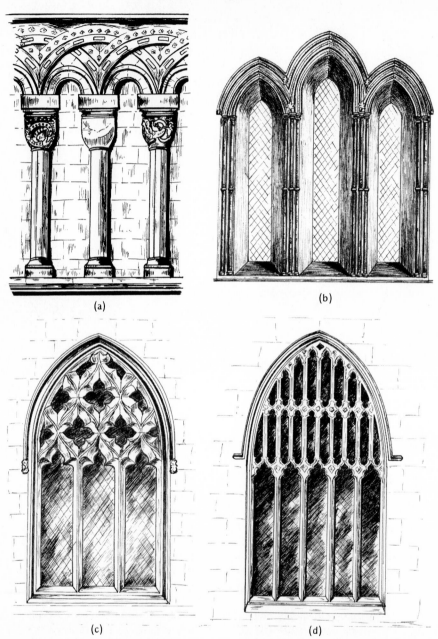

Comparative architectural styles. (a) Norman (1066-1135); (b) Early English (1135-1250); (c) Decorated Gothic (1250-1350); (d) Perpendicular Gothic (1350-1485).

The great hall of Allington Castle.

decorated. Many, because of the protection afforded by the castle's defences, were constructed of timber (another reason for their disappearance) and were riotously carved. The buildings of the bailey have better survived in courtyard castles, such as Bodiam and Allington, because a simple rectangular design was employed and all the necessary apartments were arranged around the exterior walls, thus becoming an integral part of the castle's outer defences.

Buildings (or remains) to look for when visiting castles are great halls — easily the largest and most elaborately decorated — and their adjoining rooms, stable blocks, bedrooms, offices (the last two mentioned often contained within mural chambers or towers) kitchens, withdrawing rooms and of course, chapels. In addition to the lord's own suite of rooms, those of his constable or castellan and those set aside for guests, castles also housed a small garrison and a number of retainers. Included among the latter might be a blacksmith, a carpenter, a mason, a hawker and stable hands — all of whom had their own accommodation and places of work. Most castles usually only preserve their halls and chapels but occasionally, as at Leeds, other apartments survive. The stable block there is now used as a gift shop.

When we mention the word hall we are apt to think of just one building, but really it was a collective term for a small group of rooms. The main room of the hall, the part which we more readily identify as being a hall, was divided into three sections. At one end would be either a raised platform (called a dais) or a small withdrawing room (called a solar) or sometimes both. These were for the use of the lord (or the castellan) and his family. Retainers and guests sat at long trestle tables traversing the length of the hall. At the other end of the room a wooden screen was carried across the entire width of the building. Behind this, in the outer wall of the hall itself, would be doorways into three (sometimes more) small rooms. One was the buttery — for the storage of wines and ales — one the pantry — for the storage of foodstuffs — while the other led to a passage which in turn led to the kitchen. Because of the fire risk, kitchens were usually detached from the main block.

The area between the screen and the end wall of the hall was known as the screens passage. At either end of it were usually the exterior access doors to the hall — so eliminating any draughts which might otherwise have entered the hall itself. Kent possesses many first class examples of halls, in all states of preservation from the ruined 12th century hall at Eynsford to the magnificent structures at Penshurst Place and Lympne, Allington and Starkey castles.

In most cases the screen does not survive, but at Cobham College near Rochester, both the screen and the screens passage have been preserved. It is now used as an almshouse but was once attached to the church. The elderly

The restored great hall of Lympne Castle.

52

residents who now occupy the college buildings still use the hall on special occasions and are only too happy to show visitors around.

Private chambers were often built over the buttery, pantry and solar, but the hall itself was almost always a high, single-storeyed building, usually well lit from large mullioned windows. Fireplaces in halls, as in other rooms throughout the castle, took various forms. They might be simple brazier-type affairs or open hearths (as can still be seen at Penshurst Place) the smoke escaping through a louvre in the roof. This type of heating was probably very effective, especially as braziers could conveniently be moved around the room to wherever needed. In other castles fireplaces proper were preferred, built into the thickness of the walls and the smoke emitting through shafts carried through the walls to window-like embrasures. Rochester keep provides us with many fine examples of this type of fireplace. Sometimes conventional chimneys were constructed within the walls, though these mostly date from Tudor times. It is interesting to note that most castles had a generous provision of fireplaces.

By the 13th century wood was rarely used structurally, except for roofs or bailey buildings. Internally, however, it was increasingly employed, as the domestic comforts of castles began to take precedence over military needs. The domestic architecture inside castles was continuously up-dated and made more comfortable and fashionable, much more-so than were the castle's defences.

Walls were usually plastered with burnt gypsum internally and whitewashed, or colour-washed, leaving the quoin stones around window and door arches

Allington Castle. Norman fireplace of original manor.

53

exposed as a contrast. This technique has been faithfully employed in the restorations at Allington Castle with beautiful results. The walls, once so covered, were then adorned with bright and colourful paintings, tapestries or motifs, sometimes the line of the stonework was depicted in red against the whitewash.

Wherever he could medieval man decorated his surroundings with as much light and colour as possible. Henry III, ever fastidious, is recorded as ordering Rochester Castle to be whitewashed and also for the guttering at the White Tower of London to be replaced so as not to discolour the whitewashed walls. Henry III was obsessed by the idea of comfort and colour and frequently employed the most expensive materials. His favourite design was gold stars on a green background. Furniture, especially in the bedrooms but generally throughout the castle, was considerably more elaborate than is popularly believed, as contemporary sources such as the chroniclers and royal accounts reveal. As the 13th century progressed, the demand for comfort increased out of all proportion.

From a very early date windows were glazed (excavations at Eynsford revealed glass dating from the mid-13th century) the glass often being painted, or stained, as in churches. Wooden shutters were fixed to the outside of the windows as additional protection from the elements. Unfortunately, it is impossible to tell just how extensive the use of glass was because it was a common practice for windows to be made in removable frames which could be bolted in place but removed if the lord was journeying between castles or if the castle was attacked or exposed to inclement weather.

Eynsford Castle. Remains of hall with look-out turret beyond.

If a minor castle such as Eynsford was provided with glass from an early date, there is no reason to suppose other castles to be any less well provisioned. Henry III even seems to have installed double glazing at Windsor Castle, two separate frames held one against the other with perhaps the outer one a permanent fixture. Many castles had internal windows between rooms and also small 'peep-holes' (both clearly visible at Dover keep) though no satisfactory purpose for the latter has yet been suggested. At Winchester a simple form of speaking tube connected the solar to the hall, a kind of 13th century intercom!

Other refinements were made to the roofs, with tiling and flagging replacing, where possible, thatching which though it had many qualities to recommend it, was also extremely combustible. Latrines were not only abundant, but hygienic. Most had serviceable chutes capable of being cleaned — or in some cases, flushed — again as can be seen at Dover. At Warkworth Castle in Northumberland, rain water from the roof was diverted through conduit to flush the latrines. At such castles as Rochester, where the latrine shafts emit at the wall face of the keep, raw sewage was not simply allowed to run down the outside wall, but drainpipes were connected to the openings of the chutes to carry the sewage away.

Where the sewage could not be conveniently discharged into a river, cess-pits were built into the basements of the buildings, as at Dover and Rochester Castles, which were regularly emptied. Sometimes portable toilets were provided in castles, though this was usually not necessary. To help counter the smell then, as now, air fresheners were used. Instead of merely masking the smells as our perfumed aerosols do, they sprinkled selected herbs liberally around the castle to eliminate them, a practice which we are only now beginning to reintroduce. Latrines were well provided in all parts of the castle for the use of retainers and garrison. Sometimes they were grouped together and housed within a tower as at Tonbridge, where four latrine shafts empty into the River Medway, or are built into the thickness of an external wall, as at Eynsford, where three shafts empty into the River Darenth. At Saltwood there is a tower with two tiers of latrines.

Medieval people were insistent upon high standards of personal hygiene, particularly in eating. They washed their hands frequently both before meals, at wash basins placed outside the hall (and sometimes built into the walls, as at Dover) and during mealtimes. Since knives only were preferred as a utensil they used to eat most things with their fingers and finger bowls were provided beside each person at the meal table. There is evidence in contemporary accounts to suggest that a kind of herbal soap, and certainly herbal fragrances, were freely used. Some of the larger castles had permanent baths installed, or bathrooms in which portable tubs were stood. When barons journeyed around the country these tubs were usually carried about as part of the entourage. Probably because they were wooden, they have not survived, which has led to the popularly held myth that medieval man had an aversion to cleanliness and never washed. In Kent we are fortunate in preserving one of the few stone-built bath houses ever erected, at Leeds Castle.

Quite elaborate water systems were installed in many castles, and all were provided with at least one well supplying fresh drinking water, usually from underground springs. Whilst the arrangements found in Henry II's great keep at Dover are exceptional, it is worth remarking on them to show the ingenuity of the medieval mind. A well, descending to a depth of about 600ft has its drawing place at the top level of the keep. Beside the well head is a recess which once housed a large cistern. From this, lead pipes carried water to all levels of the keep. Small hand basins emerge all over the building and each was fitted with taps to control the flow of water. The whole system operated on the simple principle of gravity, supplying a cistern at a high level with water to feed all the lower levels beneath it. A similar though less elaborate system was provided at Newcastle, another of Henry II's keeps. All of the domestic arrangements so far outlined existed by the 13th century. By the later Middle Ages they became even more elaborate.

Tonbridge Castle. The curtain wall seen from the River Medway, showing the four latrine shafts.

The Flowering of the Medieval Castle

To define just when exactly castle building reached its zenith is extremely difficult. It is generally agreed that the castles built by Edward I during his Welsh campaigns saw the culmination of defence techniques. These techniques in castle building are sometimes to be found in earlier castles in other parts of the country, but they first seem to have come together and been put to their most effective use in Wales. Certainly, the castles erected or re-fortified during the reigns of the three Edwards represent the ultimate in castle design, not only in Britain but throughout Europe. It is then to Wales that we must now turn our attention, though once again, Kent played an important part in the final stages of castle development.

At Dover Henry II introduced the concentric principle of defence into castle design. The principle is often stated as being imported from the East, but it had long been used with great effect in many Iron Age hillforts. Dover, though it became a concentric castle, was not designed as such originally. It evolved into one during the course of a hundred years or more (in this case the keep itself formed a third tier of defences).

The first castle to show a true uniform concentric design was Caerphilly in Glamorgan (built between 1268-77) which at 30 acres in extent is also one of the largest castles ever built. In this castle, and later examples, the inner and outer curtain walls run almost parallel to one another. The keeps of earlier Norman and Plantagenet castles were omitted from concentric castles, replaced by massive gatehouses. Despite their immense strength, however, few truly concentric castles were ever actually built, though certain elements of their design (eg powerful gatehouses) were adopted at other sites. By the time the principles of concentric fortification had been fully developed the medieval castle as a feudal fortress was already in decline.

A similar fate had already befallen the keeps of earlier castles. The basic principle of Norman castles had been to stack the defences one behind the other so that if one line fell, defenders could retreat to the next and continue to conduct their defence. Defenders who had already been pushed from the outer to the inner bailey ultimately, could only retreat to the keep and could do nothing to prevent the assailants from occupying the fallen parts of the castle. With the concentric principle the castle's defences were thrust outwards in all directions at once. Assailants were forced to attack the entire castle and not just a small part of it, thus spreading their forces much more thinly on the ground. Further, the outer line of walls had backless drum towers with removable floors which, as we have seen, afforded no protection or advantage to an enemy who had been successful in taking the outer defences.

The re-conquest of Wales by Edward I came in three waves (1277, 1282-3 and 1294-5). It culminated in the building of ten royal castles. They were all new, though some were on previously fortified sites, and are to be found at

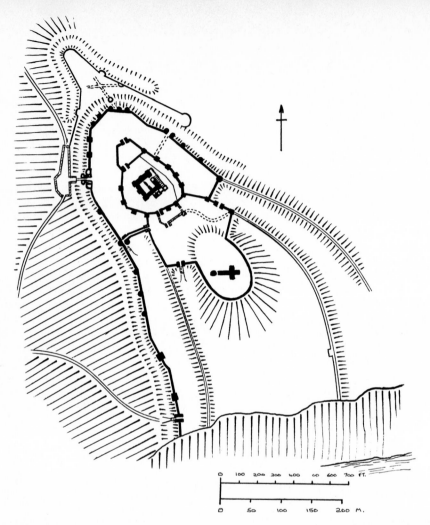

Ground plan of Dover Castle showing the massive scale of the concentric fortifications. Note Roman Pharos and Saxon Church in centre.

Builth, Aberystwyth, Flint, Rhuddlan, Ruthin, Hope, Conwy, Harlech, Caernarfon and Beaumaris. Master James of St. George, from Savoy, was responsible for their design, although Edward I always took a personal interest in their construction.

Edward's Welsh campaign cost an enormous amount of money, both in materials and manpower. Labour was brought from every corner of the land — mostly forced. The king made full use of his right to levy workmen from anywhere in the country to work on royal castles or to provide military service. Most of his army, however, was made up of mercenaries and there was never any shortage of Welsh volunteers to join him.

Everyone, of course, was paid (often quite substantially) and proper contracts existed. Workers could only be levied for set periods and were then allowed to return home. Set working hours were enforced too and the rights of workers observed, the whole system in fact being not too dissimilar to our own. Bonus money was even paid to good workers and wages policies introduced by the crown to control inflation!

Edward had planned for the new castles to quickly pay for themselves, especially those to which new towns (to encourage English settlers) had been attached — Conwy, Caernarfon, Beaumaris and Rhuddlan. He estimated that with Wales firmly held down by castles, the whole country ought then to return a good profit and so revive the royal purse. The cost, however, grew out of all proportion and became a constant drain on his resources, a fact which greatly affected the rest of his reign. The attempted conquest of Scotland was largely unsuccessful because Edward had insufficient money to mount a full offensive.

Following the building of the ten major royal castles, other new castles were built, or old ones repaired and brought up to date. The influence of Master James of St. George can be seen in a great many private castles in Wales and the border counties, and also in castles throughout the land, as at Tonbridge gatehouse and the concentric defences at Leeds Castle, Kent.

Edward's new castles in Wales were designed to be defended by as few men as possible. Conwy had a garrison of only 30, and in the rebellion of 1294, 37 men defended Harlech Castle against the entire Welsh army. Each of the castles was of a different design, but each embodied some advanced form of

Tonbridge Castle. The gatehouse seen from the bailey.

defence, later transferred to other parts of England. Beaumaris, Harlech and Rhuddlan were concentric (the former being one of the most geometrically designed of all medieval castles) while Conwy and Caernarfon (perhaps the strongest castles ever built) were large single enclosures, built to adapt to their sites.

Beaumaris was perfectly concentric — its flat site allowed it to be so — and together with Queenborough, in Kent, represents the ultimate in concentricity. It was the last of the ten to be built and suffered most from lack of money. All of Edward I's Welsh castles had palatial suites of rooms fit for habitation by the king himself. Although practically all traces of their internal grandeur have vanished, the substantial remains of the buildings themselves, coupled with detailed accounts in the royal records, allow us to reconstruct them fairly accurately. Beaumaris and Caernarfon in particular had exceptionally fine suites of rooms.

The royal accounts also tell us how gardens, complete with lawns, fish ponds and seats were laid out at each of the castles. By the end of the 13th century and throughout the later Middle Ages, such touches of comfort and domesticity had been acquired by most castles, whether royal or baronial. At Saltwood, the Archbishop's castle there shows admirably just how the residential rooms were arranged around a formal garden. The garden, known as the 'Secret Garden', is secluded and quite delightful, still preserving some of its statuary and carved stone seats. Saltwood Castle is particularly important because it preserves for us much of the real character of a medieval castle, many of its domestic apartments surviving substantially intact.

Entrance to the hall undercroft and statuary in the Secret Garden, Saltwood Castle.

60

In the later reign of Edward III, William of Wykeham, by various contrivances, became the king's building supervisor, though not a master mason as has sometimes been assumed. He had the ability to organise vast quantities of materials, labour and money from all manner of different sources and direct them to whereever they were needed, and quickly. This was particularly important for the construction of castles as it was often the practice in the Middle Ages for different parts of the building to be made at different locations, carefully numbered and then transported to the site where each was erected in its allotted place. Such building techniques required a phenomenal expertise in planning.

Wykeham was, in effect, an administrator and Edward soon promoted him through various high offices. In 1359 he was appointed the 'chief keeper and surveyor' of Windsor, Hadleigh, Dover and Leeds (Kent) castles, all important and favourite castles of Edward III. Amongst many other appointments, he was put in charge of the initial building operations at the new royal castle of Queenborough, on the Isle of Sheppey. Eventually he became Lord Chancellor and Bishop of Winchester.

Queenborough Castle was designed by John Box who may have been influenced by certain symmetrical castles built by Emperor Frederick II in Italy, the previous century. It closely resembles also, the artillery forts of Henry VIII. It was based entirely upon a circular plan and was in many ways similar to the basic design of a shell keep. The new town and castle at Queenborough cost Edward an estimated £25,000 but the town never flourished and the castle was demolished under the Commonwealth Government in 1650.

In order to carry out his immense building programme Edward III exploited his powers of compulsory service to the full. He constantly issued commissions for labour and materials (at fixed low prices) especially after the first outbreak of the Black Death in 1381, which reduced the labour force considerably. He used forced labour more than any other monarch, more even than Edward I had employed in Wales. One result of the Black Death was that labour, because of its scarcity, could command higher wages.

Because of Edward III's claim to the French throne a large number of barons restrengthened their castles or built entirely new ones (eg Cooling) in response to the threat of French retaliation. Scares of a French invasion continued, at intervals, until the middle of the 15th century (and yet again under Henry VIII) and south-east England — Kent in particular — was often subjected to lightning raids. The royal castle at Queenborough was sited in the wrong position to defend the entire Thames Estuary but the coffers were too drained to provide a new defensive system to allay a French invasion. Instead, and as something of a compromise measure, the crown allowed all castellans, private or royal, to refortify their castles and bring them up to date as they saw fit.

As a result, many old and out-moded castles were hurriedly put into some sort of repair and made defensible again. Among these was Rochester, still sound though very much in need of repair. The two rectangular mural towers, though not of the latest defensive designs, were erected at this time and still survive today. The castle at Southampton was decaying but that too was repaired. In fact, all castles on, or near the south coast were hurriedly made ready for action including Carisbrooke, Portchester, Corfe and Tintagel, in the west. One can detect a certain degree of panic in the quality of the workmanship where such repairs were made. Fortifying the south-east, however, came to be something of a national effort, with many small manor houses also being fortified (eg Starkey and Hever).

Following the expansions in domain by the three Edwardian monarchs, trade increased enormously in England. Many of these 'new' traders were not of noble birth so they were unable to build their own castles to protect their commercial interests. They tended, as a result, to settle mostly in towns. In the larger towns the traders often joined together to build a defensive wall around the town. During the invasion scares of the latter 14th century, they were positively encouraged by the king to fortify their towns. Fine examples of their work can still be seen today at Canterbury, Rochester and Sandwich, despite the inevitable growth of the towns themselves. The city walls of Canterbury are quite spectacular.

Because they were neither feudal or privately owned, town walls were usually built, maintained and garrisoned by the townspeople themselves. Often each tower or stretch of wall would be the responsibility of a particular family or section of the community. Town walls were not highly defensive and were not built to withstand a prolonged siege, more they provided protection from bandits, minor skirmishes or from possible raids by the French.

The well preserved city walls of Canterbury showing two of the many D-shaped towers which still survive.

Many traders soon became as important and powerful as the nobles themselves, storing much of their wealth within the security of defended towns, and from them grew town councils. This shift in power from the military lords to traders was also partly responsible for the erection of many fortified, or semi-fortified houses. Likewise, they were never built to withstand a siege but to protect a trader, his family and his wealth from thieves. From the 15th century onwards it becomes increasingly more difficult to define just which buildings should, or should not be termed castles.

Following a series of French raids (as for example at Rye in 1377 and Sandwich in 1438) came another intensive wave of refortifying in the south-east. Few of the castles so built, or strengthened, ever saw any military action — a constantly recurring theme in the story of castle building. Scotney Castle, near Lamberhurst, was built at this time by Roger Ashburnham. Although small it was originally more formidable than its beautiful grounds would suggest today. It consisted of two island wards in an encircling moat, itself expanded to form a small lake. The eastern ward was defended by four circular towers, only one of which survives. Local inhabitants, who helped to finance this wave of defensive undertakings, expected in return to find protection behind the walls of this, and similar castles, should the French strike.

Penshurst Place was another manor house fortified at this time. Licence to crenellate was first granted in 1341, but because Edward III was at that time winning victories, no fortifications were then made. The core of the present house was erected at that time, however. After renewed scares of invasion later in the 14th century, the house was fortified — following another licence to crenellate dated 1392. Outer walls were added and it became a fortified manor house, or small castle (though these defences were later removed to convert it back into a house). These later additions were made by Sir John de Pulteney, four times Lord Mayor of London.

Leeds Castle was also refortified at this time, most of the efforts being concentrated upon its water defences, which were greatly extended. Licences to crenellate their existing manors were also granted to John de Cobham of Cooling in 1381 (following a raid on the Thames by the French in 1379) and to Sir Edward Dalyngrigge at Bodiam. In Sir Edward's case he chose not to fortify his existing house but to completely rebuild it on new ground. The result is the beautiful and enigmatic Bodiam Castle in Sussex and, thanks to Lord Curzon's restoration work in the 1920's, much of it still survives.

Cooling Castle, somewhat unjustly, has been overshadowed by its contemporaries and has escaped serious attention from historians. All too often we read that nothing remains of it except the outer gatehouse, but in fact the remains are quite considerable, including almost the entire inner ward and substantial sections of the outer. The castle consisted of two wards surrounded by a figure of eight moat, the inner ward forming an island only accessible from the outer ward. Some of the earliest known examples of gun-loops are to be seen in its walls.

63

These later castles have come to be known collectively as 'courtyard castles'. Gone are the elaborate defences of the 13th century, replaced by a simple, four-square plan. The castles were compact and strong yet very comfortable inside and generally designed to withstand cannon fire. The changing methods of warfare brought about the change in castle design with a reversion to a more simple form; a reversion which ultimately led to the two component parts of a castle — house and fortress — parting company. Most courtyard castles were really just strongly defended manor houses, other examples of which can be found at Bolton in Yorkshire, Shirburn in Oxfordshire, Caister in Norfolk, Maxstoke in Warwickshire and Westenhanger in Kent.

Many castles put up at this time were built not only in response to the French scare, but also by rich war veterans as a kind of status symbol. In a sense, Bodiam and Scotney were of this type. Castles were largely becoming an outdated form of warfare by that time, and such heavily defended yet luxuriously suited manors can be regarded as much for their prestigious value as for their military importance. However, it was a full century and a half before the fortified aspects of castles became entirely divorced from their domestic roles.

Inner gatehouse of Cooling Castle. Note the key-hole shaped gun-loops and the draw-bar slots above gate for drawbridge.

The Years of Decline

In the 15th century, especially during the reigns of weak kings, such as Henry VI, there existed for a time a kind of anarchy amongst the barons. While these barons were in a minority, bastard feudalism — as it is called — existed in some form or other until the close of the Middle Ages. Not until the emergence of the Tudors and the changes in life which that transition brought about were such barons finally put down. It should be stressed, however, that while this state of affairs was strictly localised, it did show the one big flaw in medieval society, and that was its dependence upon a strong king to govern fairly and keep the more power thirsty barons in check. A weak king left the way open for exploitation.

In the 15th century brick began to be used extensively in preference to stone. Although earlier examples exist its use was not widespread. Tattershall is perhaps the finest example of 15th century brickwork but there are many others as at Caister in Norfolk, where a strong German influence can be felt. In Kent there are the remains of Dent de Lion Castle at Garlinge, near Margate. From what we know of it from records and old prints it followed much the same design as a typical courtyard castle and was once quite extensive. Again, it was probably not heavily defended, but constituted more of a fortified manor house. Gun-loops were provided in at least the gatehouse, which is the sole remaining portion today. It is built in flint and Thanet brick with stone dressings and arches. It stands sandwiched, somewhat incongruously, between farm buildings on one side and a modern housing estate on the other.

Gatehouse, curtain wall and drum tower of the outer bailey, Saltwood Castle.

From the early 14th century onwards there was an increasing dislike of the clergy, especially the church hierarchy, and lynchings or other acts of violence were not uncommon. The increased wealth and corruptness of the church, its special privileges and its involvement with various government misdoings, helped to make it — including the monasteries — extremely unpopular. As a result, some bishops found it desirable to fortify their palaces, as at Wells in Somerset (1331) and Otford, in Kent, a little later, though the practice was by no means universal. Other palaces in Kent of the Archbishops of Canterbury (eg Maidstone and Charing) were not fortified and Otford itself, although sometimes mistakenly referred to as a castle, was only lightly defended. Saltwood and Lympne castles, both properties of the church at Canterbury, were substantially refortified at this time. Most of the defences erected by the church, however, were built because of social unrest rather than the existence of a state of anarchy. Never built to withstand a serious offensive, most served largely as deterrents against casual marrauders.

During the years of the French scare, Hugh Herland and Richard Swift, carpenters, were very active in Kent building siege engines to be housed within castles. In the early years of the 14th century gunpowder and cannons began to be used. The first cannons were rather crude, made of timber and bound by iron hoops. They were far inferior to the mechanical siege engines then in use. The first records (both written and pictorial) of cannon being used in England appear in 1326 — at about the same time as they appeared elsewhere in Europe, China and the east. Cannon it seems, came into general use everywhere more-or-less at the same time.

By the mid-14th century, however, more sophisticated guns were being made in metal, especially at the Tower of London workshops. The first guns had been small and were held in the arms or on small tripods, but they soon became much larger. Cannon of up to 5cwt became quite common and by the late 14th century they began to be installed in castles, which were suitably adapted to take them. Some guns were mounted on rotating platforms on top of towers. Castles built after that date were usually designed from the first to accommodate them. Kent can generally be held to have been among the leaders in this country in incorporating guns into castle defences, Henry Yevelle being responsible for much of the work carried out there.

It seems there was a reluctance to use cannon to their full effect for a long time after their introduction. Perhaps because of the noise and danger element (they frequently blew up when being fired) there was a preference to use them in the open field rather than within the confines of castles. Edward III used them frequently in his French wars, employing them more in open battle than in siege warfare. By the beginning of the 15th century guns were sufficiently large and powerful enough to inflict serious damage to castles, as Henry IV showed in 1405 by quickly reducing the Earl of Northumberland's castles at Berwick, Alnwick and Warkworth.

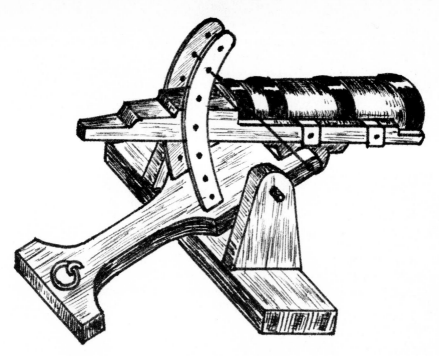

A small 15th century cannon.

From about the mid-15th century as guns became larger and more powerful few castles could stand up to a prolonged attack from them. The monarchy was able to reassert its power over the bastard-feudal lords again because few barons had the resources to afford either a large siege-train of cannon, or to strengthen their castles sufficiently to withstand a cannon attack. One of the results was that fewer castles were maintained, especially in the south and south-east, many being allowed to fall into disrepair. Yet despite this, and despite the increasing power of guns, some castles still, for a time, held their own.

The political situation in England during the 15th century, up to the advent of the Tudors, was extremely complicated, and unfortunately, no clear-cut role for castles can be traced. In theory the increased power of the crown should have rendered the barons ineffective and likewise, their castles. However, the crown itself proved ineffectual because of its weak rule under certain monarchs.

Failure by the crown to fully take command of the situation came to a climax in the civil war — the Wars of the Roses — which eventually placed the Tudors on the throne. The Tudors were powerful and wasted no time in exerting their authority, but the castles in the north and borderlands, because of the tide of events in the complex political environment, remained far more active as a result. While the true medieval castle had already seen its day elsewhere in the country, in the north existing castles continued to be maintained and even new ones built.

The Tudors' Contribution

Castles were only effective in their defensive roles if generally agreed by all parties concerned to be a key factor in warfare. Norman and early medieval warfare used castles rather as a chess board — with suitably adjusted rules. They remained the stable unit while the king, barons, knights, soldiers and villeins were moved around between them. The power of any individual rested in acquiring as many castles as possible, most of which were attained more by alliance than in siege warfare. The feudal system, by its sub-division of land under the king, made it difficult for any one baron to become too powerful, but as the system began to break up and private armies grew larger, disagreements and alliances were settled on the battlefield. Castles were no longer necessary to hold down or possess an area and so ceased to be regarded as valid pieces in political warring. They were relegated to the role of providing safe refuges or in housing prisoners — except in the borderlands where their presence was still important.

During Tudor — particularly Elizabethan — times, no serious castle building went on, except for the forts constructed for national defence (eg Deal, Walmer and Upnor) which were purely military structures. They are included within this history, however, because although not castles in the true sense, they still retain strong affinities with medieval castles.

The Tudors tended either to convert castles (where possible) into comfortable mansions — as at Hever, Leeds and Allington — or they built entirely new great houses, sometimes with the stones from ruined castles or dissolved abbeys. Often, their houses still embodied castellar principles, providing them with mock battlements and towers, such as Boughton Monchelsea Place and Knole House, both in Kent. They were employed more as decorative features and from a sense of tradition than for any real defensive value. By Tudor times also, not only was the great medieval castle redundant as a fortified home, it no longer served as a local seat of justice and administration. The nobles contented themselves to leave the defence of the country as entirely the responsibility of the crown.

Many castles found themselves being transformed into veritable palaces at this time, Kenilworth and Warwick being amongst the most well known. Perhaps the finest to be so converted, however, were Leeds Castle and Penshurst Place, again both in Kent. By the end of the Tudor dynasty any castles which had proved incapable or too costly to convert into country houses were already falling into a state of decay.

Local people often sheltered their families and livestock within the precincts of castles, erecting lean-to buildings against the walls. Such a fate befell the proud, ancient fortress at Rochester. Contemporary prints of the 18th century reveal the castle to have degenerated to little more than a shanty town. Stones from its walls and the mighty door of the keep had already, two centuries earlier, been used to construct the nearby Elizabethan blockhouse at Upnor. A similar fate befell many other castles, though Dover, because of its unique position, was maintained as a defensive outpost. So too was Queenborough, for a time, but it finally met its end at the close of the 17th century Civil War.

Dartmouth Castle in Devon was one of the earliest forts built specifically for artillery. It dates from 1481 (preceding the Tudors in fact) and was built by the townspeople to defend the Dart estuary. Even by that time the feudal element of the castle was on the wane, for Dartmouth was strictly a military fort. In many ways it was ahead of its time, for while at Canterbury as late as 1480, gun-loops of the key-hole design were still being inserted into certain stretches of the city wall, at Dartmouth the gun emplacements took the form of wide, deeply splayed embrasures to give the maximum field of fire. While no such early examples exist in Kent, there are many slightly later ones to be seen as at Deal, Walmer and Sandgate — with Upnor Castle perhaps, built in 1559 showing the new type of gun embrasure to best advantage.

Henry VII built a few fortifications, but it is to his son, Henry VIII that we owe most of the Tudor defences. They were built mainly from brick with immensely thick, low walls, faced in stone for added strength. Henry VIII brought together all the latest forms of defence in the designs for his castles. From about the 1520's on he began building his chain of coastal forts, chiefly in the West Country at that time. However, after 1538 and following Henry's excommunication, a combined French/German invasion was feared, sanctioned by the Pope to reassert papal authority in England. Henry duly stepped up his defence programme. In the course of just two years, the most comprehensive coastal defence scheme since Roman times was executed.

One of the bastions of Walmer Castle from the moat, showing the gun embrasures.

The whole of the south-eastern, south and south-western coasts were defended by Henry's artillery forts. They consisted of low, round or pointed bastions, on which heavy cannons were mounted, capable of wreaking havoc upon an approaching enemy fleet. They were usually manned by a captain and a small squad of men from the king's army, though from time to time locals might be required to lend a hand.

Henry is known to have enlisted the services of Italian, German and Scandinavian designers, regarded as world leaders in the field of artillery defences. Taken as a whole, Henry's forts represent the most sophisticated examples of their type ever built. The finest examples are to be found in Kent and Cornwall, those in Kent being not only larger but far more complex structures. While some are in ruins — eg Sandgate, Sandown — most are relatively complete, with Deal and Walmer being almost intact.

Elizabeth I further extended the defence system with the ever increasing threat of a Spanish invasion, and also maintained all those forts and blockhouses built by her father. She built Upnor Castle and again, refortified Queenborough Castle to help protect the new dockyard she had established at Chatham. One imagines that the alterations she made at Queenborough brought it close in line to Deal, which it already resembled.

Deal Castle, despite its mock battlements which date from 1732, is the most complete and unaltered of all the Henrician forts — and the strongest. It shows just how the defence system operated within it. It had five tiers of gun-ports and no less than 145 openings for firearms, and must represent one of the most strongly defended citadels ever erected during any period.

The gatehouse in one of the outer bastions, Deal Castle.

The fear of a French (and later Spanish) alliance with the Scots forced Henry to extend his chain of fortifications to defend the north of England — eg Hull, Carlisle and Lindisfarne. At Carlisle, as he had done earlier at Queenborough, he transformed the medieval castle into an artillery fort. All of the Tudor forts, though built through a number of reigns, should really be considered as a whole.

Elizabeth I's extensions to her father's defence system were concentrated in the north, where the threat of a Spanish/French alliance with the Scots was increasing. At Berwick, a particularly vulnerable point on the Scottish border, she ordered the town to be strongly refortified. The work, utilising all the latest artillery defence techniques, was pushed forward with great haste, employing forced labour from as far away as Kent to complete the task. Dover Castle and the town walls of Sandwich were also brought up to date at this time.

Elizabeth's fortifications at Berwick marked yet another turning point in the story of defence, for instead of building a mere fort, she completely surrounded the town with what was virtually an up-dated version of a town wall. After the Tudors, national defences continued to be built, but these mostly took the form of bulwarks (similar to those at Berwick) barrack blocks and other purely military structures. They tended, as a result, to stray further and further from the original principles of castellar construction.

The Fighting Finish

Although we cannot enter here into full details pertaining to the Civil War of 1642-49, between Royalist and Parliamentarian, it is necessary to make some comments because of the effect it had upon the story of castles. The Civil War was mostly a series of minor battles and skirmishes and castles served in the role of providing safe refuges for both attacker and attacked. By this time, few castles were still lived in and had to be hurriedly provisioned and made ready. Some, comparatively few in relation to the large number of castles in total, offered a stout resistance with full-scale sieges being mounted against them — such as Corfe in Dorset. For the most part, while castles played their role in the Civil War, it was mostly a minor part and did little to affect the final outcome of the war itself.

Many castles, such as Rochester, were in too ruinous a condition to be made defensible and many others offered only a token resistance, such as Deal, Walmer and Sandown. The heavy guns of the 17th century were quite capable of totally reducing a castle to a pile of rubble. A good many (again such as Deal, Walmer and Sandown) changed hands during the war on a number of occasions. Nevertheless, castles did briefly fly their colours once more and went out fighting, which is preferable to total decay.

After the Civil War the fate of many castles was finally decided. Some were deliberately destroyed by Parliament, some were made habitable again and some provided convenient quarries for building materials. The vast majority, however, were left to continue the process — albeit in a slightly more battered condition — of gentle decay.

During the 17th century the Dutch became masters of the art of defence and were in great demand, particularly during the Civil War. Great additional earthworks were thrown up around many castles, which were also adapted for the use of cannon. Dover Castle received many alterations at this time, most of which can be detected beneath still later 18th and 19th century fortifications. In many cases it was these outer bulwarks which made the castles effective again, as can be clearly seen at Carisbrooke Castle on the Isle of Wight, and not the medieval defences which were often still left ruinous behind the earthen ramparts. While many castles received some form of new outer defences, most were of a temporary nature for the duration of the war only and few were ever consolidated — fewer still survive today. Tonbridge Castle, for example, was provided with temporary wooden gun platforms, now destroyed.

It is curious to note that during the 17th century defensive ditches and ramparts came back into their own. Spiked palisades, similar to those used in the early Norman motte and bailey castles, were employed to prevent cavalry charges. Arguments arose as to which type of ditch was best. A dry ditch could be swept with gunfire from concealed embrasures in the sides of the revetment, while wet moats ensured no enemy could approach too close to the walls of the fort or castle. The ditches and ravelin at Dover Castle are amongst the finest to be seen.

Outer earthworks and great horseshoe earthwork of the Iron Age camp, from the top of Dover Castle Keep.

When the Parliamentary forces captured a castle they rendered the place indefensible or uninhabitable. Most castles in key positions were thus 'slighted', as the action was called, to prevent them from being used against Parliament again. Many castles which could never be considered a threat, however, were also badly damaged. Historians have often depicted Cromwell as being callous and un-necessarily destructive when slighting castles, but there was another reason for his actions. Castles had come to be regarded as symbols of oppression, or moreover, the symbol of aristocratic privilege. Public feeling against castles had become hostile, which was often induced and distorted by the politicians for propaganda reasons. By slighting castles and proclaiming their defence illegal, Cromwell therefore won much public support.

By the 17th century feudalism had been long dead and few of its principles were properly understood. During the Middle Ages castles were not generally considered oppressive but had become integrated into everyday life. Aristocratic privilege, however, was well out of control by the 17th century and was itself oppressive to the ordinary man. Castles, although obsolete, were still seen to be the symbol of the aristocracy and therefore, of the oppression. One can see the logic behind Cromwell's reasoning then, for by removing the apparent symbol of oppression, he was seen to also remove the oppression itself — which of course he did not.

The slighting of castles might be only light and later repaired. It might be considerable, as at Corfe, or it might be total destruction. Many castles, however, such as Leeds in Kent, escaped slighting altogether. It would seem that those castles which received the highest degree of slighting were those held by the Royalists during the Civil War. Public opinion generally was in favour of pulling castles down so many suffered considerable damage at the hands of locals in search of building materials. Stones taken from castle walls can usually be found in abundance in the houses and walls within the immediate vicinity, as a brief tour of the backstreets around Rochester Castle reveals.

Not until castles had become romanticised in the late 18th and 19th centuries were serious attempts made to preserve them. A few were maintained by their owners and restored or extended as living conditions changed (eg Leeds) and some were acquired in a ruinous state and made habitable again (eg Allington, Hever and Saltwood). Most of them were allowed to gently slumber away as forgotten ruins, hidden behind later buildings in towns or buried beneath undergrowth in the countryside. In the circumstances, it is quite remarkable that so many castles have survived, and in many cases, in such good overall condition.

It is perhaps a final irony that the Victorian society which was responsible for handing down to us a falsified image of the Middle Ages, was also responsible for rescuing vast quantities of our medieval architecture — churches and castles — and restoring them. We should therefore be careful when criticising some of their over-enthusiastic restoration work, for without it, there might be few buildings preserved at all.

The Memory Lives On

In many respects castellation, as an architectural style, was never really dismissed. Henry III is noted for putting 'fake' battlements on some of his unfortified houses and hunting boxes as long ago as the early 13th century. Battlements were also incorporated into church designs as a decorative feature. Even the Tudors, who were keen to dissassociate themselves from the Middle Ages, continued to put medieval embellishments onto their buildings. The large and noble Tudor residences of Knole and Boughton Monchelsea Place, though they appear to be semi-fortified, are purely residential, the defensive features being used for their aesthetic value only.

Throughout history, no age has entirely divorced itself from the picturesque aspects of the Middle Ages. The age of chivalry has been preserved, albeit romantically, right up to the present day, there still existing a certain fascination and affection towards it. The medieval atmosphere has been beautifully captured at Chilham Castle near Canterbury, where banquets are held in the great keep, free-flying birds of prey are on display and jousting tournaments are staged in the grounds.

The Renaissance, as a building style, did not last very long and by the 18th century there was already a strong reaction against its rigid, symmetrical lines. Architects reached back to the Middle Ages once more for their source of inspiration. Soon, it seems every nobleman or gentleman of repute had built himself a

The new Jacobean 'castle' at Chilham.

74

castellated mansion. Mock castles mushroomed all over the country — the age of castle building was back. One of the reasons for the revival was that classical style buildings, like modern architecture, no matter how artistically conceived, stand out harshly against the landscape. Gothic styles better reflected the irregularities of nature herself in their shapes, colours and textures.

Some of the revivalist buildings were merely houses with mock battlements and arched windows and doors. Others, such as Peckforton Castle in Cheshire, were genuine attempts at reviving the medieval concept, closely resembling real castles. Kingsgate Castle near Broadstairs, though obviously a sham, preserves many medieval features and looks every bit a real castle. As the medieval revivalism continued, the 'gothicising' became more and more elaborate, nowhere moreso than at Hadlow Castle, near Tonbridge. Here Walter Barton May deliberately exaggerated the Gothic principles of design.

Another trend was to label a house with the suffix 'castle' purely for prestigious reasons, often where no part of the building in the least bit resembled a castle. Mereworth Castle near Maidstone, although it stands on the site of a semifortified manor house, is in fact a Paladian mansion complete with a classical domed roof. By no stretch of the imagination does it resemble a castle, yet the title of its predecessor lives on — albeit in memory only.

The same architects who built the 'mock' castles were also commissioned to restore or rebuild ruined ones, John Nash and Anthony Salvin being amongst the most respected. One castle, Penryn, was designed along Norman principles even to the extent of having a keep, using Rochester as its model. While many of these romantic revivalist castles were good reproductions and genuinely medieval in appearance, others were heavy and overdone. The interiors of all of them tended to be rather flamboyant, sometimes an elaboration of medieval interiors, while others were strictly Georgian or Victorian. Tonbridge, Whitstable and Stone — all in Kent — fall into this latter category.

At Cardiff and Castell Coch, both in Wales, authentic rebuilding programmes were carried out within the shells of ancient castles so that there is a blend of original and restored work. The interiors of both castles are a riot of colour and decoration in the true medieval manner.

There developed a kind of competitive spirit among gentry (the wealthiest now no longer being the aristocracy but industrialists) to build castles ever more authentic in appearance. This was partly inspired, no doubt, by a strong desire to reintroduce colour into the drab Victorian world, and partly by the novels of Sir Walter Scott. The whole trend of medieval revivalism began as a kind of social snobbery, but by the mid-19th century castellated features had been introduced into humble terraced houses for decorative effect. Many new churches were also built in medieval style.

The revival was widespread, even reaching as far as Scotland (eg Culzean Castle) where castle building proper had never really died out. Civic buildings, such as the Houses of Parliament, were rebuilt in Gothic style and even the royals became caught up in the trend, erecting such structures as Balmoral Castle and

Stone Castle as it appeared in 1829 from a drawing by Fussell   (Aylesford Galleries)

adding many 'mock gothic' embellishments to Windsor Castle, already a genuine medieval castle. Even as late as the 1930's medieval looking houses were being built into the ruins of castles, as at Leybourne near Maidstone, representing a charming marriage of styles.

Some architects believed that there should be no attempt at completely reviving the Gothic style, but that they should merely borrow from it. Anthony Salvin, on the other hand, was a purist. It was he who designed Peckforton Castle in the mid-19th century and which is reckoned by some authorities to actually be defensible. He also built the 'new' castle at Scotney. Salvin, however, was not a romantic, he genuinely understood medieval engineering.

Even today the medieval revival cannot be said to be truly over, for while we no longer actually build castles, we meticulously restore and preserve them as part of our proud heritage. Such governmental bodies as the Royal Commission on Historical Monuments record and catalogue their minutest details, and the Department of the Environment (probably the finest conservation group in the world) go to extraordinary lengths to keep many castles in their original condition.

The National Trust care for a small number (eg Scotney and Sissinghurst in Kent) and tend their grounds with care and devotion. Many of course are still in private hands or are cared for by a local authority — most of these are also well preserved — but just a few remain as neglected, overgrown ruins. My heart still misses a beat with sheer excitement when confronted by a half-forgotten, ivy-clad ruin, such as Westenhanger Castle, for the first time. Truly, the 'Age of Castles' is still alive and well!

76

PART TWO

A GAZETTEER OF CASTLES AND CASTLE SITES IN KENT

GAZETTEER: A Note on the Entries

While every effort has been made to ensure accuracy of opening times, readers are advised to check beforehand if intending to visit any of the castles listed to avoid possible disappointment. Where castles are stated as not being open to the public, please respect the privacy of the owners. All map references given refer to Ordnance Survey 1:50 000 Series.

Standard opening hours of castles administered by the Department of the Environment are as follows:

	Weekdays	Sundays
March—April & October	9.30—5.30	2—5.30pm
May—September	9.30—7.00	2—7.00pm
November—February	9.30—4.00	2—4.00pm

Allington Castle in 1828 prior to restoration, from a drawing by Burford.

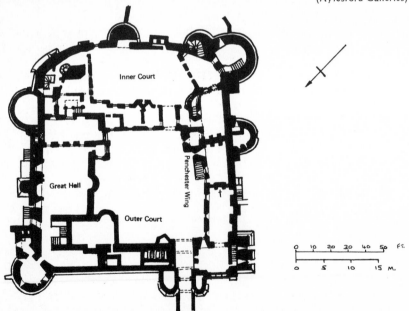

Inner Court

Penchester Wing

Great Hall

Outer Court

Ground plan of Allington Castle.

ALLINGTON CASTLE

Allington Castle is a personal favourite of mine, perhaps because, like Saltwood Castle, it remains elusive and still comparatively unknown. It stands near Allington locks on the southern bank of the River Medway, tucked away behind a row of poplars. It is surrounded by 50 acres of delightful woodland and looks every part a fairy-tale castle standing beautifully preserved behind its moat — now shrunken to a mere stream but still fed by the river.

The castle site has a long and chequered history dating back at least to the Bronze Age. The River Medway was fordable at Allington and finds have been made nearby of a settlement and burial ground of about 700BC. The Romans quarried stone hereabouts and 100 yards south-west of the castle is the site of a Roman villa. In Saxon times the manor of Allington was held by Ulnoth, King Harold's brother, and traces of fortifications erected by him have been uncovered.

After the Norman Conquest it was added to the vast Kentish estates of Odo, Bishop of Bayeux. From him it passed to William de Warrene and then, during Stephen's reign, to Osbert de Longchamp. At this time a timber motte and bailey castle was constructed on the high ground to the south of the present structure. This was destroyed by Henry II, however, on his accession to the throne because it had been erected without royal licence.

In Edward I's reign the manor of Allington was owned by Stephen de Penchester, Lord Warden of the Cinque Ports and Constable of Dover Castle. He rebuilt his house at Allington, most of it still surviving in the present castle as the Penchester wing. In 1282 he was given a licence to crenellate his house. The original licence still survives and a copy of it can be seen hanging in the entrance porch to the chapel.

Penchester surrounded his house with a strong curtain wall, eight towers, a gatehouse, and possibly an outer bailey to the south, now gone. It gradually evolved into an early example of a courtyard castle, though it was never as strong as such later examples as Bodiam or Cooling. It was later listed among the seven chief, or royal, castles of Kent but earned its place on the list more for its residential qualities than for defensive ones. One of the remarkable features of Allington is the early use of bricks in its construction — largely because the Penchesters had estates in Essex where bricks had been made since the mid-13th century.

When Stephen de Penchester died Allington passed to his daughter, who later married into the Cobham family, and it remained in Cobham hands until the reign of Edward IV. The castle was acquired in 1492 by Sir Henry Wyatt, a Yorkshireman and ardent supporter of Henry VII. It is to him that we owe most of the Tudor additions to the castle including the long gallery — which bisected the courtyard into two separate courts — and the charming little plaster and lathe house in the south-east corner, replacing an earlier tower.

Allington Castle from the south, the site of the original motte and bailey castle, showing Soloman's Tower far right.

Allington received many distinguished guests at this time — Henry VII, Henry VIII and Cardinal Wolsey, to name but a few — keeping Sir Henry Wyatt in strong royal favour. When Henry VIII stayed there he took the precaution of having himself walled in to his bedroom each night. The room, now known as the Royal Room in the north-east tower, was reached by its own spiral staircase and its doorway was closed off by a dry-stone wall. Such was Henry's obsession for the safety of his life.

Sir Henry's son, Sir Thomas Wyatt, inherited the castle in 1537. He was born at the castle in 1503 and became something of a diplomat and courtier, enjoying the same royal favours as his father before him. He was one of Anne Boleyn's lovers prior to her marriage to Henry VIII, but his chief claim to fame is that he first introduced the sonnet form into English verse from Italy. He later married Elizabeth Brooke, daughter of Lord Cobham.

In 1536 he was imprisoned in the Tower of London after confessing his affair with Anne Boleyn to Henry VIII and was afterwards banished to Allington. He seems to have passed back into royal favour, however, for in 1538 when the abbeys of Boxley, Malling and Aylesford were dissolved, he was given their estates.

He died in 1541 and was succeeded by his son, another Thomas, who was created Earl of Kent by Edward VI. It was he who led the famous Wyatt Rebellion in 1554 in protest of Queen Mary's marriage to Philip of Spain. The first meeting of the plotters was held at Allington Castle, but the rebellion soon failed and Wyatt was later executed at the Tower of London.

Allington Castle from the south-west.

Queen Mary dispossessed the Wyatts, who later emigrated to Virginia, in America, and Allington then became crown property for a short while. Elizabeth I gave it to Sir John Astley, Master of the Crown Jewels, in 1570. The Astleys, however, never lived at Allington preferring their other property, the Archbishop's Palace in Maidstone. Allington was leased to the Best family in the 17th century who had Catholic sympathies and it is they who are believed to have constructed the 'priests hole' in the entrance room next to the chapel. Later on in the 17th century a serious fire badly damaged the north-east wing and great hall. It seems the damage was never properly repaired, but a second storey added instead to the north and west wings.

The castle was purchased in 1720 by Sir Robert Romney — a distant relative of the Wyatts — but again, he never lived there. The castle was allowed to deteriorate and soon became used as a farmyard. A great many shacks and agricultural sheds littered the courtyard and the gatehouse suffered the ignoble fate of being used as a barn. A later descendant of Sir Robert's, in the 19th century, wanted to demolish the castle for its building materials, but local opposition to the move prevented him from carrying out his plans.

A Mr. Falke rented the Penchester wing in 1895 and carried out a series of basic repairs, after which he contented himself with the growing of roses. An advertisement in a newspaper then changed the fate of Allington Castle, which was by this time a sadly neglected ruin. In May 1905 Sir Martin Conway advertised in 'The Times' for an old manor house. He received a reply from Lord Romney telling him of Allington Castle. Sir Martin and his wife visited Allington and fell in love with the place from the start. They bought it for £4,800 in June of the same year.

Lord Conway, as he later became, and his American wife, spent the next thirty years restoring Allington Castle to its former splendour. He was careful to retain all of its remaining features and to blend any re-building with the original stonework. He was supported financially in the venture by Mr. Manston Marble,

81

Allington Castle. The Penchester steps on the right are part of Stephen de Penchester's manor. The centre arch is Tudor.

Allington Castle. Exterior of great hall.

his wife's step-father, and also by the architects, Mr. Caroës and Philip Tilden. A local building firm, Corbens, provided all the masonry skills required to restore the castle.

The restoration of Allington Castle became Lord Conway's life work and as each section of the castle was completed so he installed there some of his valuable art treasures, gathered from all over the world — a number of which still remain, such as the Persian tiles. Philip Tilden later landscaped the grounds. He turned the old tilting yard into a rose garden and screened the castle from view by planting a row of poplar trees along the river bank. A great deal of the original fabric remains at Allington and the new work is so perfectly blended with it that even an expert could not tell it apart without difficulty.

Lord Conway's daughter, Agnes, inherited the castle on his death in 1937 but she, and her husband George Horsfield, did not move in until 1946. Agnes died a few years later, however, so Mr. Horsfield decided to sell Allington. It was purchased in 1951 for £15,000 by the Carmelite Order of nearby Aylesford Priory. The Order had recently (1949) returned to their old home at Aylesford. It is one of the ironies of history that Allington Castle, once owned by Sir Thomas Wyatt who acquired Aylesford Priory after the Dissolution, should now be owned by that very same order of priests.

Allington Castle became a satellite to the priory and was first occupied by an order of Carmelite nuns and, after 1958, by the friars. The Carmelites have continued to bestow their care and love upon the castle. They have made it available for public use, not simply by opening it to visitors, but by turning it into a Christian retreat centre so that anyone may go and stay there. In addition the Carmelites hold seminars and conferences there and also stage various functions within its walls. These are usually of a cultural nature such as poetry readings, theatrical events or musical evenings. There can be no more fitting role for a castle to play than that presently acted out by Allington.

To the casual visitor there is a great deal to see here for practically the entire castle can be viewed — though in guided parties only so as not to disturb the guests staying there. The gatehouse is a magnificent structure still preserving its portcullis groove (now blocked at the top), the recess for a drawbridge and a very old door, probably of Tudor date. The machicolations are modern replacements. A gift shop is housed in the room to the left of the gate passage. The door to the right gives access to a small room now called the 'Open Door' where the 'priests hole' is situated. The chapel, in the next room, is modern and occupies part of the old Penchester wing.

The next two rooms are also of the original Penchester manor house and of particular interest is the Stone Hall. Solomon's Tower in the south-west corner has, by the addition of a forebuilding, evolved into what is virtually a small keep, though it clearly was not designed as such. Originally it housed the castle garrison while the lord occupied rooms in the north range. Emerging from Solomon's Tower — which takes its name from one of Allington's 12th century owners — brings you to the inner courtyard where, on the opposite wall, is Sir

Henry Wyatt's Tudor house. The east wall adjoining this house is the only remaining ruined wall in the entire castle — except for the barbican in front of the gatehouse — and still preserves a huge Norman fireplace. It is a survival from the first stone manor house to occupy the site. A colony of brown pigeons brought over from Italy by Sir Thomas Wyatt have been bred at Allington since the 16th century and are believed to be unique in England. They live in the old kitchen area of the inner court.

Passing back through the arch under the Tudor long gallery, you re-emerge at the outer courtyard. The great hall is shown next, a magnificent structure indeed. Although restored it is almost entirely original. The screen at its southern end has now gone, but it still preserves the doors that led to the old kitchen, buttery and pantry — now the refectory. At the other end of the hall is the solar. The north-west tower opening off from the hall block contained the principal bedrooms.

There is much more to see at Allington to which I can do no justice here but a visit is to be strongly recommended. Few castles anywhere have been so excellently and faithfully restored to show the layout of rooms and the comfort afforded by them. As in most other castles, because of the deeply splayed internal recesses of the windows, an extraordinary amount of light is admitted to the interior.

The castle is handsomely furnished and creates one of the most authentic medieval atmospheres I have ever encountered. The presence of the friars in the castle also gives it the religious and slightly mystical feel of a monastery.

There are two approaches to the castle — one by foot from the opposite side of the river, the other by car from the main A20 road. Perhaps the best approach and the one which truly captures the atmosphere, however, is the one by foot.

After crossing the lock gates at Allington near the Malta Inn, if you walk back along the bank towards Maidstone, you come to a concealed gate beside a small shed-like building. It leads to the woodland that surrounds the castle. At first, the castle cannot be seen, but as the path gently fingers its way between the trees and climbs to higher ground, it suddenly appears before you. It squats on low ground amidst gently rolling meadows, its gatehouse majestically framed by the branches of willow trees growing on the banks of its moat.

I first visited Allington Castle during winter-time. A fine mist enshrouded it and a log fire was burning in the great hall. The whole scene was, and still is, quite enchanting. Although much smaller in stature and more humble of purpose, Allington I feel ranks among the finest castles in England, alongside such mighty piles as Leeds, Dover or Rochester castles.

Access: By road from the A20. Just outside Maidstone, at the traffic lights by the Tudor Garage, is a signed road to the castle. Care should be taken when entering and leaving the grounds. Open every day of the year between 2—4 pm. Free car and picnic park. Excellent toilet, gift shop and refreshment facilities.
Map Ref. 752579

BAYFORD CASTLE

Bayford is the central one of an interesting trio of castles near Sittingbourne. Taking Bayford as the apex of an imaginary triangle, it is exactly 1.4 miles distant from both Castle Rough and Tonge Castle. The significance of this, of course, remains a mystery, but ancient sites and earthworks are often found to either align in perfectly straight lines or to form geometrical patterns on the ground — evident from a close study of Ordnance Survey maps.

Another puzzle, this time an historical one, also surrounds this trio of castles (see separate entry for Castle Rough). The Anglo Saxon Chronicle tells us that in 893 the Danes (under Haesten or Bjorn Iaernside — both names are given) invaded this part of Kent and, after landing at Milton Creek, set up an earthwork camp. The site of this Danish camp was long held to be Castle Rough on the opposite bank of the creek at Kemsley, but recent excavation has shown that earthwork to be of medieval date. The Danish settlement now seems certain to have been situated elsewhere at an as yet unlocated site.

In response to the Danish invasion of these shores, King Alfred marched a large army into Kent and erected his own, counter fortifications just over a mile from the Danish camp. The site of Alfred's earthworks is believed to be that now occupied by Bayford Castle.

The stronghold erected at Bayford was evidently maintained throughout the later Saxon times for in 1052 Earl Godwin — who owned Goodnestone Manor to which Bayford became attached — sought shelter there following his rebellion against Edward the Confessor. We do not know if the castle at this time was still built of wood or whether it had been rebuilt in stone.

Later owners of Goodnestone and Bayford manors were the Leybourne family, but by Edward I's time Robert de Nottingham was in possession. Bayford later passed to the Cheyneys and was sold off by Humphrey Cheyney in Henry VI's reign. It eventually became the property of the Lovelace family and in 1555 it was owned by Sir William Garrard, Mayor of London. By the end of the 15th century, however, Bayford Castle had ceased to be a viable defensive structure and is believed to have been already reduced to the role of farmhouse. Known today as Bayford Court, it still fulfils that function.

The castle itself is no longer in existence, but a large white house and out-buildings standing on the site possibly incorporate some of its materials. Up until the beginning of the 19th century there were still visible remains of the castle walls. Most of the earthworks are still in evidence, however, despite their some-what incongruous location amidst a vast industrial estate.

The castle was a quadrangular enclosure about 250 ft square surrounded by a 30 ft wide moat; still fed with sea water on occasion by Milton Creek. The enclosure was divided approximately in half by a cross-ditch and rampart creating two courts. Although it is known to have been rebuilt in medieval times it is

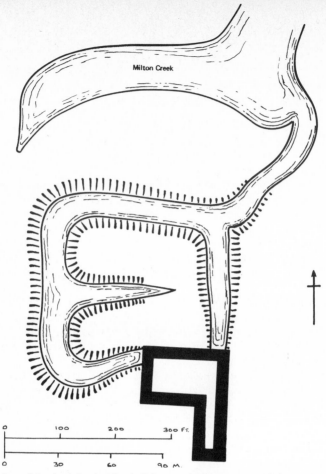

Milton Creek

Ground plan of Bayford Castle. The building marked is not part of the original castle but represents a farmhouse and its various outbuildings.

most certainly of earlier origin for its shape is most uncharacteristic of early medieval castles.

The castle site still clings tenaciously to its agricultural background, though it is in constant danger of being swallowed up by the encroaching industry. Up until 1907 it was cultivated as a small orchard but when I last visited, horses were grazing in the outer court. The earthworks have been considerably damaged but parts of the ditches still survive and a hawthorne hedge marks much of the course of the ramparts.

Access: On private land. However, if you turn down Crown Quay Lane in Sittingbourne and take a track near to the Dolphin Sailing Barge Museum entrance, the house and fields of Bayford Court mark the site of the castle.
Map Ref. 911639.

86

BINBURY CASTLE

Alternatively known as Bonbury or Stockings Wood Castle, Binbury is situated 1¼ miles from Thurnham and 2½ miles from Stockbury castles, with which it has close affinities.

In William I's reign, the manor of Binbury was part of the vast Kentish estates of Bishop Odo. When his lands were confiscated it passed to Gilbert de Magminot, who held it from the king by knight service. It then, together with nearby Thurnham, came into the possession of the Northwood's (or Northwode's) who held it continuously until the reign of Henry V. The Northwood's seem to have preferred their other property at Thurnham to Binbury as their principle residence, and it soon fell into decay.

The castle was built away from main roads and had a very uneventful history. The only recorded incident there occurred during Edward III's reign, and that was an accident rather than an historical event. A landslip at the castle buried Lady Alice de Northwood alive. The manor contributed 60 shillings towards the knighting of the Black Prince in 1347.

Binbury was of the motte and bailey type and comparatively small. The mound was originally about 160ft by 95ft in overall dimensions and surrounded by a wide moat, 60ft across. The mound, however, has been considerably reduced in height and the earth thrown down to infill the ditch. A house and farm buildings now occupy much of the bailey area.

It is unusual in that, despite being a very minor castle, it seems to have acquired stone defences from a very early date — perhaps from the first. The single bailey appears not to have had any earthworks attached but was surrounded by a flint-built, defensive wall, some small traces of which still survive. The remains of a tower, complete with one lancet window, though much altered, are incorporated into the present agricultural buildings. The walls, however, were very slightly built, being only about 2ft thick.

Access: Situated on farmland. Strictly private, though the remains can be seen from the farm approach road, off the A249 near Detling.
Map Ref. 812603.

BRENCHLEY CASTLE

On a hill about 1 mile north-east of Brenchley village can be found a double-defensive ringwork, marking the site of Brenchley Castle, sometimes known as Knowle Castle. What remains today are the mutilated earthworks of a mound, once measuring some 200ft in diameter by 80ft high. The site is so badly damaged that it is difficult to say whether or not it once had additional earthworks attached to it.

The mound is almost certainly of pre-Norman date. There are signs of later alterations to the original embankments, possibly made by the Normans when converting it into a motte and bailey castle. The entrance was to the south-east, as revealed by gaps in the embankments, and the ditch around the base of the mound was once filled with water.

Virtually nothing is known about Brenchley Castle and practically nothing survives. In fact, it is questionable whether this ever really was a castle, or if it was another of the prehistoric earthworks that was not converted into a motte and bailey, later historians perhaps tacking on the label because it resembled an early Norman Castle. Some evidence to support this view can be found in tracing the history of the manor of Brenchley.

At the time of the Domesday Survey it was non-existent as a manor. It was held during Henry III's reign, however, by Richard de Clare, but even as late as 1274 it was worth only one mark because no rents were payable under it. De Clare had estates at Tonbridge and if a castle ever did exist at Brenchley, it must have been very minor and probably deserted at a very early date in favour of the much larger and far more important castle at Tonbridge.

There is, however, also a castellated mansion at Brenchley dating from about 1524. When its moat was cleared in 1860 an old drawbridge was discovered, so presumably it did have some defences. Perhaps a certain amount of confusion has arisen between these two sites at Brenchley — as it so often has elsewhere — and their histories have become confused.

Access: On B2162 take the turning to Brenchley village, then take the first right turn. About ½ mile up this road, on the left, is a footpath through some woodland which passes right by the earthworks.
Map Ref. 693427.

BROMLEY CASTLE

Not a castle proper but a small, fortified manor house. The manor itself dates back to 862 but did not become fortified until the early 14th century. Licence to crenellate his manor, known as Simpson's Moat, was granted to Sir John de Banquel about 1302.

The house he built was rectangular — about 100ft by 45ft overall — and surrounded by a moat. It was of a simple, courtyard design similar to Hever Castle, and built of flint and ragstone rubble.

It stood near to the site presently occupied by Bromley Railway Station. By Henry VIII's time the original manor was already ruinous and was replaced by a brick-built, unfortified house. By 1869 however, this too had fallen into ruins having stood empty for many years, and was finally pulled down.

No trace of it survives today, though materials pillaged from its walls may well have been used for other buildings in the area. Part of the mound and moat still survive, however, amidst the buildings of modern Bromley.

Access: The castle has been destroyed and the site largely re-used for modern buildings.
Map Ref. 407691.

CANTERBURY CASTLE

Famed more today for its magnificent Cathedral, few people are aware that Canterbury also has a castle. Situated in the south-west corner of the Roman City walls, only the keep survives, and that in ruins. It is, however, one of the earliest stone keeps in England, dating from about 1080, and is roughly contemporary with the Tower of London. References in the Chancery Rolls for 1173-75 (once thought to be the date of the keep's construction) refer merely to repairs being carried out on an already existing stone castle. The keep was already in existence by the time of the Domesday Survey.

There is a popularly held view that the nearby Dane John Mound was the site of the original castle at Canterbury and that the name of this mound is a corruption of the word donjon — meaning a keep. Had the mound always appeared the way it now does, this would have been a viable suggestion, but the original mound is really only a low burial mound. It was shaped up into its present conical form by Alderman Simmons in 1790 as part of his scheme for the new Dane John gardens he was creating. The castle is also known to have been near to St. Mildred's Church — where it now stands.

There were originally four such mounds at Canterbury, two of which were outside the line of the city wall. It is possible that the castle occupies the site of another, which may or may not have been adapted for use as a timber motte and bailey castle. If it were, then it was only a temporary interlude, for as we have seen, only fourteen years after the Conquest, Canterbury Castle was begun in stone.

The castle once covered an area of about 4½ acres, surrounded by a strong rectangular curtain wall with a tower at each angle. The city wall itself formed the south-western boundary. The line of the Roman city wall was different to that of the present walls and enclosed a much smaller area. A curious point about the castle defences is that, right up until 1548, a public road passed through the castle bailey via the Worth Gate, which must have been an obvious weakness. In that year, the Worth Gate was blocked off and the road diverted, and a new gate into the city — Wincheap Gate — was erected.

Canterbury Castle was used as the county gaol from very early times — at least since the 12th century. It became also the centre of policing activities and was the official residence of the Sheriffs of Kent. Usually holders of this office also had their own castles elsewhere in the county.

There are many stories told of the terrible conditions endured by prisoners in the castle which have rather tended to sour the popular conception of what a castle was. Canterbury was an exception in that it became the county gaol, for in reality, few castles ever contained prisoners in their dingy dungeons. Most castles never actually had a dungeon, usually just a guard room. Perhaps it was Canterbury Castle's reputation as a prison which turned the inhabitants of that

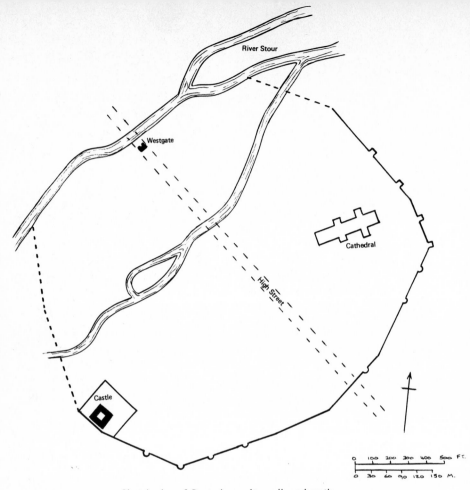

Sketch plan of Canterbury city walls and castle.

fair city so bitterly against it and why they also tore it down at the earliest opportunity.

Hamo (or Haimo) was the first Constable of Canterbury Castle — he was also Sheriff from about 1070 until at least 1086. Hubert de Burgh was Constable in 1215 and again in 1223. In 1232 he accompanied Henry III to Gascony and had to surrender his constableships of Canterbury, Dover, Rochester, Windsor, Odiham, Hertford and Colchester castles and also the Tower of London. There can be few men of his day who were allowed to amass so much feudal power.

Throughout its history, Canterbury Castle received more money for the safe keeping of its prisoners than for repairing its defences. The crown, it seems, was more intent upon keeping its prisoners from getting out than in preventing an assailant from getting in. In consequence, the castle walls and outer defences were allowed to fall into a deplorable condition. As early as 1359 a Royal Commission was set up to discover how it was that residential houses and gardens

90

Canterbury Castle showing the massive proportions of the keep.

had been allowed to be set against the castle and city walls — both within and without — and in the city ditches. The castle and city walls, despite their early erection in stone and obvious potential strength, were never really taken seriously as a fortification.

In the 1370's and 1380's, however, the Lollard uprisings and general unrest caused the city defences to be repaired. The present city wall and magnificent West Gate date from this time and are believed to have been built by Archbishop Courteney, who also strengthened his castle at Saltwood. Some authorities believe Archbishop Sudbury, who was murdered by the mob, was responsible for the work, but it seems more likely for Courteney to have erected them as a result of his predecessor's murder.

When Canterbury acquired its new, up-dated city defences — which were built and maintained by the church and townspeople, not the crown — the castle seems to have fallen even further into decay. The city walls were maintained in a good condition throughout the remainder of the Middle Ages and still survive in an excellent state of preservation. Close to two-thirds of their circuit still remains and a walk along the ramparts provides a fine view of the ancient city. The towers in the circuit of the walls were provided with gun-ports of the key-hole type.

The West Gate is like a self-contained fortress in its own right and stands astride the main street of the city in a near perfect condition. Inside it is fitted out as a museum of arms and instruments of detention. It took over from the castle as gaol and still preserves the condemned cell in one of its towers. It was protected by a drawbridge and a row of machicolations above the gate. In many ways it is similar to the inner gatehouse at Saltwood Castle. While the West Gate

One of the towers in Canterbury's circuit of 14th century city walls.

The West Gate Canterbury from the field displaying one of the earliest known uses of gun-loops.

is built from ragstone, the city walls are constructed almost entirely from flints.

Returning now to Canterbury Castle, we find that by the reign of Elizabeth I it had so fallen into disrepair that it ceased to be used as a prison. It was almost called into action in 1648 during the Civil War, but a treaty was signed before it could be put to the test. By that time the castle was not capable of offering anything but a token defence.

James I granted it to Sir Anthony Weldon, whose descendant Walker Weldon, was responsible for removing much of the fabric of Rochester Castle for its materials. From then on, the history of Canterbury Castle is one of gradual erosion and demolition. Stones taken from its fabric were sold off as building materials. Between 1770-1792 most of the castle walls and towers were demolished to make way for a new road, the keep then being left in isolation.

An attempt was made in 1817 to demolish the keep, but it was so massively built it was given up after only the top storey had been removed. A great deal of the finely-dressed Caen stone facings were removed, however, revealing the solid rubble core consisting of a mixture of flint, ragstone and re-used Roman tiles.

In 1826 the Canterbury Gas, Light and Coke Company purchased what remained of the castle site from its then owner, John Gostling. They installed pumping machinery in the old keep and later still, used it as a coal-store. In 1928, after a century of such ignoble uses, the castle was sold to the City Council. It is still owned by the council, the bailey now laid out as a small public park. The keep is normally locked but the key is available on request.

Externally, the keep measures about 88ft by 76ft — excluding its wide, battered plynth. Two of its three storeys survive and parts of its internal cross-walls — originally it had two main and several small, additional cross-walls

92

The West Gate Canterbury from within the city.

dividing it into various sized apartments. The walls are, on average, about 9ft thick. There are a number of window embrasures, fireplaces and the like built into their thickness, but the more extensive mural chambers and galleries, found at the later keeps of Rochester and Dover, are absent here.

Originally it had a forebuilding on its west side, traces of which were discovered during excavations in 1971. Entry to the keep was at second storey level, as at Dover. The kitchen area at basement level had a rather unusually placed well situated part-way between the outer wall of the keep and one of the cross-walls, within the thickness of the wall. There is also an unusual fireplace at this level contrived within one of the corner turrets. It is round backed and continues, undiminished, a full 20ft up into the wall, where it is topped off with a dome. Its flues emit at the re-entrant angles of the corner buttresses.

The upper levels of the keep were well lit but unusual in that their recesses were not splayed internally but were stepped back in a series of plain orders, or stages. Three of the rooms at basement level received no light at all and were probably used for storage. There was a spiral staircase in the north-east corner which rose to battlement level and another, shorter stair in the south wall connecting to the basement.

Although very ruinous, Canterbury Castle keep is an extremely important example and has much to offer the historian or keen student of castellar construction. Perhaps because it has little of interest to show the casual visitor, it remains largely unknown. Recent demolition to the north of the castle has opened up a fine view of the keep.

Access: Grounds open to the public until dusk every day. Access to the keep on application for key at the Royal Museum in the High Street. Can be clearly seen from Canterbury Ring Road. Council Car Park nearby. Map Ref. 146575.

CASTLE ROUGH

After landing at Milton Creek in 893 the Danes, under Haesten, erected an earthwork fortification, long thought to be the site of Castle Rough (see also entry on Bayford Castle). However, objections were raised to this popularly held view in 1908 in the pages of the 'Victoria History of the County of Kent'. An excavation in 1972 by the Sittingbourne and Swale Archaeological Research Group confirmed these doubts and revealed the Castle Rough earthwork to be almost certainly of medieval date.

The excavation revealed little evidence of any buildings ever having been erected within the earthwork. A small fragment of a jug was found — dated to the 13th-14th centuries — and a silver penny of Henry VI's reign, issued between 1454 and 1460, was discovered in the topsoil. The only other artifacts to be discovered were several sherds of Romano-British pottery alongside distinctively 13th-14th century pottery.

Castle Rough consists of a rectangular mound approximately 145ft by 130ft surrounded by a wet moat, fed from a tributary stream of Milton Creek. Attached to it on its south side is a small, oval mound. The rectangular mound is constructed of alternate layers of brickearth, sand and blue clay. The presence of both medieval and British pottery alongside one another in the lower levels of the mound indicates the re-use of materials from another site during medieval times.

This discovery now casts considerable doubt upon Castle Rough's claim to be the Danish earthwork erected by Haesten. The site may, of course, have been completely remodelled during medieval times — but such upheaval of the then existing earthworks seems unlikely. The materials used could also have come from a nearby earthwork, which may have been the site of the Danish camp. Alternatively, the camp may have been on the site of Bayford Castle, the presumed site of Alfred's counter earthworks. Perhaps none of these is correct and the site of Haesten's camp has been destroyed or lies elsewhere, as yet undiscovered.

It would appear that there is to be no easy solution to the Castle Rough mystery, and it does not end merely with determining the site's origin. Since it can be claimed with reasonable certainty to be of 13th-14th century date, we are now faced with the problem of ascertaining its original use. Though it resembles a moated manor house, it does not appear to have either contained a habitable residence or to have been defended by a wall. Perhaps it was an industrial site in some way connected to the brickfields nearby which were in continuous use from the Middle Ages up to the last century. A more extensive excavation may reveal more information.

The site today is scheduled as an ancient monument and is still very well preserved. The moat, though choked with vegetation in places, is still filled

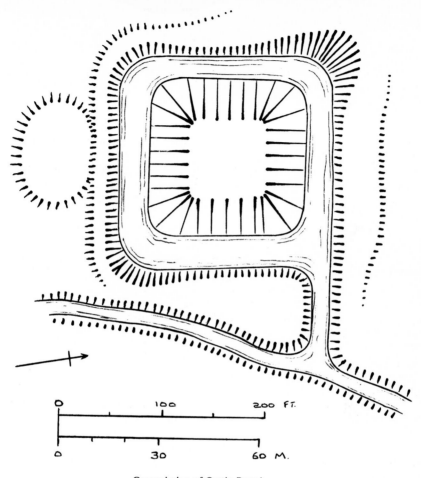

Ground plan of Castle Rough.

with water. Grazing animals from the farm on whose land it stands, however, are damaging the outer embankment. Strangely, the 1972 excavation failed to show any obvious trace of a substructure ever having bridged the moat to give access to the earthwork itself.

Access: Castle Rough is situated on farmland owned by Kemsley Mills (Bowaters) and is private property. The area is generally highly industrialised. A disused and ancient track runs across the land passing close by the west side of the earthwork.
Map Ref. 919660.

95

CASTLE TOLL

Castle Toll, near Newenden, was long held to be the site of Roman Anderida, but this belief has largely been dismissed in recent years. The claimant now, and probably the rightful one, is Pevensey in Sussex. While Roman finds have been made in the area, none were made at Castle Toll itself.

The castle earthworks occupy the apex of a vast triangular earthwork which covers an area of about 18½ acres. It was once surrounded by a wet ditch some 65ft wide fed by the Hexden stream. The outer earthwork has been claimed to be of both Saxon and Danish date, but it is almost certainly of much earlier origin. The castle, occupying a mere 1¾ acres, consists of a mound originally 125ft in overall diameter and a roughly rectangular bailey. Both sets of earthworks have been badly damaged by weathering and agriculture in this exposed region of the county.

It has been argued in 'The Victoria History of the County of Kent' that Castle Toll was not a castle at all. However, I feel this probably is one of the earthworks of undoubted prehistoric origin which was converted by the Normans into a motte and bailey castle. Although no record of its building or destruction survive, nor does any masonry remain, documentary evidence would seem to point to the site being inhabited for at least part of the Middle Ages.

In the years immediately following the Norman Conquest it was considered to be almost impregnable. The manor of Newenden, as it was then known, was held by the Archbishop of Canterbury until 1540 when Thomas Cranmer exchanged it with the crown for other lands. In 1080 it was held for the Archbishop by the FitzAuchers. In 1241 one of their descendants founded a Carmelite Priory at Newenden which, like the castle, has also disappeared.

Ralph de Seyntleger held the manor in 1272 when Edward I came to the throne. Edward is known to have made many hunting trips to this part of Kent and to have stayed at Newenden — presumably at Castle Toll. The manor is recorded again, briefly, during Edward III's reign but after its exchange in 1540 to the crown, nothing more is heard of it. It has been argued, however, and with some authority, that the references to Newenden manor do not refer to Castle Toll at all but to one of the other manors in the area, of which there are several.

The earthworks today are difficult of access, sited well away from any road, but they are still impressive. Their height, however, is exaggerated by the relative flatness of the land hereabouts. An excavation into the mound revealed nothing, except to prove that it was constructed of layers of earth and other materials and was not simply a pile of dirt, as is so often assumed of all mounds and earthworks.

Access: Situated on farmland. Go to Newenden village on A28 and take public footpath for approximately 1½ miles which leads directly to Castle Toll. Map Ref. 852285.

CHIDDINGSTONE CASTLE

Situated in the delightful village of Chiddingstone — which is largely owned and protected by the National Trust — is Chiddingstone Castle. Though obviously a sham castle, it is never-the-less important because it represents one of the few really serious examples of the Gothic castellated revival in Kent. Unlike most other sham castles, however, Chiddingstone began as an ancient manor house and still preserves part of a 16th century Tudor house as its nucleus, around which the present castle has grown.

The manor at Chiddingstone (of which there were once six separate manors) dates back to at least 1200. The site of Chiddingstone Castle was occupied by the Streatfield family from the early 1500's right down to 1938. Nothing of the pre-Tudor dwelling is known and in 1679 Henry Streatfield pulled down most of the then existing Tudor house. He built in its place a red-brick Caroline mansion which, together with its extensive formal gardens became known as High Street House. Old drawings of the house are still in existence.

The great-grandson of Henry Streatfield, another Henry, and who became High Sheriff of Kent in 1792, decided to modify the house in the currently fashionable trend of Gothic revivalism. In 1808 he spent what would be an equivalent sum today of £250,000 on refacing the house in sandstone blocks and adding certain castellated features such as towers, turrets and mock battlements. A lake was added and the formal gardens swept away to provide a landscaped setting. From this time on the house came to be known as Chiddingstone Castle.

Henry Streatfield's son, yet another Henry, carried the gothicisation a stage further and called in Henry Kendall, a prominent 19th century architect. He installed the long windows in the ground floor rooms and added more towers and mock battlements. He also built the gatehouse and the buttressed garden wall. The alterations as finished in about 1838 have remained largely unaltered to the present day. In addition to the Tudor core much of the wood panelling, furniture and interior decorations remain from the 17th century house.

When Col. Sir Henry Streatfield (Private Secretary to Queen Alexandra) died in 1936, the castle was converted into a school. Chiddingstone has the rare distinction, denied to most other sham castles, of being occupied for a brief spell in World War II by the armed services, thus almost becoming a castle proper! General Montgomery was at the castle on a number of occasions prior to taking command of the Eighth Army.

For a few years after the war the castle again became used as a school until 1955, when it was purchased by Mr. Denys Eyre Bower. He transferred to the castle his marvellous historic collections and in 1956 opened it to the public.

Included among the exhibits is the largest collection of Japanese lacquer outside Japan (the collection also includes swords, armour, netsuke and many other interesting items). In addition, there are on display collections devoted to the

Chiddingstone Castle from the park.

Royal Stuarts and the ancient Egyptians, including items from pre-Dynastic to Roman times — both the largest collections of their kind in private hands.

The castle interior is quite fascinating, stocked full with antique furniture and paintings. Of particular interest are the carved bosses of the ceiling timbers. The exhibits are displayed in glass collection cases and are well documented, both at the castle and in the guide book, and practically the entire house is open to view.

Chiddingstone Castle looks very impressive and attractive from almost every vantage point but the view from the back, where the public entrance through the gatehouse is situated, is perhaps the finest. Fishing is allowed in the castle lake on payment of a small fee — in 1945 the largest Common Bream then caught in British Waters (13lb 8oz) was landed. On the other side of the lake are a series of caves, said to have been used for smuggling.

The best approach to Chiddingstone is probably from Tonbridge. All the roads in this area are narrow and twisting — but well surfaced — and above all quiet, except perhaps at weekends in high summer. There is delightful panoramic and woodland scenery in almost every direction with large outcrops of natural rock much in evidence in the countryside generally.

Access: Open to the public. March 25th—October 31st. Daily (except Mondays) 2—5.30. Saturdays, Sundays and Bank Holiday Mondays 11.30—5.30. Free Parking. Toilets. Refreshments.
Map Ref. 494452.

CHILHAM CASTLE

To me Chilham is perhaps the most visually attractive village in England, certainly in the south-east. It crowns the top of a hill near Challock Forest and consists of a delightful square — now alas turned into a car park — with black and white houses lining two of its sides, the church on another and the entrance gates to Chilham Castle on the fourth. Each of the roads leading up the hill into the village is likewise lined with fine old houses. It sets the scene beautifully for any intending visitor to the castle.

The hill, or if not this one certainly one nearby, was the scene of powerful British resistance to the Romans under Julius Caesar in 55BC. Roman finds have also been made within the castle precincts, including the possible site of a camp. The great keep itself possibly stands on Roman foundations and there are traces of Saxon defences in the grounds.

There are two castles at Chilham, a magnificent Jacobean mansion and the keep and inner bailey of a Norman castle. The grounds and the courtyard around the keep are open to the public but the Jacobean house is not. Access can be made to the interior of the keep, however, but only by attending one of the highly popular medieval banquets regularly held in its great hall.

The medieval scene is further enhanced at Chilham by the free-flying displays of eagles and falcons and by jousting tournaments, staged by a group of enthusiasts in the grounds. If visitors are lucky enough to see these events, full of the colour and pageantry of the Middle Ages, Chilham will for many years hold a special place in their memories.

Hasted states that Chilham Castle began as a motte and bailey castle, originally covering an area of some eight acres. Although later rebuilding and landscaping have greatly mutilated these earthworks, it is interesting to note that they are located more to the convenience of the ancient track, the Pilgrims' Way, than being sited in the most suitable and strategic defensive position. This possibly is an indication of their prehistoric, and pre-defensive origin. When excavations were carried out beneath the keep in 1927 a pre-Norman dwelling house was discovered.

The first Norman castle to occupy the site was erected by order of Odo, Bishop of Bayeux and Earl of Kent, and half-brother to William the Conqueror. Fulbert de Lucy held the castle from Odo. When Odo was banished and his lands confiscated in 1082 because of his revolt against the king, William I entrusted Chilham to de Lucy. As part of the conditions stipulated by William, de Lucy had to provide soldiers to help garrison Dover Castle. In addition to extending the fortifications at Chilham, de Lucy is supposed to have also built one of the towers at Dover.

An entry in the Pipe Rolls dated 1171 states that work on Chilham Castle was begun in that year, but this refers to its rebuilding in stone. Up until then

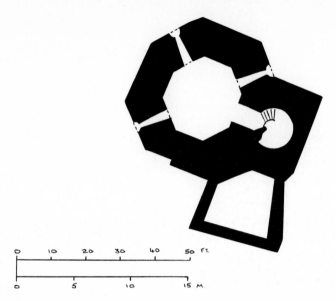

| 0 | 10 | 20 | 30 | 40 | 50 | FT. |

| 0 | 5 | 10 | 15 | M |

Ground plan of Chilham Castle keep.

the fortifications had been of timber. Some authorities, however, claim that the keep was built in about 1160.

The keep at Chilham is similar in design to that at Odiham Hampshire, but is much smaller. It is octagonal in plan with two projections — the larger one is a forebuilding, the other a stair turret. Originally it had flat, pilaster buttresses supporting each side but these have been mostly cut away. It stands within a small, rectangular courtyard, the curtain wall of which is relatively complete. Although of a slightly later date than the keep it stands on older foundations.

Internally the keep has been considerably altered — two of its lower floors were thrown together to form a single, lofty apartment — but it remains in good condition throughout. It is interesting in being the only example in Kent of a multiangular keep. Compared to the mighty keeps of Rochester or Dover, it is comparatively small. The battlements are missing and it has been roofed over with a flat roof in recent times. The keep and curtain walls are covered in ivy, left growing there for its picturesque effect. The walls are built predominantly from flint with a kind of plaster covering still remaining in places. An interesting feature in the courtyard is the ancient draw well, while in an underground chamber beneath the mound on which the keep stands, is an armoury.

In 1202 the de Dover family purchased the castle from the Exchequer and later, King John granted it to Foulke de Bréant. By marriage it eventually passed back to a descendant of the de Lucy's. From then on the owners of Chilham reads like a 'Who's Who' of the medieval hierarchy. Among its more notable owners were Richard de Chilham, Alexander de Baliol and Bartholomew de

The 'new' castle at Chilham from a drawing by J.P. Neale of 1825.   (Aylesford Galleries)

Badlesmere, later of Leeds Castle but who was born at Chilham. In 1322 Badlesmere suffered the most brutal and gruesome execution for his part in the revolt against the king — he was publicly hanged, drawn and quartered.

In 1542, after briefly becoming royal property again, Chilham Castle was granted to Sir Thomas Cheyney, Treasurer and Warden of the Cinque Ports. It was he who pulled down most of the castle and transported the materials along the River Stour to the Wantsum Channel and then up to the Swale. Here they were carried inland to Shurland, on the Isle of Sheppey, and used to construct Shurland Hall. His son, Henry, sold Chilham to Sir Thomas Kempe. When he died he left the estate to his four daughters, one of whom eventually bought the other three shares to become sole owner. She later married Sir Dudley Digges.

It was Sir Dudley who had the Jacobean 'castle' built between 1603-1616. The plans are still in existence and are believed to have been designed by Inigo Jones. The house is built in brick but with stone dressings and remains largely unaltered externally. Internally, however, little of the original decorations and furnishings remain, being altered and added to considerably over the years.

In 1724 the castle was sold to James Colebrook under whose ownership many alterations were carried out. During the 18th and 19th centuries, cricket developed into a favourite pastime of the gentry in England and many of the early matches were held in the grounds of Chilham. It was the setting in 1878 for one of the first matches staged between England and Australia.

In 1918 the castle was purchased by Sir Edmund Davies who commissioned

Chilham Castle keep from the grounds.

Sir Herbert Baker to restore the house and castle keep to their original condition. More recently the castle was purchased by Viscount Massereene and Ferrard, the present owner, who can trace his ancestry back to Norman times.

The gardens at Chilham were first laid out by John Tradescant soon after the Jacobean mansion was completed. The gardens today, however, are largely the work of Capability Brown, the eminent landscape gardener, and contain many rare trees and shrubs — some of considerable age. It was Brown who created the terraces and the lake, famous for its carp which can be hand fed. A number of the trees in the grounds are of historical interest. For example, Chilham Castle claims to have the first wisteria to be planted in England.

Lord Massereene re-introduced the birds of prey at Chilham in 1971. In medieval times they would have been a familiar sight, though now they are used for free-flying displays only and not for hunting. Lord Massereene is an ardent supporter of conservation in all its many forms and has taken many noteworthy steps in conserving the natural flaura and fauna of this corner of Kent.

A more recent attraction to the grounds — and alas one soon destined to disappear because of difficulties over planning permission — is the Battle of Britain Museum in the dis-used swimming pool building. It is a collection of relics, chiefly from fallen aircraft, in commemoration of the Battle of Britain, and is quite stirring — if a little sad.

Access: Entrance is from Chilham village square. Grounds only. Open to the public April to October from 2.00—6.00pm. Daily except Mondays and Fridays. Free Car Park. Excellent gift shop and catering facilities. Toilets.
Map Ref. 066535.

COLDBRIDGE CASTLE

A farmhouse now occupies the site of Coldbridge Castle, about 2 miles west of Egerton. It stands within a small, rectangular earthwork and is surrounded by a much larger, triangular outer earthwork. Nothing of the castle itself survives, but the N.W. side of the outer ditch and ramparts (once quite considerable) and much of the inner earthwork remains.

The castle stood on level ground on the southern slopes of Quarry Hill. Mention of a Colebridge Manor first appears during Henry III's reign, when it was held by Fulk de Peyforer. He received a licence to crenellate his manor in 1314, but shortly afterwards we find it in the possession of the Leybourne family.

When Juliana de Leybourne died in 1367 all of her estates, this one included, passed to the crown. Ten years later Coldbridge was granted to John, Duke of Lancaster. In 1398, it passed to the Dean and Canons of the College of St. Stephen at Westminster, with whom it remained until 1545. The estate then passed, through successive families, to Sir Edward Wotton, the Stanhopes and finally, the Cornwallis family.

The castle was roughly triangular in overall plan and may have been inspired by the design of Caerlaverock Castle, in Dumfriesshire. William de Leybourne is known to have fought under Edward I at the siege of Caerlaverock in 1300 so he may have borrowed the design and added the triangular, outer ward to his castle at Coldbridge, perhaps surrounding de Peyforer's much smaller castle, which then became the inner ward.

It is generally claimed that nearby Boughton Malherbe Place was built from the stones of Coldbridge Castle. Boughton Malherbe was owned in 1363 by a Robert Corbye, and in that year he received a licence to crenellate his house. The Leybourne's were at that time owners of Coldbridge, and as far as can be ascertained, the castle was then still in a habitable condition. If the contention is correct then it must be to the later portions of the house to which reference is made and not the original house — as is sometimes claimed.

Nothing, however, remains of the masonry of Coldbridge Castle today, though some of the materials from the inner ward may be incorporated into the present farm buildings. The earthworks are also considerably reduced, but still impressive. The entire enceinte can still be traced on the ground. Part of the once extensive water defences can also be detected.

Access: On private land. Not open to the public.
         Map Ref. 884478.

COOLING CASTLE

Cooling Castle preserves one of the finest gatehouses of any castle in Kent, its twin towers top-heavy with their machicolated parapets. There are considerable remains of the rest of the castle too, which was built in the 1380's in response to the French threat of invasion.

Both Roman and Saxon settlements have been located near the castle site and a manor house has stood there at least since Norman times. Sir John de Cobham acquired the manor in the early 13th century, which was then known as Coolyngg. The Cobham's held the castle, by knight service, from the heirs of the Countess of Aumarle. It later became customary for tenants of the castle to pay a fixed sum of money instead of fulfilling knight's service.

In 1380 Richard II granted a licence to crenellate his manor at Cooling to a later Sir John de Cobham. French and Spanish ships had, the previous year, sailed up the Thames estuary and pillaged the north-west coast of Kent, especially on the Hoo Peninsular, reaching as far up the river as Gravesend. Cooling Castle was built in response to the threat of a more extensive attack. It was then much nearer to the sea and really served a dual purpose. In addition to being able to offer some kind of resistance to a renewed attack, the outer ward was made sufficiently large to house and protect all of the neighbouring community.

The splendid outer gatehouse at Cooling Castle showing the machicolations on the towers.

104

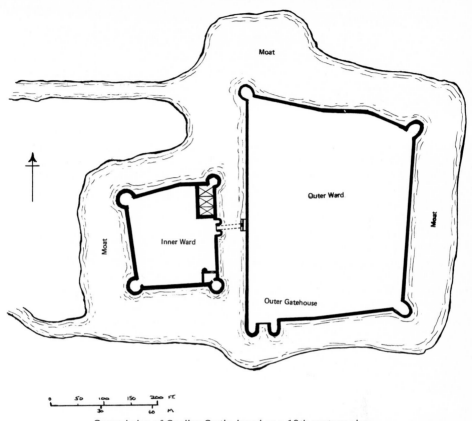

Moat

Outer Ward

Inner Ward

Moat

Moat

Outer Gatehouse

0   50   100   150   200 FT.

30   60   M

Ground plan of Cooling Castle, based on a 19th century plan.

The inner ward was built first and was occupied throughout the building operations. The castle seems to have been largely complete by as early as 1385 (the building accounts survive almost in their entirety). Within thirteen years, however, Sir John de Cobham was banished to Guernsey because of his part in a baronial dispute with the king. When Richard II died a few years later his successor, Henry IV, allowed Sir John to return and reclaim his estates. He died in 1408.

Sir John's only child, a daughter, had died before him so Cooling passed to his grand-daughter, Joan. She married four times, on the fourth occasion to Sir John Oldcastle, but he was killed before she herself died. Although the title Lord Cobham remained, the estates passed to other families through the female line.

The most famous event to take place at the castle was the siege of 1554. It lasted for only a day — 30th January. The then Lord Cobham was George Brooke whose sister was married to Sir Thomas Wyatt, of nearby Allington

Castle. Wyatt led a rebellion in Kent to protest at the proposed marriage between Queen Mary and Philip of Spain.

On January 28th Lord Cobham went to Gravesend to meet with other royalist nobles and the Duke of Norfolk. The Duke had brought an army of 600 'Whitecoats' and 6 guns from London to crush Wyatt's rebellion but was defeated by Wyatt, at Strood, the following day. Many of the Whitecoats deserted the Duke and joined Wyatt who then marched, with his newly captured guns, against his brother-in-law, Lord Cobham, at Cooling Castle.

Cobham had only a handful of men (some reports say as few as 8) and virtually no arms with which to defend his castle. When Wyatt arrived at Cooling on January 30th he trained two of his cannons against the main gate and four against the curtain wall. Within a very short space of time he succeeded in taking the outer ward and then set his guns against the inner gatehouse. A few hours later, Cobham surrendered. The siege, which had begun at 11 am that morning, was all over by 5 pm the same day.

Some of Cobham's men were dead, most were wounded, and the castle was badly damaged. He wrote a letter to Queen Mary explaining what had happened and that he had been unable to stop Wyatt. Later, when the rebellion had been squashed, Mary had Lord Cobham and his sons imprisoned in the Tower of London. Thomas Cobham, the youngest son, carved his name on the wall of their prison in the Beauchamp Tower, which can still be seen today. The Cobhams were restored to their estates, however, by 24th March of the same year.

After the siege Cooling Castle was never fully repaired and the Cobhams never again lived there. Their other property, Cobham Hall, became their chief residence and Cooling Castle was allowed to gently fall into disrepair. The castle estates soon reverted to their original use of farmland and in the 19th century tenant farmers erected a number of agricultural buildings in the outer ward.

More recently the castle was acquired by the Knight's, a local shipping family, the present owner being Mr. Christopher Knight. He and his father have been responsible for much of the restoration work at the castle. There are considerable remains, especially of the inner ward, and in fairly good condition.

The castle consists of two rectangular wards, separated from one another and surrounded by a figure of eight moat. The larger, outer enclosure contained the principle gatehouse and was connected to the mainland by a drawbridge. The inner ward, however, stood on an island in the moat and was only accessible from the outer ward. The castle buildings themselves occupy about 3½ acres but including the water defences this area extends to double that.

Henry Yevelle is known to have been at the site during building operations and is reputed to be the designer. In order to speed up the building, John de Cobham employed the services of a number of different masons, allotting each one a specific section of the castle to build. Both William Sharnall and Thomas Crump, a Maidstone man, have at various times been credited with the design and construction of the outer gatehouse. The building accounts show that it was completed by 23rd July 1382 and cost £456.

The gun loops in the outer gatehouse — and also found elsewhere at the castle — would appear to have been provided from the start. They are of two types; key-hole shape loops for small hand guns and larger plain, circular port-hole type openings. In the latter examples, guns were mounted in the internal embrasures behind the openings and trained onto certain fixed spots on the ground outside the castle. They could not be elevated and consequently could only be fired when an attacking force were within its limited range.

The inner ward at Cooling was much higher than the outer one so as to over-look and command it. Being in a rural position there was rarely sufficient man power available to effectively defend the castle. The idea was that a small number of men could man the inner ward and to some extent protect the outer ward. Because the inner ward could not be reached from the mainland, the outer ward had first to be taken by an attacker seeking entry. The main gatehouse and corner towers of the outer ward were backless so that if it was captured it would afford no protective cover to an assailant — who would also be exposed to fire from the walls of the inner ward.

All of the residential apartments were confined to the inner ward, the build-ings being arranged around its four sides in the typical fashion of a courtyard castle, such as Scotney or Bodiam. The outer ward was reserved for outbuildings, livestock and, as mentioned, the local inhabitants in times of trouble. The gate-house in the south-west corner was the only substantial building in the outer ward. It stands virtually complete to a height of about 40ft. It was 50ft wide

Cooling Castle showing inner gatehouse with chequer-work effect on curtain wall.

overall and about 25ft deep including its D-shaped towers. The actual gateway was 9ft wide by 15ft high and was protected by a drawbridge, a pair of folding doors and machicolations, but there was no portcullis.

The gatepassage originally had a vaulted roof. There are 12 machicolations encircling the west tower and 11 on the eastern tower, with a long slot divided into three similar openings above the gateway itself. Attached to the side of the eastern tower is an inscription by Sir John de Cobham on a copper plate, giving his reasons for erecting the castle. It is written in English (rare for the time) and in rhyme, and reads:

Knouwyth that beth and schul be
That I am mad in help of the cuntre
In knowying of whyche thyng
Thys is chartre and wytnessyng.

It is possible, however, that the inscription was put up after the siege of 1554 by Lord Cobham to please Queen Mary. Considerable portions of the curtain wall and corner towers remain from the outer ward.

Remains of the inner ward are even more substantial. Of the four corner towers one survives almost in its entirety, one is half ruined, one is reduced to its lower levels only and one has been demolished, though its internal features can be seen on the curtain wall. On the western side is a small postern, near to the north-west tower and protected by a row of machicolations. A row of exotic palm trees also line this wall. Not only are the walls of the inner court higher

Cooling Castle. Inner court and outer gatehouse from the moat.

than those of the outer, the ground level inside is also higher — perhaps embodying an earlier mound.

The inner gatehouse is much smaller than the outer one but is almost as well preserved. A bridge is connected to the outer ward with a drawbridge at its inner end. The inner gatehouse was also provisioned with key-hole shaped gun-loops (as are the remaining towers) and it had a portcullis. The drawbridge was of the type where two timbers passed out horizontally through slots which, when drawn in, pulled up the drawbridge.

In the north-east corner of the inner ward is a delightful room which was either the undercroft for a hall above, or a chapel. It is a highly decorative room and may have been either. Its outer walls are decorated with a chequer pattern, an effect created by the alternating use of flint and stone in rectangular blocks. The room originally connected to one of the corner towers, but this has now gone. There are niches in the outer wall, possibly for holy vessels if the room was a chapel, which would originally have been inside the tower. The walls of the inner court are built from Kentish ragstone with ashlar dressings, but with a chalk core. Part of the vaulting in the chequered room survives revealing the squared, chalk blocks.

The south-east tower, the most complete one, has a basement with loops in the wall to protect the moat and the area between the two wards. Unfortunately, none of the other buildings of the inner ward have survived, but corbels jutting out from the wall faces show where they were positioned.

Part of the outer moat still survives — now frequented by herons from a nearby nature reserve — while the rest has been partly filled in and laid to lawn. Mr. Knight has removed ivy from the castle walls and planted out the grounds in a very tasteful fashion. He lives in a house standing in part of the outer ward. The remaining part of this ward is still occupied by farm buildings.

Access: On private land. Not open to the public, but much of the castle can be clearly seen from the road, especially the outer gatehouse and inner ward.
Map Ref. 754759.

DEAL CASTLE

Following his divorce from Catherine of Aragon and the formation of the independent Church of England, Henry VIII's position in Europe became very precarious. European politics was dominated by Emperor Charles V of Germany and King Francis I of France and only with their help could the Pope be successful in re-establishing Catholic authority in England. Henry knew this and sought to keep the two at loggerheads, as it were, and so thwart the proposed invasion. In June 1538, however, the Pope succeeded in reconciling the German and French leaders thus making the threat of a combined invasion of England imminent.

In the years immediately prior to this Henry had strengthened the coastal defences in the south-west, but now this new threat of invasion left the south coast — and the south-east coast in particular — exposed and vulnerable. Within the space of just two years — 1538-40 — he built a chain of forts from Hull to Cornwall on a scale even surpassing that of the Roman Shore forts. A number of bulwarks and blockhouses were constructed between the forts, several at Gravesend and Dover, but little of these fortifications remains today. Other castles near the coast, such as Queenborough on the Isle of Sheppey, were strengthened at this time also.

Of the chain of new castles (although technically they were not castles in the true sense but military forts designed specifically for defence by cannon) four were built in Kent. Of these, one has almost entirely disappeared — Sandown — and one survives in a mutilated condition — Sandgate — while the other two, at Deal and Walmer, are in a splendid state of preservation. Deal Castle is the most complete and unaltered in the entire chain; it is also the biggest.

The three castles at Sandown, Deal and Walmer were spaced one mile apart on the east coast overlooking the Goodwin Sands. In the 16th century the sands formed a safe harbour for shipping, known as the 'Downs'. The castles became known as the 'Three Castles which keep the Downs' and were linked together by earthen bulwarks.

Although most of Henry's castles and other fortifications were built within two years, Deal, Walmer and Sandown castles were actually built simultaneously in just 18 months. Remarkably, the buildings did not suffer because of the restrictions imposed by the threat of invasion and they display a high standard of workmanship. Materials and money from the recently dissolved monasteries largely financed this mammoth enterprise. The castles were mostly constructed in brick but were encased with a thick layer of stone as extra protection against gun shot.

The three castles of the Downs were not only built simultaneously, but their histories also have close affinities. Once thought to have been designed by Henry himself, it is likely that they were built by a German designer, Stephan von

Aerial view of Deal Castle. (Kent Messenger)

Haschenperg. It was also generally believed that the three castles were designed in the shape of the Tudor rose, but this is pure romanticism. Their shape and defensive features largely followed examples in Europe designed by Albrecht Dürer in 1520-21.

None of Deal, Walmer or Sandown castles saw much action and when they did, they did so together. Usually this took the form simply of firing cautionary shots across the bows of passing foreign ships. The threat of an allied invasion of England soon passed and the castles saw little real action until the 17th century Civil War. The three castles began the war in Parliamentary hands but in 1648 there was a mutiny in the Downs fleet and a Royalist uprising in the south-east. Sandown declared itself for the king and, after a brief skirmish, involving a combined land and sea attack, Deal and Walmer castles soon followed.

Parliamentary troops quickly squashed the rebellion and then turned their attentions towards the three castles. Colonel Nathaniel Rich with 2000 men and only a handful of large guns besieged all three castles in turn, beginning with Walmer. Despite the harassments of sorties from the other two castles, attempted relief from the Royalist fleet and being seriously hampered by a lack of artillery, he succeeded in taking Walmer Castle without too much difficulty. Deal and Sandown castles also surrendered after similar brief skirmishes.

Following the Civil War the three castles were not 'slighted' by Parliament but were instead repaired and garrisoned as they still provided valuable protection for the fleet. Despite this, they were able to offer no defence at all when the Dutch fleet sailed across to the north Kent coast in 1667 and sacked the English fleet lying in anchor in the River Medway. During the wars with France in the 18th and 19th centuries, the castles were again garrisoned but they served more in the role of military bases and training grounds than in actually offering any serious defence.

In the early 1730's a residential house was built at Deal Castle, partly on top of one of the outer bastions and partly filling the courtyard. It was the residence for many years of the Captain of the 'Cinque Ports Volunteers' and later became known as the 'Governor's Lodgings'. In 1802, to make way for Lord Carrington's anticipated residence, the house was rebuilt, but in a most undistinguished style. A bomb dropped by the Germans during the last war fortunately did little damage to the main fabric of the castle but happily, destroyed the 'Governor's Lodgings'. The house has since been entirely removed from the courtyard and the castle now looks much as it did in Henry VIII's day.

The only notable differences are the battlements. Many of the original deeply splayed gun embrasures were replaced by the present medieval style battlements when the first house was built in the courtyard in the 18th century. Although they have mellowed the stark military look of the castle, they do not detract from its overall appearance. Guardianship of the castle was handed over to what is now the Department of the Environment in 1904, which authority has continued to care for the fabric, maintaining it to its now customary high standard.

Deal Castle has a sexfoil plan arranged in three tiers. It consists of a large, central tower (known as the keep) which rises through three storeys with a central stairway connecting to all floors. Attached to this are six lobes, or lunette shaped bastions, rising through two storeys. This central block is surrounded by a circular courtyard, attached to which are six lunettes, or outer bastions, rising through one storey only. A dry moat following the contours of the outer chemise surrounds the entire castle.

Deal Castle. The inner-face of the gatehouse bastion, from the courtyard.

112

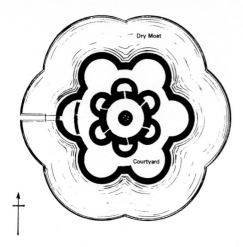

Ground plan of Deal Castle.

Cannon mounted on the roofs of the keep and inner and outer bastions could thus fire at three levels simultaneously. A fourth level of hand gun emplacements in the basement of the inner bastions protected the courtyard. A similar series in the outer bastions raked the moat. The castle could then, bring five tiers of gunfire into action at once if need be, giving a total of 145 firing positions.

Although larger in plan than Walmer, Deal has a lower profile, an impression exaggerated by the heightening of the entrance bastion at Walmer in 1874. The entrance is housed within the westernmost outer bastion. In addition to housing the present ticket office it also contains a small museum of local archaeological finds. The original iron-studded oak door still hangs in the entrance passage which was also protected by a drawbridge, a portcullis and a series of five meutrierrés, or murder holes, in the vault above.

From the gatehouse the visitor emerges in the courtyard and, before entering the keep, it is recommended that a tour of the outer bastions be made. These are mostly solid at ground floor level but by climbing onto their upper levels a good view can be had of the basic layout of the castle. Unfortunately, few of the original massively constructed gun embrasures remain.

Entrance to the keep is by way of a door in one of the inner bastions placed about one-third of the way round the courtyard. Inside the keep and bastions is a warren of corridors, rooms and passageways. You tend to walk round in circles and are never entirely sure whether or not you have completed the circuit. Especially interesting is a tour of 'the Rounds'. This is a narrow passageway that encircles the outer bastions at basement level to protect the moat. Access to it is either from the basement of the keep or from a staircase in the courtyard.

While some of the castle's exterior has lost its Tudor appearance, internally it is almost entirely original and largely unaltered. All of the gun embrasures can be observed. Of especial interest are the smoke outlets and small compartments for lamps, ammunition and stores beside each one. None other of Henry VIII's coastal fortifications display quite so much of their original layout as Deal Castle, and practically all of it is open to view. Still preserved there are ovens for both domestic use and for making bullets and cannon balls.

Housed in part of the keep is an exhibition outlining Henry VIII's entire coastal defence system. A small collection of arms and armour is also on display. The upper levels of the keep still show traces of decoration and wood panelling from the 18th century when the castle was used as the Captain's (or Governor's) lodgings.

Elsewhere in the castle much of the Tudor interiors remain. Timber and wattle partitions still survive and there are many exposed beams, the intervening plaster being painted white in typical Tudor fashion. A few brick fireplaces can also be seen. Despite all of this, however, there is a marked contrast between the stark, purely functional interior of this castle and that of a castle proper, even though certain medieval features can still be observed.

Of this whole fascinating interior, one feature stands out for particular attention — the central newel staircase in the keep. Originally it consisted of a double stair, both climbing the same central column, but at different levels. An assailant, on gaining entry to the keep, would ascend the stairway in front of him. The garrison could at the same time descend via the other stair and surprise him from behind. One can imagine the chaos and bewilderment this might have caused if it had ever been put to the test. One of the stairways is still in use while only the lowermost stairs of the other remain.

In all, Deal Castle is a most fascinating place to explore and is situated right on the sea-front. Deal itself is a pleasant old seafaring town with much to offer the visitor.

Access: Department of the Environment. Open Standard Hours. Toilets. Parking in adjoining street.
Map Ref. 378522.

DEPTFORD CASTLE

The castle at Deptford has long since been deserted and its site built upon — now lying beneath the extensive docklands in the area. William the Conqueror granted lands at Deptford to Gilbert de Magminot, who built a castle there, roughly contemporary with the Tower of London itself, only four miles away. It commanded both the River Thames and the Dover Road (Watling Street).

The Magminot's died out in 1192 however, and ownership of the manor was allowed to lapse. The castle seems to have fallen, or been allowed to fall, into ruins at this early date, for no mention is made of it again. Perhaps it was considered too close to the Tower of London for the king's comfort.

Access: The castle site now lies buried beneath modern dock developments and its exact location is uncertain.

DOVER CASTLE

Dover Castle is arguably the most impressive castle in England. It embodies all the popular conceptions of what most people think a medieval castle should be. Its history is one of continuous occupation from the Iron Age down to modern times. Even as late as the Second World War troops were stationed there and top level military plans hatched within its walls. It has thus continued, throughout its long and chequered history, to be the first and perhaps strongest obstacle to any intending invader of these shores. Even more remarkable is the splendid condition in which it has been handed down to us, despite centuries of purely functional and military use.

The castle crowns the cliff top on the eastern side of the town and encompasses within its outer walls not only the largest medieval castle in southern England but remains from all periods in history. These include a Saxon fortified township and church, a Roman lighthouse (the Pharos) and an Iron Age hillfort. The massive earthworks of the hillfort can still be seen embodied in the later works.

When the Romans built their lighthouse — they also built a similar structure on the western heights — they most likely protected it with a small fort. The Roman town and Saxon Shore Fort were sited below on the ground now occupied by modern Dover, but a community of sorts certainly lived on the cliffs here in Roman times.

The Saxon works consisted of a fortified township, or burgh, which stood on the site of the present inner bailey, and a more strongly defended citadel. This occupied the large horse-shoe shaped earthwork on which the church and Pharos stand. It is likely that both these enclosures were defended by stone walls, for the Saxons made more use of stone in their buildings than is generally assumed. The church of St. Mary in Castro, although heavily restored, still preserves many Saxon features. The fact that so large a church was built away from the town and harbour below suggest that a fairly large community occupied the site in Saxon times.

It seems that the fortified citadel developed into a castle in the more popular sense, at quite an early date. In 1048 the Anglo Saxon Chronicle tells us that Eustace, Earl of Boulogne, attacked the castle at Dover. It also states that Harold strengthened the defences of Dover Castle in 1064, just prior to his leaving for Normandy. After the Conquest the Normans made certain additions, but did not consider any further restrengthening was necessary for over a hundred years.

Such is the early history of Dover Castle. Most of the present remains, however, are of the medieval period, beginning in about 1180 with the replacement of the Saxon and early Norman fortifications by Henry II. The castle he superimposed upon the earthworks at Dover far exceeded, in both scale and cost, any

Dover Castle in 1832, from a drawing by H. Gastineau   (Aylesford Galleries)

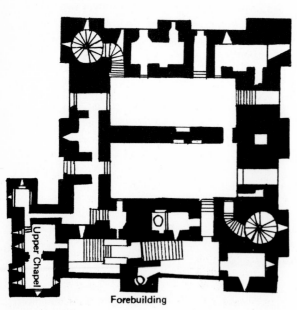

Plan of Dover Keep at 2nd storey level.

Upper Chapel

Forebuilding

other castle then built. It consisted of the massive keep and inner bailey, occupying the central earthworks, and at least part of the vast outer curtain wall and towers and its attendant ditch.

The castle thus created was so strong that remarkably, it has remained virtually intact. It was also the forerunner of a type of defence later fully developed in the 13th century — the concentric castle — and is the earliest example known in Europe.

Richard I spent another large sum of money between 1189-90 completing the work started by his father and extending it. In John's reign came the threat of a French invasion and between 1205-1214 a great deal more money was spent on the castle. The circuit of outer walls and towers was completed, new gatehouses added and the whole castle generally brought up to date. John's work can be distinguished from that of Henry II by the rounded or D-shapes of the towers — Henry's towers were rectangular. Entrance to the castle then was not through the Constables Gate, as it is now, but through a gate, now blocked, marked by the Norfolk Towers at the northern extremity of the outer bailey.

Following the siege of 1216 by Prince Louis of France, certain flaws in the defence system were highlighted. Henry III, between 1217-1256, spent a comparable sum of money to that which Henry II had expended when first beginning the castle. This work mostly took the form of blocking the old entrance and building the magnificent Constables Gate between 1221-27 further to the west.

The castle was maintained throughout the Middle Ages in a good state of repair. Henry VIII adapted the defences to carry cannon when he, in his turn, feared invasion. The next substantial wave of refortification — and in many respects, the most damaging — came during the Napoleonic wars, again in response to the threat of a French invasion. The underground works, begun in the 13th century, were extended and various outworks constructed, principally on the north and west sides and in the castle ditch, on which large guns were mounted.

Unfortunately, in order that guns could be mounted on top of the towers, many of them were reduced in height. The curtain wall was similarly reduced in height and earth embankments piled up against them for protection from heavy gun-fire. A number of subterranean casemates and batteries were constructed within these embankments. The most noticeable effect of the alterations has been the loss of many of the medieval battlements. The roof of the keep was also replaced with the present 'bomb-proof' brick vault. Over 200 cannons were installed at Dover at this time.

Fortunately, Dover was seldom put to the ultimate test of having to withstand a prolonged siege. The only major siege to take place there occurred at the end of King John's troubled reign in 1216. Many of his barons rebelled against him and they invited Prince Louis of France to take the throne of England. Louis responded almost immediately and was soon laying siege to Dover Castle, the most powerful fortress in the kingdom.

Hubert de Burgh defended the castle for the King. Louis attacked the castle

Forebuilding of Dover Castle keep.

vigorously and made two breaches in its defences, one at the old outer gatehouse and the other by a mine dug beneath the west wall in the outer curtain. This mine now connects to part of the underground works and can still be seen. The castle was on the point of surrender when the siege was halted by John's rather untimely — some say convenient — death. The barons changed their loyalties to the infant King Henry III and sent Louis back to France. The weaknesses highlighted by the siege were put to rights, but Dover was never again attacked so fervently.

Dover Castle has remained a royal fortress throughout its long history, the constableship being coveted in the Middle Ages as one of the most prestigious titles. It carried with it the title Lord Warden of the Cinque Ports and the responsibility for defending the seaways of the English Channel against possible invaders. The title is still conferred upon dignitaries today, though now, purely for prestigious reasons.

Below is a list of some of the more notable Constables:

1066-1084 — Odo, Bishop of Bayeux and Earl of Kent.
1202-1232 — Hubert de Burgh.
1265-1298 — Sir Stephen de Penchester.
1409-1413 — Henry, Prince of Wales — later King Henry V.
1493-1505 — Henry, Duke of York — later King Henry VIII.
1792-1805 — William Pitt.
1828-1852 — The Duke of Wellington.
1860-1865 — Lord Palmerston.
1941-1965 — Sir Winston Churchill.
1979-   — Her Royal Highness, The Queen Mother.

The centre of attraction within the castle is undoubtedly the keep. It is one of the largest and certainly the finest of its type ever constructed anywhere in England or on the Continent. Excluding the forebuilding, plinth and buttresses, it measures some 98ft by 96ft and is 95ft high — almost a cube. Its walls are built from Kentish ragstone with Caen stone dressings and are an incredible 21ft thick at the base. They are not solid, however, for contained within their thickness are a multitude of ingeniously contrived rooms, mural passages, latrines, cupboards and other compartments.

The keep was designed not only to serve as the place of last resort should the rest of the castle be taken, but also to provide sumptuous living accommodation. The level of domestic comfort, sanitation and decoration is consistently high. The plumbing arrangements within the keep have already been discussed in Part One of this book, but equally worthy of mention are the latrines. Expertly positioned so as to empty into cess-pits, which were regularly cleaned, each of the principle bedrooms had its own separate latrine.

Dover Castle. The Palace Gate and inner bailey curtain wall with the keep behind.

A cross-wall divides the keep into two roughly equal sections providing each of the two main residential floors with a separate suite of hall and great chamber, off which opened the smaller rooms contrived within the walls. Beneath these two floors was a basement, used mainly for storage and as a kitchen area — one of the ovens still survives complete. There is a postern at this lower level of the keep, unusual if only because of its obvious weakness. Inside the keep at second floor level is a fine collection of arms and armour, and on the floor below is a model of part of the battlefield at Waterloo.

Entrance was by way of a forebuilding ranged along the east and south faces of the keep, giving access to the interior at second floor level. It survives in its entirety and contains within it three flights of steps and a drawbridge (replaced by a modern bridge) spanning a deep pit. In the lower vestibule of the forebuilding is a beautiful little chapel. This was presumably for the use of the castellan, or lesser mortals of the castle, for an even more sumptuously appointed chapel is contained within the keep itself at second storey level for the use of the constable. Both chapels contain a wealth of Norman architectural detail. Spiral staircases in the north-east and south-west corners connect to each floor of the keep and to the battlements. The view from the roof is magnificent, looking out over the entire castle precincts, the town and harbour below and, on a clear day, across the sea to France.

Decorative detail of Upper Chapel on 2nd floor of Dover keep.

Although most of the medieval buildings that once lined the walls of the inner bailey have gone, the walls and towers themselves remain almost intact. All of the fourteen towers remain. The two at the north end and the two at the south end were drawn closer together than the others to form gatehouses, themselves protected by barbicans — the northern one still survives. All were rectangular and backless so as to be defended from the keep and to be of no value to an assailant gaining entry to the inner bailey. The interior of one of the towers can be viewed from inside the castle restaurant.

Most of the outer bailey is accessible though, regrettably, not the interior of the Constables Gate. Especially worthy of a visit are the Saxon church and Roman Pharos. The lower stages of the Pharos are Roman while the upper ones are medieval. At one time it served as a bell tower to the church, connected to it by a covered passageway.

There is an extensive system of underground tunnels and defence works beneath Dover Castle, parts of which are open to the public. Following the breaches made during the siege of 1216, Hubert de Burgh blocked off the old outer gatehouse and constructed an outwork in the castle ditch. Access to this outwork, which was partly underground, was by way of a series of underground tunnels. Whilst tunnelling, the builders discovered the mine dug by Louis' engineers, revealing just how close they had come to gaining entry to the castle. A small chamber has been constructed in the tunnel wall opposite the mine. The mine itself was left open after the repairs had been carried out at the castle. The

Dover Castle. The splendid Constable's Gate.

121

Outer curtain walls, towers and defensive ditch of Dover Castle, with Napoleonic defences beyond.

shaft may have been allowed to remain so as to serve as a postern, or a trap perhaps, for any future besiegers. The tunnels and underground works were extended during the Middle Ages and again during the Napoleonic wars. An ingenious system of trap doors was added at this time. The tunnels and underground works have also been extended in modern times and were in active use during World War II.

Intending visitors to Dover Castle should allot themselves at least a day to ensure that they see it all. The grounds are extensive and pleasantly laid out, and are wholly contained within the precincts of the mighty walls. Without doubt, this is one of the premiere castles in England.

Access: From the A2 turn off for the castle before entering Dover town centre. The road encircles the castle giving entry via Canons Gate. Pedestrian entrance via Constables Gate. Department of the Environment. Open Standard Hours. Large coach and car parks (fee). Excellent gift shop, refreshment and toilet facilities.
Map Ref. 326418.

EYNSFORD CASTLE

In about 970 Archbishop Dunstan established a title on the manor of Eynsford, beginning a long association with Christ Church, Canterbury. Sometime prior to the Conquest the Church lost it, but it was recovered again by Lanfranc, the first Norman Archbishop. In the Domesday Survey (1086) the castle appears among the lands of archbishop's knights, and was held by Ralph, son of Unspac. A castle may well have existed even then, in basic form — a timber watch tower on stone foundations and a hall, surrounded by a timber wall and ditch.

Odo, Bishop of Bayeux and Earl of Kent, had vast estates in Kent, particularly this corner of the county, and Lanfranc was constantly aware of his presence. Ralph settled permanently at Eynsford and took the name of the manor as his surname. All later direct descendants of the Eynsford's were, for some unknown reason, christened William. Ralph's son, William de Eynsford I, built the present curtain wall in about 1100, away from his father's original hall and on the site of the watch tower.

William de Eynsford I had strong connections with Gundulph, Bishop of Rochester. He was also literate and a prominent local administrator — though not in Kent — and in about 1135 retired to Christ Church as a monk. Christ Church was then given the right to appoint the resident parish priest at Eynsford, an act which was later to have dire consequences.

His son, William de Eynsford II, built the present hall on the site of the timber watch tower and extended the curtain wall to its present height of about 30ft. This refortification of Eynsford was carried out by permission of its overlords — the Archbishopric — during the troubled reign of Stephen when many private castles were built or extended without royal permission. When Henry II came to the throne he destroyed most of these adulterine castles, but Eynsford was allowed to remain.

Between about 1175-1200 William de Eynsford III is believed to have built the kitchen and forebuilding attached to the hall. A curious train of events occurred in his time. He was supposed to have been faithful to the Archbishop, and generally he was, but at the same time he openly aggravated the ill-feeling between Becket and Henry II.

In 1163 the monks at Christ Church allowed the appointment of a priest at Eynsford to lapse. Thomas Becket decided to make the appointment for them but his supposed friend, William de Eynsford III, refused to allow the priest to enter the church. Becket, in his usual forceful manner, immediately excommunicated de Eynsford. The king intervened, however, and demanded that Becket reverse his decision — which he did, though reluctantly. It was a build up of minor squabbles such as this which eventually led to Becket's murder in December 1170. De Eynsford is then supposed to have reconciled his dispute with the Archbishop, but on Becket's death he retired to the sanctity of Christ Church

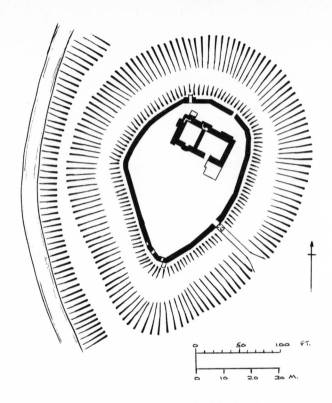

Ground plan of Eynsford Castle.

monastery — perhaps out of a feeling of remorse or guilt for his part in the proceedings.

William de Eynsford V was another in the family line with divided loyalties. In his early career he actively supported King John, even taking part in John's expedition to Ireland in 1210. In 1215, however, we find him among the rebel barons at Rochester Castle under William de Albini. When John successfully took that castle during his famous siege (see entry on Rochester Castle) he wanted to hang all of the surviving rebels, but was persuaded to imprison them and hold them all to ransom instead. De Eynsford's ransom was not paid until after John's death the following year. He later recovered all of his estates and became Constable of Hertford Castle. He died in 1231.

Eynsford Castle then passed to his grandson who became William de Eynsford VI and his son, William VII, was the last direct descendant. In about 1250 he reconstructed the hall of the castle following a disastrous fire — glass from the windows of this period has been found on excavation and is amongst the earliest known. He died in 1261, the Eynsford estate then being divided among the descendants of William V's sisters — William Heringaud and Nicholas de Criol (or Kiriel).

Eynsford then became uninhabited for a while. During the barons' wars of 1264 both Heringaud and Criol supported de Montfort, against the king. Afterwards their lands were confiscated, Ralph de Farningham seizing Eynsford Castle on behalf of the king. Eynsford should, on their reinstatement, have been equally shared between Heringaud and Criol but Farningham had somehow acquired Heringaud's share which he passed on to Ralph de Sandwich, a judge. He in turn sold his share of the manor to another judge, William Inge.

The rightful possession of Eynsford Castle thus became very complicated, for not only was it a joint property but each half had a separate existence. The Criol's continued to inherit their half of the estate, but the old Heringaud share was freely sold and purchased at will. The situation finally came to a head in 1312.

Ralph de Sandwich had no desire to live at Eynsford so he had co-operated with the Criol's and allowed them to live there — for a payment — though not, it is thought, continuously. When Inge acquired a share in the ownership, however, he refused to co-operate with the Criol's and became deliberately obstructive. In 1312 Nicholas Criol and his supporters ransacked Eynsford Castle and also Inge's other manors at Ightham and Stansted. A great deal of damage was done to Eynsford — doors were ripped off, windows broken and the place generally vandalised. Recent excavations have substantiated the story for remains from that period were discovered in great disarray.

Eynsford Castle. The ruins seen from the west with fallen stretch of curtain wall in foreground.

Various court actions followed but no compromise to equally share the manor could be reached. The castle was repaired but was never again lived in, though it continued in use for some time as a manorial court. Very gradually, however, its buildings fell into disrepair. The manor of Eynsford eventually became united under one owner in 1461 when the last of the Criol's was beheaded. The Criol's share of the estate then passed to the Zouche's, who had inherited Inge's share.

It was afterwards acquired by the Hart's of nearby Lullingstone Castle, later the Hart-Dyke's. In the late 18th century they used the castle as kennels for their hunting dogs. These were later removed, and in 1835 Mr. Edward Creasy was able to carry out some excavations there. In 1872 a stretch of curtain wall on the riverward side collapsed and is still lying recumbent on the marshy slopes of the castle earthworks.

A Tudor house was erected near to the castle, known as Little Mote, which may occupy the site of the first hall. This house became the occupancy of later tenants to the castle, which included the Sybill's and Bosville's. A man named E.D. Till leased the site early this century and began to take steps in the castle's preservation. Lady Fountain soon afterwards purchased the freehold and handed the castle over to the Society for the Protection of Ancient Buildings, who subsequently gave it to the then Ministry of Public Building and Works — now a part of the Department of the Environment.

Eynsford Castle is of a rather unusual design. Unlike most other early Norman castles, it did not start out in life as a motte and bailey, though it probably did use an ancient mound as its nucleus. Originally it consisted of two enclosures. A hall was built to the east of the present enclosure and surrounded by a wall — possibly only ever of timber construction. Attached to this was an outer ward, the site of the main castle today. In the centre of this outer enclosure stood a wooden watch tower, with stone foundations, on a mound. It was then surrounded first with a timber wall and later by the present, stone one. The wall revets an earthen mound so that the level inside is higher than that outside.

Excavation has revealed that when the tower was built in the centre of the enclosure it was erected on a wide, low mound which was then completely surrounded by the curtain wall. The gap between the mound and the curtain was then filled in to provide a raised, earthen platform — as was also done at Saltwood.

The original residence was in the now vanished eastern enclosure, the western and surviving one being a purely defensive feature to carry the watch tower. When the castle was reconstructed and the present hall built in the outer enclosure, however, the inner enclosure seems to have been demolished.

The castle thus created is a single, oval enclosure some 200ft by 150ft at its widest points. The curtain wall is a most striking feature being constructed almost entirely from flint rubble with squared flint facing stones and tuffa dressings. Roman tiles have also been freely reused as a decorative feature in the walls and in the round-backed hearth of the fireplace, or oven, in the undercroft.

The curtain wall, as noted previously, was erected in two stages. The original wall, constructed in about 1100, was about 20ft high and had a plain, continuous parapet. It was heightened in the mid-12th century, the line of the original wall top being just discernible inside the castle. The enclosure contained within the curtain appears to be oval, but in plan it is really polygonal, consisting of a number of short, straight lengths of wall. Although it was exceptionally well built, the wall was comparatively thin for its height, being only about 6ft thick, and is entirely plain having no arrow loops or mural towers. The watch tower on the north side is a later addition and housed a latrine, but even this is still flush with the wall-face, as is the turret near the gate tower.

At the eastern extremity of the curtain is a narrow opening in the wall which was originally the entrance and connected to the inner bailey, now vanished. A well, built beneath this opening in the 18th century, is a somewhat confusing addition. The gate tower (which projected internally, not externally) was not added until the new hall was built within the walled enclosure. It has mostly been destroyed but a large gap in the south wall marks its position.

It is intended to restore the original entrance path for general admittance to the castle, entry at present being by way of a modern staircase passing through one of three latrine openings in the south-west corner. Recent excavations by Mr. Rigold revealed that a range of timber lean-to buildings once lined the west wall. Traces of the timber watch tower were also revealed. Another interesting feature is to be seen on the external face of the south-west corner of the curtain.

Present entrance of Eynsford Castle, through latrine shaft.

A series of holes remain at parapet level which once carried a wooden hoarding.

The hall-block is a most impressive structure, even though it has been reduced to its foundation and lower courses only. The hall was entirely free standing and was protected on its west side by a forebuilding. It had a well in its basement — still containing water — a large fireplace, or oven, and an impressive array of windows. It was first built in the early 12th century but was reconstructed following a fire in about 1250.

The hall was a 'first-floor' hall, which means that the main residential rooms were contained on the first floor, raised above an undercroft, which might have been used by the lord's retainers or for storage. The hall was subdivided by a cross-wall to create a solar, this wall also extending down into the undercroft.

The hall has sometimes been termed a small keep, but it would have resembled more a house than a fortified keep. It had a hipped, tiled roof — as revealed during excavations — in common with many ordinary houses in Kent in the early Middle Ages and in consequence, probably did not have an embattled parapet. Even the castles of the early Norman period lent more towards domestic comfort than defensive requirements. A right-angled stair in the solar undercroft and a spiral stair in the hall undercroft gave access to the solar and hall respectively.

In the north-western corner of the enclosure was the kitchen, immediately beside a large well. In keeping with early medieval houses and castles it was built away from the main residential rooms, which contained a great deal of timber

Site of the original entrance, Eynsford Castle.

and must always have been a fire hazard. In the mid-13th century a new, smaller kitchen was built between the eastern side of the curtain wall and the hall block, which then ceased to be a free standing structure.

Eynsford, despite its chequered, if uneventful history, displays many of the domestic arrangements lost in many other castles. Its early abandonment as a residence has ironically been responsible for so much of its structure surviving in an unaltered condition. It is possibly the most complete and important castle of its type in England.

Despite its being virtually unknown by the majority of the public, the castle stands in the main street of Eynsford village, behind a row of houses. A little further down the road is a delightful group of medieval buildings and a stone bridge crossing the River Darenth. The river, now reduced to a mere stream and famous for its trout fishing, once washed the walls of the castle and fed its moat.

Access: Department of the Environment. Open standard hours. Small free car park. Entrance signed between houses in main street of Eynsford village on right bank of River Darenth.
Map Ref. 658542.

FAIRSEAT CASTLE

From a footpath near to the famous Coldrum Stones can be seen the scanty remains of Fairseat Castle. They consist principally of a mound occupying one end of a rectangular earthwork enclosure. The site was excavated in 1964 and remains of a wooden tower were found.

Although there is no documentary proof of a castle ever having existed here, the tower was taken to be the remains of a timber motte and bailey castle. The site itself appears to be very much older — perhaps a prehistoric burial mound considering its close proximity to certain other megalithic remains and ancient trackways. It may have been one of the adulterine castles erected during the troubled reign of King Stephen but deserted soon after Henry II came to the throne.

Access: From A20 take A227. Turn off for Fairseat. A footpath leads to the castle site.
Map Ref. 629614.

FOLKESTONE CASTLE

Folkestone was already a place of some importance on the arrival of the Normans in 1066, possessing its own small harbour. Apparently the Normans established two castles here, though both were not in use at the same time and it is not entirely certain which one was occupied first.

William de Arois built a castle near to the harbour soon after the Conquest. The sea undermined its foundations, however, and it was washed out to sea at a very early date, together with a nearby nunnery. With the continual encroachment of the sea at Folkestone, the site of this castle is believed to now be about half a mile off-shore.

On the landward side of Folkestone are two especially high hills — 'Caesar's Camp' and 'Sugar Loaf Hill'. The latter, though it has not yet been thoroughly excavated, shows traces of prehistoric occupation — not necessarily of a defensive nature. The westernmost of the two hills, confusingly named 'Caesar's Camp', is the site of Folkestone's other castle.

The name 'Caesar's Camp' has often been tacked on to prehistoric earthworks in post Roman times, but they have no resemblance to any Roman earthworks, nor do they usually reveal Roman finds on excavation. This 'Caesar's Camp' is no exception. Last century, General Pitt-Rivers (and others following on this

The earthworks of Folkestone Castle — 'Caeser's Camp' — occupies the hill in centre of photograph. The hill in the foreground is 'Sugar Loaf Hill'.

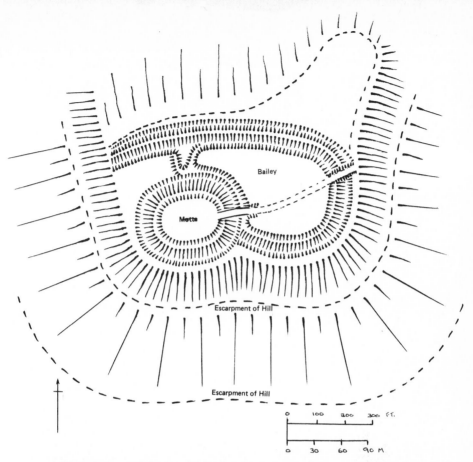

Labels within figure:
Bailey
Motte
Escarpment of Hill
Escarpment of Hill

0   100   200   300 FT.

0   30   60   90 M

Ground plan of Folkestone Castle showing the impressive array of earthworks.

work in later years) carried out an extensive excavation of the site and came up with some interesting results.

He found no trace whatever of Roman occupation but he did find considerable remains of the ancient British, mostly in the form of pottery, and a number of early medieval coins. He concluded that the earthworks were undoubtedly of prehistoric origin but that the Normans had considerably enlarged and altered the site. They strengthened the mound and inner earthworks by making them defensible (previously it seems they were constructed for another use) and added an outer, defensive earthwork.

General Pitt-Rivers found no evidence of there ever having been stone walls or buildings erected on the site, so presumably the castle never expanded beyond its basic motte and bailey form. It may have proved to be too far removed from the town or too difficult of access for the occupants, who may then have moved to a more convenient site.

131

Medieval barons, it should be remembered, invariably had more than one castle or manor and frequently moved around between them. Though originally provided with two castles, Folkestone now possesses none — one being washed away by the sea, the other being reduced to earthworks only and neither it seems, were permanently built in stone.

The remaining castle site, however, is easy to reach and is still impressive, commanding a marvellous view over the town and harbour. To reach it take the A260 road out of Folkestone to Canterbury, then take the first left turn and left again. The roads here are very narrow but a cleverly worked out 'one way' system is in operation. The road, before dropping down to meet the A20, encircles the castle hill. For those brave enough to cross a field of bulls, the North Downs Way long distance footpath passes right through the centre of the castle earthworks. It is certainly worth the walk for only by standing amongst the ramparts does one feel the full impact and impressiveness of the earthworks, which seen at a distance appear to be insignificant.

Access: Although the castle stands on farmland, the North Downs Way passing through its ramparts makes it freely accessible.
Map Ref. 214379.

GARLINGE CASTLE

Many castles in the south-east were built, or refortified, in response to the threat of a French invasion during Edward III's reign — Cooling, Bodiam and Scotney are examples. Fifty years or so later came another threat of invasion, this time from the Flemish people of the European lowlands.

In 1435 England's Flemish allies turned against her and in response, a new wave of refortification passed through the south-east. The defences at Sandwich were strengthened at this time. John Dent de Lion (Daundelyon or Dandelion) fortified his manor at Garlinge, near Margate, in 1440 with an eye to the Flemish threat.

Dent de Lion was a disreputable Kentish gentleman who, though a farmer, had links with the smuggling trade. When the threat of invasion passed, he used his new castle as a base from where he conducted his illicit businesses. He was the last male heir of the family, and when he died in 1445 he was buried at Margate Church.

His only child, a daughter, inherited Garlinge, which then passed by marriage, to a man named Petit of Shalmesford, near Chartham. Later descendants of the Petit family sold the castle and its estate in the 18th century to Henry Fox — Lord Holland — who was responsible for erecting the sham castle and other follies at Kingsgate, near Broadstairs. His son, Charles James Fox, then sold Garlinge to John Powell. His nephew, John Robert Powell of Quex and nearby Birchington, later acquired it.

Garlinge Castle. The impressive brick gatehouse of the Dent-de-Lion stronghold near Margate.

Many alterations were made to the castle during the 18th century and it subsequently became less of a castle and more of a country house. When Margate first became popular as a seaside resort the castle was frequented by a great many visitors, acting almost in the capacity of a hotel.

Its new found popularity was short-lived, however, and sometime in the 19th century practically the entire house was taken down, the site then reverting to its original use as a farm. The sole remaining part of this once magnificent structure is the gatehouse, but materials from the other buildings have been re-used in the adjoining farmyard.

The gatehouse, though sandwiched somewhat incongruously between the farm and a modern housing estate of bungalows (and looking to be in the way of both) is still a remarkable building. It is built of alternating layers of brick and flint to give a wasp-like effect, with dressed stone arches and quoins. It is roughly square with four corner turrets rising high above the battlements of the main structure, each one containing a spiral stair.

There are two entrance arches, alongside one another, to front and back, one being very lofty, almost the full height of the building, and the other much smaller, presumably for foot travellers. The roof and entrance passage are missing, but otherwise it is in very good condition.

Although built more as a fortified manor house, it still preserves a number of defensive features — arrow and gun loops, and at one time a portcullis. Unfortunately, nothing else of the castle survives, so none of its features are known. A stone-carved shield above the doorway bears the family coat of arms of the Dent de Lions'.

During the rebuilding programme carried out at the castle in 1703, a most unusual discovery was made. Whilst digging near the gatehouse, a stone-lined vault was uncovered, said to be large enough to hold 8 to 10 people. It contained funerary urns of pottery and glass, believed to be of Roman date. Close by was also discovered a curious chamber of unknown purpose. It had a narrow neck, opening out into a circular room — not unlike the chambers found in caves, dene holes and other subterranean works.

This chamber was immediately labelled by historians as a well-prison — whatever that is supposed to be. However, I prefer to keep an open mind, for until we have more evidence to show for what purpose such things were constructed, it is best not to ascribe conjectural uses to them, but to admit that we do not know their purpose.

Access: Turn off the A28 coastal road to Margate at the junction signed to Garlinge. Take next right, 'Dent de Lion Road'. A little way down on the left is a farm on whose land the castle ruins stand. Although the farm is strictly private, the gatehouse can just be viewed from between the bungalows of the nearby housing estate, which occupies part of the castle site.
Map Ref. 333697.

GRAVEL CASTLE

The Ordnance Survey map clearly shows a castle here near Barham, on the Downs, but all I have been able to find on the site marked is a rather attractive thatched cottage. I have also been unable to locate any historical evidence for the existence of a castle here, so it would appear to be a castle in name only.

The Downs are littered with prehistoric remains — tumuli and the like — and it is quite likely that the word 'castle' applies here to its more ancient definition i.e. an earthwork. Ancient tradition often carries on a name, its origins lost in time and mythology, attaching itself to the site regardless of the type of building to later occupy it.

I would suggest that this is such a site and never was a castle proper, but only an archaeological excavation will reveal its true origins and use. Extensive ploughing to the rear of the site, however, may have destroyed any earthworks which may once have been attached.

Access: Just off the A2 near Barham. A private house occupies the site but it is encircled by adjoining roads and a public footpath.
Map Ref. 213498.

Hadlow Castle as it appeared in 1830 soon after its construction, from a drawing by W.H. Bartlett.
(Aylesford Galleries)

HADLOW CASTLE

The manor of Hadlow once formed part of Bishop Odo's Kentish estates. Although no medieval castle is known to have occupied the site, it takes the name 'castle' from the Gothicised mansion erected there in the mid-19th century.

Hadlow Court Castle was built by Walter Barton May during the 1830's, and between 1838-40 he added the 170ft high tower we see today. The tower, thought to have been designed by May himself, is octagonal in plan with gabled projections and surmounted by a slender, four-storeyed upper stage. An octagonal lantern crowns the whole thing.

The rest of the castle has mostly disappeared, though it was once quite extensive, but the entrance gateway and its attached lodges still stand, as does the stable range. The castle is built in brick but covered with cement, the tiny windows of the gate lodges, now deeply recessed behind extensive ivy growth, peering out as if searching for daylight.

Old prints, such as the one shown here, reveal the castle to have been a magnificent structure. Today, the remaining tower is regarded as something of a folly, but when the castle was complete it formed but one small part of an extravagant whole. It was a deliberate exaggeration of Gothic principles, presenting a fantastic panorama of battlements, arched windows and pinnacles.

Access: On private land, but a fine view may be had of it from Hadlow High Street, and the tower can be clearly seen for miles around.
Map Ref. 634497.

HEVER CASTLE

Hever ranks alongside Scotney and Sissinghurst for the splendour of its gardens, but here there is an added bonus, for standing beautifully preserved within its moat is Hever Castle. The manor of Hever is very old but there are no records of its early owners. In about 1200 we find reference to a family who took their name from the manor and village. William de Hever was created a sheriff by Edward I. He built the central keep/gatehouse on the entrance front in the late 13th century.

In 1340 another William de Hever was granted a licence to crenellate the manor and it was he who probably added, or extended, the surrounding courtyard wall. When he died Hever was divided between his two daughters, who married respectively, Sir Reginald de Cobham and Sir Oliver de Brocas. Joan, the eldest daughter, later bought her sister's share of the estate which then became the property of the Cobhams.

In 1380 Sir John de Cobham was in possession and in 1384 another licence to crenellate was issued, at about the same time as Cooling Castle, another Cobham residence, was being built. He is believed to have strengthened the courtyard walls and remodelled the living accommodation. The key-hole shaped gun-loops inserted into the gatehouse and turrets on the entrance front were probably his work too. The larger, port-hole types in the two turrets are probably of Tudor origin.

When Sir John de Cobham died Hever was sold to Sir Stephen Scrope, who came from a northern family. When he died in 1408 he left a son, still in his minority. His widow married Sir John Fastolf and between them they managed — or rather mismanaged — the estate. When he came of age and wished to fight in the French wars, the young Scrope had to sell Hever to finance the expedition.

The castle was sold in 1423 to Sir Roger Fiennes, a Suffolk man. It then passed to his brother James, 1st Baron Saye and Sele and in 1462, the 2nd Baron Saye again sold it. The purchaser this time was Sir Geoffrey Bullen of Norfolk. He had been Lord Mayor of London in 1459 and it is with his family's ownership that Hever entered its most notable period in history.

The Bullens (later Boleyns) had a number of properties, including Blickling in Norfolk, and were very much in royal favour. It is thought that Sir Geoffrey bought Hever to be within easy travelling distance of London. Although he probably intended originally to use the castle as a temporary residence, he came to spend more and more time there. He converted the castle — which was really a fortified manor house — into a splendid Tudor country house. Henry VIII often visited Sir Thomas Bullen, Sir Geoffrey's grandson, at Hever and it was here that he first met — and later courted — Anne Boleyn, a meeting that was to change the course of history.

Henry's association with Anne began through her elder sister, Mary, who was

136

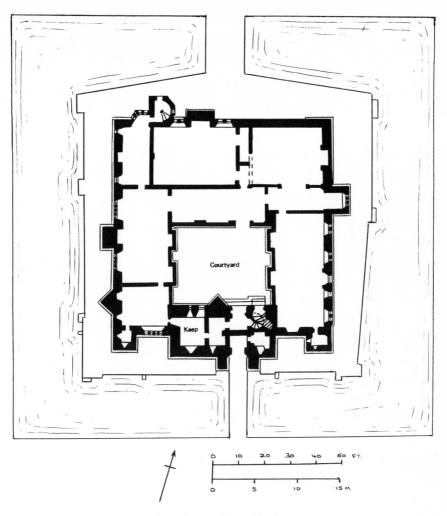

Ground plan of Hever Castle.

Lady-in-Waiting to Queen Catherine. The king made amorous advances toward Mary but soon tired of her. He next focused his attention on her younger sister, Anne. The Bullens were an extremely power conscious family and Sir Thomas took full advantage of his daughters' influence over the king to elevate his own position in court.

Anne was, by nature, a flirtatious woman. She had an affair with Sir Thomas Wyatt, of Allington Castle, and was later accused of committing incest with her

Hever Castle as it appeared in 1829 from a drawing by G. Shepherd. (Aylesford Galleries)

brother George — a crime for which he was beheaded. She became Lady-in-Waiting to Queen Catherine but determined that being simply the king's mistress was not enough — she wanted to become queen herself. Without entering too deeply into what is now national history, Anne was the instrument which first of all led to Henry VIII becoming divorced from Catherine of Aragon and latterly, as a direct result, to the split with the Church of Rome.

Anne, who changed the family name to Boleyn in 1533, was found guilty on four separate cases of adultery — including that with her brother. As a result, she was executed at the Tower of London on 19th May 1536. Her ghost is still reputed to haunt the grounds at Hever each Christmas.

Anne's parents lived out the remaining years of their lives at Hever, shunned by society. The castle afterwards passed to the crown. Henry VIII granted it in 1540 to Anne of Cleves, his divorced fourth wife, and she lived there until her death in 1557. After that time the castle seems to have been largely forgotten. It became a centre of smuggling activity in the 18th century and by the late 19th century had diminished to the humble role of farmhouse.

In 1903 Hever Castle was purchased, and rescued, by Mr. William Waldorf Astor, an American but of German descent. He became a naturalised British subject and in 1917 was created Viscount Astor of Hever Castle. The castle is now owned and lived in by his grandson, Gavin Astor.

It is to William Waldorf Astor and his architect, Frank L. Pearson, that we owe the present splendid condition of the castle and grounds today. The restoration programme lasted four years. The first steps taken by him were to

The impressive entrance front of Hever Castle. Note the different types of arrow and gun-loops.

remove the clutter of farm buildings and restore the castle to its former glory. This done, he then turned his attentions toward the gardens. The course of the River Eden was altered and made to fill a newly excavated lake covering some 35 acres, but which includes a large island, and the whole, extensive grounds landscaped. Within this overall scheme a series of individual gardens and walks were created.

Now, after seventy years of slow maturing, the gardens rank among the finest to be seen anywhere. Visitors come from all over the world to this tiny corner of Kent just to see them. Great use has been made of natural stone outcrops in the grounds and the view looking back from the Golden Stairs and Anne Boleyn's Walk is unforgettable. The castle looks particularly attractive in spring when daffodils girth its moat, creating an idyllic scene.

One other feature remains to be seen at Hever that makes it unique among English castles. When Mr. Astor embarked upon the restoration of the castle he was faced with the problem of how to provide extra accommodation without destroying the atmosphere of the castle. He overcame the problem by leaving the basic fabric of the castle unaltered but added to it a splendid, single storey house, but so expertly designed as to resemble a Tudor village.

It blends perfectly with the castle and while from outside it appears to consist of a number of separate dwellings, inside it was one continuous house. In 1962, however, it became necessary to convert it into a number of self-contained apartments. Unfortunately, the castle and village have been seriously flooded on a number of occasions causing considerable damage each time.

Hever Castle showing the inner moat and 'Tudor Village' beyond.

The castle as we see it today is largely as it would have looked in Tudor times. The interiors are magnificent and despite the somewhat ignoble uses to which it has at various times been subjected, the fabric is in very good condition. A small armoury is contained within the keep. Most of the castle dates from the Tudor period but the keep/gatehouse and exterior walls are medieval. In medieval times the stonework was covered with brightly painted plaster, which has long since gone, and now reveals the beautiful soft tones of its honey-coloured stone.

The gateway is one of the finest still existing of any castle, and it still preserves two of its original three portcullises. The outer one of these is believed to be the only original portcullis in England that is still in working order. The drawbridge is modern but it has already acquired a look of antiquity about it. The entrance front at Hever with its machicolations above the gateway is most imposing. Although it is termed a fortified manor house, it was of considerable strength and rightly deserves the suffix of 'castle' that has been added to its name.

Access: From Hever village, near King Henry VIII public house. Best approached from Penshurst direction. Open to the public April 1st—Sept. 30th. Separate admission to castle and gardens. Castle: Tues. and Fri. 1.30-6.00pm. Wed. and Sun. 1.30-7.00pm. Gardens: Tues., Wed., Fri. and Sun. 1.00-7.00pm. Large free car park. Excellent gift shop, refreshment and toilet facilities. Farm produce shop.
Map Ref. 478452.

KEMSING CASTLE

Two houses, themselves dating back to at least the 16th century, stand on what is believed to be the site of Kemsing Castle. They are appropriately named, 'Castle Bank House' and 'The Keep'. The latter may be a late medieval, three-bay hall-house. The castle site is in a position just south of the Pilgrims' Way, which passes through the village near the school.

During King John's reign, the castellan appointed was Fulk de Brent. Following the depletion in population brought about by the Black Death in the second half of the 14th century, the castle seems to have diminished in importance and fallen out of use, for nothing is heard about it after that time.

Opposite the castle site is an ancient holy well, dedicated to St. Edith, and there was once also a shrine in the churchyard to her. It attracted a large number of pilgrims en route to and from Canterbury.

The village itself later revived from the effects of the plague and prospered, but the castle appears never to have regained its importance. Nothing survives today, except for one or two slight traces of earthworks, and these so altered by later buildings as to be almost unrecognisable. The proximity of these earthworks to the ancient trackway, the Pilgrims' Way, does suggest, however, that perhaps they are of pre-Norman origin.

Access: The site is freely accessible, though later, privately owned buildings now occupy much of the area.
Map Ref. 554589.

KINGSGATE CASTLE

Kingsgate Castle stands majestically on top of the cliffs between Margate and Broadstairs and, from the landward side at least, looks every bit a medieval fortress. It is, however, a sham castle, a folly erected partly by Lord Holland, father of Charles James Fox, in the 18th century.

As originally built it was called Holland House, but he then proceeded to surround it with follies. One of these follies was a stable block, brilliantly disguised as a ruined Edwardian castle. One tower only of this 'castle' remains for in the 1860's the rest of it was transformed into a habitable residence. It was a full-scale reproduction of a castle — the sham castle we see today — and replaced Lord Holland's original house.

The castle today is a quadrangular building with square towers at the angles and round entrance towers. It is built from brick but is entirely faced with flint and dressed stone, and at first glance looks to be quite authentic.

Today, the castle has been divided into a number of separate residences, each forming a self-contained apartment, and the grounds pleasantly laid out as a communal garden. It looks both commanding, perched high on the cliff edge, and very romantic with the sea and sandy beach below as a backdrop.

The impressive facade of the 'mock gothic' Kingsgate Castle.

Another of Lord Holland's follies lies in ruins on the cliff top here, a tower built in the style of Henry VIII's coastal forts. Holland, however, claimed that it was supposed to have been erected by King Vortigern in the 5th century. Nearby are at least two more towers and remnants of his other follies — he was obviously determined to confuse historians and archaeologists of the future!

Access: On the B2052 cliff-top road between Margate and Broadstairs. Private property but the residents are usually willing to allow passers by to view and photograph the entrance front.
Map Ref. 397705.

KNOX BRIDGE CASTLE

Knox Bridge Castle, near Frittenden, consists solely of a small mound. No traces of an attached bailey or any other earthwork have yet been discovered — nor in all probability are they likely to be. The mound is entirely artificial and was surrounded by a wet moat, fed by a channel from a nearby stream.

One wonders if this ever was a motte and bailey castle, as it is claimed to be, or whether it is one of the many prehistoric mounds that the Normans did not fortify and convert into a castle. This I feel is the danger in ascribing all such mounds as castle mottes. When we encounter a mound, it is now customary to infer that it is of Norman origin, and search for adjoining earthworks or documentary evidence — both of which are usually lacking.

The 'castle' at Knox Bridge is unrecorded and is only a very slightly constructed mound — not I feel, very defensible.

Access: The mound stands in fields about ½ mile east of Knox Bridge but a footpath passes close by.
Map Ref. 784407.

LEEDS CASTLE

Without doubt, Leeds is one of the most romantically situated castles in England and quite justified in its claim to be 'the loveliest castle in the world'. Set majestically like a jewel within the girth of its watery moat, it is a sight to behold, a perect fairy-tale castle.

The River Len formed a natural lake in a hollow between the hills here and created two rocky islands, upon which the castle was later built. A third island, partly artificial and partly natural, now forms the barbican in front of the gate-house.

In 857 Ledian, or Led — Chief Minister of Ethelbert IV King of Kent — built a wooden castle on the two islands, connected to each other and to the mainland by drawbridges. Soon after the Norman Conquest, William I gave Leeds Castle to his half-brother Odo, Bishop of Bayeux and Earl of Kent. In 1084 following Odo's exile, William then gave Leeds to his cousin, Hamon de Crevecoeur. At this time the castle was still built in wood.

The castle was first rebuilt in stone in 1119 by Robert de Crevecoeur, who also started the building of nearby Leeds Priory. The priory was once quite extensive and became one of the richest in Kent, intrinsically linked with the castle. Thirty of the de Crevecoeur family were buried there.

The Crevecoeurs were a rebellious family. Hamo de Crevecoeur took part in the barons' revolt against King John in 1215. The family fell in and out of royal favour until finally, during Henry III's reign, Robert de Crevecoeur was forced to hand over Leeds Castle to Sir Roger de Leyburn. Sir Roger was a good friend of Prince Edward (later Edward I) and was generally held in favour by the king.

In 1272 Sir Roger's son, William de Leybourne (Leyburn), gave the castle to the newly crowned king, Edward I. Leeds became a great favourite of Edward and his queen, Eleanor of Castile, and they frequently lived there. Entries in the royal accounts show not only the numerous occasions on which they stayed there, but also the elaborate preparations made for their arrival. Even then the castle had a vineyard, fishponds, gardens and a park. The fountain in the court-yard of the Gloriette is fed from a natural spring in the park. A conduit carries the water, which is fresh and drinkable, into the heart of the fortress.

Edward I not only improved the residential accommodation but greatly enlarged the defences of the castle. He extended the gatehouse — though he left the original Norman arch and did not impose one of his great, characteristic gate-houses — and provided it with machicolations. He also strengthened the Gloriette, or keep. At this time the Gloriette was of one storey only with a small, central courtyard, not unlike a shell keep in appearance.

The most significant change that he made, however, was to add an outer bailey. This he did by encompassing the ground immediately outside the Norman wall on the larger island with a further wall, rising sheer from the waters of the lake.

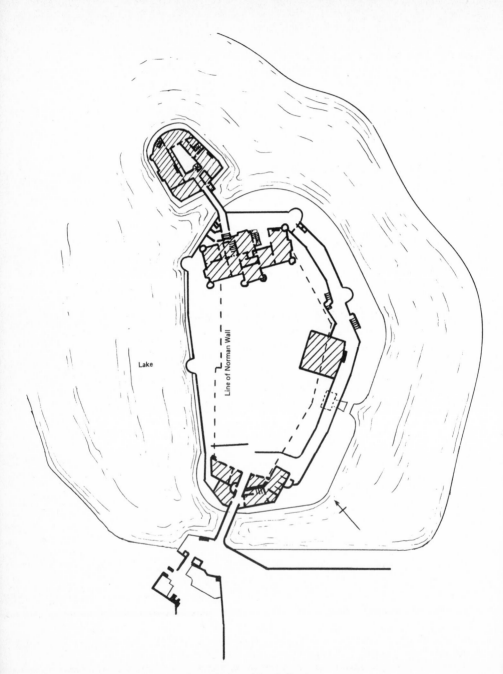

Lake

Line of Norman Wall

Ground plan of Leeds Castle.

He thus created a concentric castle, though not very obvious now because of the removal of much of the original, Norman wall and the lowering of Edward's outer wall and bastions. Originally of course, these would have been much higher than they are at present. Edward I also built the bath-house, now used as a boathouse.

Edward gave the castle as a dower to Eleanor and it subsequently became the possession of most queens of England, earning itself the reputation of being a 'ladies castle'. The queen died young, however, and at Leeds Edward established a charity for her soul in the castle chapel. Edward later remarried taking Margaret, the King of France's sister, as his queen. They honeymooned at Leeds Castle which, as for Eleanor before her, became part of her dower. Edward II temporarily broke the tradition of granting the castle to the queen and gave it instead to Lord Bartholomew de Badlesmere — for reasons not entirely clear.

In 1321 Queen Isabella sought shelter at the castle — it is presumed to test Badlesmere's loyalty — but was refused entry by the castellan. Edward II raised a huge army of 30,000 men and besieged the castle, which eventually fell, and on 1st November of that year the entire Badlesmere family were sent to the Tower of London. Later, Bartholomew Badlesmere was executed and his head displayed on the walls of Canterbury as a warning to others.

Following Edward II's suspicious death in 1327 Queen Isabella installed herself at Leeds, claiming her rights under the dowry. She died in 1358 whereupon Edward III decided to take a hand in further extending and beautifying the castle. He appointed Henry Yevelle, the master mason, in charge of works there. Richard II also favoured Leeds Castle as a royal residence and again bequeathed it to his queen, Anne of Bohemia, in 1382. In 1394 Froissart, the European Historian, stayed at the castle and wrote a praiseworthy account of it in his chronicles. Even then, he refers to Leeds being more of a palace than a fortress.

In 1403 Henry IV gave the castle to his queen, Joan of Navarre. Nine years later she gave it to Thomas Arundel, Archbishop of Canterbury and in 1416 it served as a meeting place for Henry V and Sigismund, the Holy Roman Emperor. They stayed there for a whole month negotiating an alliance. Henry V's wife, Queen Catherine of Valois, was the last queen to personally own Leeds Castle as part of her dower, receiving it in 1423.

There are considerable records and inventories extant of all the royal owners of Leeds, too many and too detailed to mention here, but which do show the very high standard of living enjoyed there.

Henry VIII made considerable changes to Leeds, mostly of a domestic nature. He built the upper storey of the Gloriette and the large Maidens Tower in the middle bailey, and generally updated the castle adding many large, Tudor style windows and internal decorations. He is claimed to have transformed it from a fortress into a palace, but by all accounts, it had already assumed palatial proportions long before his day, as has been noted. Henry VIII granted Leeds Castle to his trusted friend and statesman, Sir Thomas St. Ledger and so, after nearly 300 years of being a royal castle, Leeds passed once more into private ownership.

The St. Ledger's fell upon less fortunate times, however, and were later

The gatehouse of Leeds Castle from a 19th century print.   (Aylesford Galleries)

forced to sell the castle to one of their relatives, Sir Richard Smith. He again sold it to one of his relatives, Sir Thomas Culpepper of nearby Hollingbourne. A later owner, Sir John Culpepper, was granted an enormous area of land, by the exiled King Charles II, in the new colony of Virginia, in America. By marriage, the castle and the entire English and American estates passed to the Fairfax family.

Many Jacobean alterations and additions were made to the castle including many of the outbuildings still standing. The beautifully timbered Fairfax Hall, originally part of the stable block and now used as a restaurant for the visiting public, dates from this time. After much legal wrangling on both sides of the Atlantic, the 6th Lord Fairfax eventually emigrated to Virginia in 1745. He became very successful in his new homeland and was befriended by George Washington.

Most of the Fairfax family resided in America and Leeds Castle, the last remaining part of their English estates, subsequently passed through the female line to the Wykeham-Martins. In 1822 Fiennes Wykeham-Martin spent £30,000 — left by General Martin — on repairing and renovating the castle.

Leeds Castle escaped the usual slighting following the 17th century Civil War, but instead received many Stuart and Jacobean additions. These were swept away by Wykeham-Martin during his rebuilding programme and replaced by the rectangular, mock-Tudor block which today dominates the middle bailey of the castle.

While he has often been criticised for these actions, Fiennes Wykeham-Martin did at least restore the medieval look of Leeds Castle which had for long been lost, hidden beneath later work. He was also responsible for lowering the outer bailey wall and adding many of the 'medieval' embellishments that we see today.

Despite all this rebuilding, however, a great deal of what remains today is original to the castle. Apart from the removal of certain buildings from the middle bailey, most of the 19th century work is confined to the main, rectangular block and even that preserves its original basement. Many writers in the past have mistakenly credited Wykeham-Martin with destroying much of the medieval work, but considerable portions remain. A good many of the embellishments credited to him are really of Tudor date.

In 1926 Lady Baillie (of Anglo-American descent) purchased the castle and at once set about restoring it. Firstly, the outer structure was consolidated and then she turned her attention toward the interiors. It is largely due to her that the internal rooms are once again seen in their medieval splendour. She spent a lifetime filling the castle with antique furniture, paintings and tapestries and redecorated it entirely in keeping with its age and surroundings. Within the castle, however, a great many original features remain, especially the woodwork displaying exquisitely carved floor joists and intricately jointed floorboards.

She bestowed the same care and devotion upon the grounds as on the castle itself, creating many of their most beautiful features — including the Wood Garden, the duckery and water fowl lakes and the waterfalls. She also stocked the grounds with rare birds from all over the world. Many breeds of duck and water fowl inhabit the lakes including a large breeding colony of black swans. The aviaries house pheasants and other exotic breeds of bird while strolling around the grounds are countless peafowl — including some albinos — resplendent in their colourful feathered coats.

During World War II Lady Baillie allowed the castle to be used as a top-level military headquarters and later as a military hospital. After the War she devoted the rest of her life to consolidating the fabric with the express intention of handing it over to posterity. She determined that, on her death, it should be opened to the public and also used to further medical science. So it was that when she died in 1974 the estate was turned into a charitable trust — The Leeds Castle Foundation — one of the patrons of which is Her Royal Highness Princess Alexandra.

The castle today is a haven of peace and tranquillity, a sanctity against the world. Medical seminars, conferences and other functions are held at the castle when it is not open to the public. It is occasionally used by the Government for top-security talks. For some years also, the Bearsted Golf Club have had their

Leeds Castle from across the lake showing the Maiden's Tower on the left and the 19th century block on the right, with the two lines of curtain wall between.

course in the castle grounds. A recent addition to the facilities at Leeds is a museum of dog collars, dating from medieval times.

To even begin to put into words the beauty of the grounds surrounding Leeds Castle (extending to about 500 acres) is an almost impossible task. From the moment you pass through the entrance gates you enter a whole new world. There is a vast, free car park in the outer limits of the grounds, itself a popular picnic spot beneath the shade of mighty oaks, elms and beeches.

A tractor-drawn trailer is on hand to transport the old or infirm the half mile or so to the castle, but for the more able bodied it is worth taking a rather lengthy stroll through the grounds first. Passing down a sunken road to the right, through woodland, you emerge at the banks of an extensive lake, home to many rare ducks, geese and other water fowl. A wooden catwalk carries you across to the other side where you pass smaller water courses and waterfalls.

The Wood Garden confronts you next. It is quite enchanting, mostly left to its wild, natural state but skilfully planted out with daffodils, bluebells, anemones and ferns, and continually bisected by little streams, tributaries of the River Len.

The timber-framed summer house is now used to provide refreshments, the white tables and chairs on the lawn creating a perfectly English scene. If you visit in early summer the scent of rhododendrons and azaleas hangs heavy in the air at this point, the vast banks of flowering shrubs squatting at the far edge of the lawn.

148

Leeds Castle gatehouse. It is of simple design but note
machicolations and recess for drawbridge.

Throughout your approach to the castle you will have seen tantalising glimpses
of the majestic pile through the trees, carefully landscaped to provide breath-
taking vistas. From now on the castle is firmly held in view. Instead of joining
the road at this point and walking up to the castle gatehouse, walk down the
bank to the left, parallel to the crystal clear waters of the River Len which looks
for all the world like a mountain stream as it cascades over the rocks in its path.
From here, climb up through the ruins of the 13th century millhouse (deliberately left so) picturesquely planted out as a wild and rambling rockery.

Next, the castle awaits to be explored. An excellent gift shop is housed in the
stable block adjoining the well preserved gatehouse. It is worth calling in before
venturing down to the waters edge of the outer bailey and entering the castle
proper. Inside the castle visitors are left to wander around the rooms on their
own but guides are stationed in each room to highlight the interesting points.

The castle is still run as an estate and some of the employees actually live in
converted outbuildings. All money raised from the estate and from public

The ruined mill and barbican, Leeds Castle, now a rock garden.

support is ploughed back into the trust. I once had the privilege of working at the castle whilst researching for this book. Though only a brief interlude in my working life, it was certainly a memorable experience. I shall long carry with me the memory of working in such beautiful surroundings.

I must here take advantage of my position as author and pay tribute (as I promised I would) to the happy and hardworking bunch of employees at the castle. Most people are quite unaware of the sheer volume of work involved in opening such a place as Leeds Castle to the public. I salute them all, and all others similarly employed at the many stately homes and castles throughout the land.

At the time of writing, the peace and tranquillity of the castle is threatened by the proposed extension to the M20 motorway — planned to pass right through the grounds, carving it up into two separate pieces and destroying its unique scene forever. It is hoped that the authorities concerned have the foresight to see the folly of such an enterprise.

Access: Open to the public from March to October every Tues., Wed., Thurs., Sun., and Bank Holiday Mondays. 13.00-17.00pm. Separate admission to castle and grounds. Excellent catering, toilet and gift shop facilities. Free car and coach park. Entrance is signposted from A20. Care should be taken on entering and leaving the grounds.
Map Ref. 836534.

LEYBOURNE CASTLE

Leybourne is another of those castles that seems to be a speciality of Kent, standing close to a main thoroughfare yet remaining virtually unknown. Taking the slip road off of the M20 motorway to West Malling, the village of Leybourne nestles quietly among wooded hills. Immediately beside the church and crowning a hill are the remains of Leybourne Castle.

The present castle dates from the 13th and 14th centuries, but the site is much older. William the Conqueror granted the manor of Leybourne to Bishop Odo. When he was dispossessed and his lands confiscated, however, it became crown property and was then granted to Sir William de Arsick. At this point there is a gap in the records and we next find the manor in the possession of the Leybourne family, in the reign of Richard I. It is not certain when its owners adopted the name of the manor for their surname, or indeed, who that family were prior to the adoption.

The present castle occupies only part of a quite extensive series of earthworks. There are only scanty remains of these earthworks now, the central portion of which is a wide, low mound originally a motte and bailey castle. Sir Roger de Leybourne rebuilt the castle in stone in about 1190 and the following year accompanied Richard I to Palestine on crusade.

When he died in 1198 he left a son, another Roger. He had great honours and offices bestowed upon him by Henry III, becoming Warden of the Cinque Ports. The peoples of the Cinque Ports were then openly defying the king, but he brought the seas back under royal control again. Sir Roger also went on crusade, with his great friend Prince Edward (later Edward I). He died whilst in the Holy Land in 1272. There is an interesting story told of him concerning a heart shrine in Leybourne Church.

When a soldier died in a foreign land it was a medieval custom to have his heart embalmed, sealed in a leaden casket and returned to his homeland. When Sir Roger died, his heart was embalmed and returned to England in 1274 by Edward, then king. The following year he visited Leybourne Castle and deposited Sir Roger's heart in the church. A shrine was built around the casket which can still be seen in the parish church — though it has been repositioned. When the casket was opened in the 19th century it was found to contain an embalmed heart.

Sir Roger's son, William inherited Leybourne and, like his father before him, became a trusted friend of Edward I. Edward is known to have stayed at the castle in 1286 on the anniversary of Sir Roger's death. In 1287 Sir William de Leybourne was created the King's Admiral and Constable of Pevensey Castle. Two more of the Leybourne family, Henry and Simon, received honours from Edward I and were knighted for their services at the siege of Caerlaverock Castle in 1300.

Interior of entrance tower, Leybourne Castle.

The hall/chapel block in Leybourne Castle.

Sir William's son, Thomas, died before him leaving no direct heir, so the castle passed to another in the family, John de Leybourne. The last Leybourne to live at the castle was Juliana de Leybourne. She was three times married, first to John de Hastings, then to Thomas le Blount and finally to Sir William de Clinton, of Maxtoke. Each time her husband died without leaving an heir. When she herself died in 1370 there was still no heir to her estates and Leybourne then passed to the crown.

Edward III granted it to his newly founded Cistercian abbey, St. Mary's Graces, in London, who rented it to Sir Simon de Burley — Knight of the Garter and Warden of the Cinque Ports. He was executed for high treason by Richard II and in 1399 it was given back to the abbey, along with Leybourne Church. The castle remained in possession of the abbey until the Dissolution, when it was given to Thomas Cranmer. He later gave it back to Henry VIII and in 1546 it was granted to Sir Edward North, Chancellor.

After that time the castle and estates passed through a long line of owners, finally being converted into a farmhouse. By the late 18th century it belonged to the Hawley's, vicars of Leybourne Church. Later owners were the Golding family, who replaced the farmhouse with a mansion after a disastrous fire there, but it also was later burned down. For a long time the castle and house remained a gaunt ruin. In 1930 the present house was built into the ruins by Walter Godfrey

The modern house built into the remains of Leybourne Castle. Although not castellated, it blends perfectly with the ruins.

153

Leybourne Castle from a 19th century print showing the first house built into the ruins prior to its destruction by fire. (Aylesford Galleries)

and it is now owned by the Harris family. Mrs. Harris informed me that she is continually visited by descendants of the Leybournes from all over the world, tracing their old family home.

The house fits snugly into the castle ruins and blends perfectly with it. The castle was never very substantial, despite the importance of the Leybourne family. Parts of the castle date from the late 12th century, but the remains are chiefly from the 13th and 14th centuries. For a small castle, however, it was provisioned with a large number of buildings in its roughly rectangular courtyard. One of these is substantially intact, though restored, and was probably a hall, but part of it may have been a chapel. It stands on the west side of the courtyard opposite the house.

The principal remains are of the gatehouse, which survives to about two-thirds of its original height. It is notable for the chute over its gateway (as discussed in Part One) which acted as a kind of machicolation, emerging internally in the sill of the large window above the gate. The gate passage was originally vaulted, the corbels supporting the stone roof still remaining and though the original doors have gone, the iron bolts on which they were hung still survive.

The gatehouse contains one more curious feature which I have not encountered anywhere else in Kent. The portcullis groove, instead of connecting to an upper room in the gatehouse to allow the portcullis to slide up into it at first floor level, is here continuous on the outside of the gatehouse. When the portcullis was raised, therefore, it remained on the outside of the castle, passing in front of the window above the gateway. There is an arch high up on the outside wall above the window, supported on corbels, the portcullis running behind it.

The gatehouse is generally very impressive, especially as seen from the road, and has two circular towers astride its gateway. The right hand one of these has an additional lobe-shaped tower attached to it. It is well provisioned with arrow loops — the right hand tower internally consists of a whole row of embrasures with arrow loops about 3'6" long — and is well lighted with large windows.

The modern house stands between the gatehouse and a ruined tower to the south. No attempt was made to castellate the house, which is built in sympathy with, rather than in immitation of, the castle. The curtain wall on the west side of the courtyard was lowered to open up a better prospect from the house. Throughout the castle can be seen the familiar putlog holes — so called — but unlike those at Saltwood, most are inaccessible.

The castle is built of Kentish ragstone with Caen stone dressings around some of the windows and door arches. I also detected the use of megalithic stones in the fabric, which would indicate that a prehistoric stone structure probably once occupied the mound before the castle was built. The Castle, like the one at Stockbury, stands remarkably close to the church and both buildings may once have formed part of the same earthwork.

There are many stories told at most castles of tunnels existing below ground, but most are confined to folk memory alone. At Leybourne, however, the stories can be substantiated for at least two tunnels still survive, believed to have once connected to Leybourne Church and Malling Abbey. One is situated in the ruined tower near the house, but was blocked off when the house was built. The other can be found beneath the right-hand tower of the gatehouse and extends a little distance before it too, becomes blocked.

Some of the locals from Leybourne village and West Malling can still remember picnicking in the castle ruins prior to 1930 and playing in the tunnels. They became unsafe, however, and were later blocked off.

Access: On private land. Not open to the public but the gatehouse and modern house can be clearly seen from the road.
Map Ref. 688589.

LULLINGSTONE CASTLE

To speak nowadays of Lullingstone Castle is a little confusing, for really there are two castles here. The older, original castle is incorporated into a farmhouse about a mile down the road, and now known as Shoreham Castle. What is presently called Lullingstone Castle used, prior to 1738, to be known as Lullingstone Park, but the then owners, the Hart family, transferred the title of 'castle' to it as a kind of status symbol.

In the past this has led to a great deal of confusion among historians, many assuming the present Lullingstone Castle to be built on the site of the ancient castle, and for Shoreham Castle to have always been known as such. Hasted was the first person to draw the distinction between the two. All records referring to Lullingstone Castle prior to 1738, should rightly be applied to Shoreham Castle (see separate entry).

The manor at Lullingstone has origins almost as old as the original Lullingstone Castle itself. It first appears in the Domesday Book (though doubtless it is older still) and soon after became the property of the Rokesle family. The last in the family line, John de Rokesle, died in 1361, the manor then passing to John Peche, Alderman of London. A later descendant of his, another John Peche, was responsible for building the two original brick gatehouses (only one of which survives) and the core of the present house which stands hidden behind the Queen Anne mansion we now see.

Sir John Peche — he was knighted in 1497 at the age of only 24, following his part in the Battle of Blackheath — was a prominent character at Henry VII's Court. In 1494 a Royal Joust was held at Lullingstone, in honour of the king, in the field lying to the west of the gatehouse. Sir John's jousting helmet still hangs above the fireplace in the dining room.

The following year he was appointed Sheriff of Kent and was responsible for delivering the Pretender, Perkin Warbeck to the King in London. Henry VIII also befriended Sir John and the two became great companions, the king staying at Lullingstone whenever he could.

Lullingstone then passed to Sir John's nephew, Sir Percival Hart, who lived to the age of 84 and became Knight Harbinger and Chief Server to no less than four Tudor monarch's — Henry VIII, Edward VI, Mary and Elizabeth I. He died in 1580 but Lullingstone remained in the Hart family until 1738, when Percival Hart died without male issue.

The estate then passed to his daughter, Anne Hart and her husband Sir Thomas Dyke, in whose family it still remains. It was Sir Thomas's son, John Dyke, who pulled down the other great gatehouse and filled in the moat, now the site of the lawn immediately in front of the house. Before he died, however, Percival Hart had added the imposing Queen Anne style facade to the front of

The Tudor brick gatehouse of Lullingstone Castle.

Lullingstone Castle. The Queen Anne facade hides a Tudor manor house.

the house — Queen Anne herself was a frequent visitor — and as noted earlier, transferred to it the title of castle.

The remaining gatehouse was built during Henry VII's reign in 1497 and is believed to be one of the earliest of its type in England. It is a fine structure of three storeys, complete with a row of mock battlements and still preserving a great deal of its original woodwork, particularly the doors and window frames.

The castle is still lived in, the interior displaying a wealth of fine furniture and portraits. Most of the beautiful wood panelling dates from the Queen Anne period, as do the high and very ornate plaster ceilings. Glimpses of the original, stone-built manor house can be seen from the upstairs windows.

The church of St. Botolph — a parish church and not a private chapel — standing on the castle lawn, is a curious structure indeed. It is of Norman origin, rebuilt in the 13th century, but with many 16th and 17th century additions, making it a strange yet oddly fascinating blend of Gothic and Renaissance styles. The castle grounds are pleasant, though not spectacular, situated amidst farmland and with a large reservoir lake to the right of the gatehouse.

Access: Taking a narrow, signed road from Eynsford, you pass beneath a spectacular railway viaduct. At Lullingstone Roman Villa, take another signed, private road to the castle. Open — April to Sept. Wed., Sat., Sun. and Bank Holidays. 2—6pm.
Map Ref. 529644.

158

LYMPNE CASTLE

The history of Lympne Castle dates back to at least Roman times. When the Roman Shore Fort was built on the lower slopes of the cliffs the sea still came in to them. A watch tower was constructed on the high ground now occupied by the castle. It is believed that this watch tower has been incorporated into the present structure — certainly the castle is built from re-used materials from the Roman fort.

The word 'Lympne' itself has an interesting story. It comes from the Celtic word meaning 'elm' and was the original name of the River Rother. The Roman fort, and later the town on top of the cliffs, took its name from the river. Before the Roman fort began to subside the town prospered, but when the Romans left these shores in the 5th century it fell into decline. Within a few centuries the town had shrunk to a small village clustered around its church. Hasted tells us that the church and site of the present castle were inhabited in Saxon times by an order of monks, but that these were disbanded by the Normans sometime after 1085.

The church and manor of Lympne remained in the possession of the Archbishop of Canterbury until Lanfranc gave it to the Archdeaconry. Just as the archbishops built themselves a castle at nearby Saltwood, so the archdeacons erected a small castle, or fortified manor house, at Lympne. This explains why the castle was built so close to the church. Parts of the castle date from Norman times but most of it was rebuilt about 1360 during a lull in the Hundred Years War.

In the Middle Ages the church was not only a large landowner but was also a powerful political force, so it was important for it to contribute to the country's defence. Like most castles, Lympne was built partly for the protection of its inhabitants and partly for national defence. On this exposed and vulnerable stretch of the Kent coast, Lympne Castle was very strategically placed. The castle was never put to the test, however, and seems to have enjoyed a relatively quiet existence.

In later years successive archdeacons added bits to the original core and it developed into quite a substantial house. It became quite a wealthy one too, collecting tithes from the rich farmland in the area around it. In the 18th century it was leased to William Glanville Evelyn and later in the 18th and early 19th centuries, to the Bridger family. By this time the castle was being used as a farm, its buildings suffering greatly as a result. When Archdeacon Croft died in 1860 it passed out of the possession of the Archdeaconry for the first time since the days of William I. It was sold to Major Lawes of Old Park, Dover. He never lived there but leased the castle and farm to a Mr. Stonham.

During the 19th century the great hall had been converted into a two storey house. It was partitioned into a number of separate rooms and a floor inserted

159

Lympne Castle viewed from the garden showing the round tower to the right and the new wing on the left.

The entrance porch and front of the great hall, Lympne Castle.

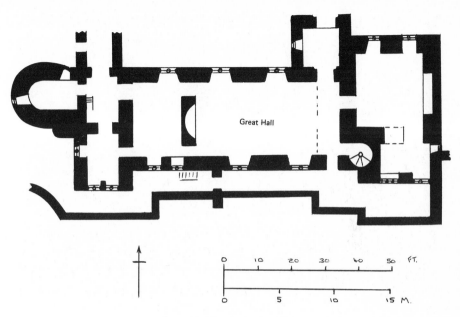

Great Hall

Ground plan of Lympne Castle.

at about half-way up the walls to provide sleeping accommodation above. Many of the outer buildings and much of the surrounding curtain wall had by this time fallen into ruin. In 1905 the castle was bought by Mr. Tennent who immediately set about the task of restoring it. He commissioned the architect Sir Robert Lorimer to carry out the work and also to build a new wing to replace certain of the buildings which once adjoined the present hall-block. The castle is now owned by Mr. Harry Margary.

Lympne Castle played a prominent part in the smuggling activities that were rife in this part of Kent in the 18th and 19th centuries. The castle again saw active service during World War II. Just as the old watch tower had kept guard over the Roman fort for Saxon invaders, in the 1940's an observation post was constructed on top of the east tower to watch for German bombers.

The castle today consists of a hall-block, complete with all its various apartments, with a square tower at its east end and a much larger round, or D-shaped tower at its west end. The new wing to the north occupies much of the old court-yard area. The curtain wall which once surrounded this complex of buildings has largely disappeared, though traces of it can be seen in the gardens on the west side.

Sir Robert Lorimer's restorations were just in time to save the castle from total ruin. The new wing, which he also designed blends well with the older parts of the castle, but his work has one serious flaw. During the restoration work a

161

Lympne Castle and Church in 1829 from a drawing by G. Shepherd.   (Aylesford Galleries)

great many finds were made but not recorded. For example, mention is made of the discovery of a 13th century hall but its position was not marked. Much of this 'evidence' now lies buried beneath the modern wing and is therefore unlikely to come to light again in the foreseeable future. This flaw in Sir Robert's work is a blot in an otherwise praiseworthy restoration programme.

The partitions and false floor were removed from the great hall and the windows provided with tracery. Sir Robert's restorations were so expertly carried out it is hard to tell them apart from the original work. He made good the roof timbers and generally consolidated the fabric. He also inserted windows into certain of the rooms in the two towers and provided them with individual fireplaces. The fireplace in the great hall was restored. Prior to its insertion in 1420 the hall had been heated by a central hearth, similar to the one still in existence at Penshurst Place.

Despite these restorations, there is a great deal of original work at Lympne, especially the timber. The rooms are mostly unfurnished but there are some interesting pieces and a fine collection of pictures, prints and displays. Practically the entire castle is open to view — except the new wing — and it gives a very good impression of life in a medieval house. The great hall of course, is of singular importance and is a fine example.

There is a fascinating arrangement of interconnecting rooms within the castle,

162

some with vaulted ceilings. They are surprisingly large and airy with well placed windows to admit the maximum possible light. Although a number of these windows were inserted by Lorimer, the castle must always have offered comfortable accommodation.

Access can be had to the battlements of the west tower and to the observation post on top of the east tower, now roofed over. The outlook from the top is magnificent, affording a fine, uninterrupted view over Romney Marsh and out to sea. The scattered remains of the Roman fort — Stutfall Castle — can also be made out on the slopes below. From this height it is just possible to discern its original layout. There is a small, pleasant garden to the west of the castle. A footpath leads down the slopes here passing close to the Roman fort, and from it, Lympne Castle looks its most impressive.

The approach to Lympne Castle from the A20 is beautiful. The castle, village and church nestle snugly alongside one another forming a delightful group of medieval buildings. The castle car park is also rather picturesque contained within a clearing in a small patch of woodland.

Access: Take the signed road from A20 just outside Hythe. Open to the public April—October. Suns. 2.30—6.00pm. July—Sept. Daily 10.30—6.00pm. Free car park. Toilets inside Castle.
Map Ref. 119347.

NEWNHAM CASTLE

Newnham is another of those sites shown on the O.S. maps as possessing a motte and bailey castle, but today all that remains is the mound. As with similar mounds, historical evidence is also lacking, so again we must ask whether this was a castle. It may have been another of those mounds of ancient origin which was not converted into a castle, but incorrectly labelled as such on old maps.

Hasted mentions a Newnham Manor, sometimes known as Champyn (or Champion) Court, which seems the most likely candidate if a castle ever did exist there. The owners of this manor took their name from the estate. When Fulk de Newnham died without male issue sometime during Stephen's reign, his daughter Juliana succeeded to the estate. It then passed, by marriage, to Sir Robert de Campania (Champyn or Champion). It remained in that family until the end of the 16th century, after which time it passed through a succession of farming families.

It may well be that what is now shown on O.S. maps as Newnham Castle was originally the site of the first Newnham Manor, which may have been rebuilt on a new site during the Campania's ownership.

Access: On private land. Not open to the public.
Map Ref. 955581.

Mereworth Castle in 1821 from a drawing by I. Hawkesworth.   (Aylesford Galleries)

MEREWORTH CASTLE

So often referred to as a castle in name only, there was in fact a fortified manor house at Mereworth in Norman times. At the time of the Domesday Book, it was owned by Hamon de Crevecoeur (William the Conqueror's cousin and of Leeds Castle fame) and later passed to the Clare family. In Edward II's reign we find reference to a 'Mereworth Castle' and while nothing remains today, its namesake lives on.

The building presently bearing the name castle is in fact, a Palladian style villa, built in 1723 by Colin Campbell for John Fane (who in 1736 became the 7th Earl of Westmorland). It is a direct copy of Palladio's famous villa at Vicenza, Italy — the villa Rotunda — and is generally agreed by most scholars to actually surpass it in magnificence.

It takes the form of a large square with 90ft sides, is 55ft high and surmounted by a huge dome, itself topped off with a latern. A decorative moat, perhaps a remnant of the original manor, once surrounded the house, but it is now filled in.

The entrance lodges now stand on the opposite side of the A26 road to Tonbridge, which road also provides a fascinating glimpse of the house. The countryside all around Mereworth is heavily wooded and right up until the time of Elizabeth I wild boar could be found in abundance.

Access: The house is strictly private, but grounds open from time to time through the year.
Map Ref. 668533.

PENSHURST PLACE

Throughout the gazetteer section of this book I have refrained from including stately homes or manor houses which do not bear the name 'castle'. Space precluded me from mentioning all ancient houses, so a criteria of sorts had to be adopted. So it is that such vast piles as Knole House find themselves excluded because at no time were they fortified or did they resemble castles proper — despite the presence of mock battlements. Penshurst Place, however, finds mention because it represents something of a unique case. It developed from a manor house into a castle in the 14th century, but was later de-fortified, as it were, to convert it back into a house.

A manor house has stood at Penshurst at least since the time of the Domesday Book, but Sir Stephen de Penchester, of Allington Castle, is the first recorded owner. In about 1338 Penchester's son-in-law sold the manor to Sir John de Pulteney, four times Mayor of London. He received a licence to crenellate his manor in 1341 but seems not to have acted upon it. Instead, he built the fine range of 14th century buildings which still form the core of the present house. Pulteney died of the Black Death in 1349 and Penshurst passed to his descendants and those of his widow. One of these was Sir John Devereux, who became Constable of Dover Castle and Warden of the Cinque Ports.

Devereux received a second licence to crenellate in 1392. He surrounded his manor with a strong, rectangular curtain wall with towers at each corner and mid-way along each side — those on the north and south sides being enlarged into small gatehouses. The Garden Tower (the southern gatehouse) survives relatively intact. The north gatehouse and the south-west, north-west and north-east towers may be incorporated into the present building, as are parts of the north and west curtain walls.

The medieval block, consisting of the great hall and its attached apartments, survives almost complete. The south and east curtains and towers have been largely destroyed, while the west and north walls have been replaced by ranges of buildings, built in waves in each of the 15th, 16th, 17th and 19th centuries. The medieval core, once free-standing in the middle of a rectangular defensive enclosure, is now at the centre of a zig-zag shaped stately mansion.

Following the Devereux ownership, Penshurst passed successively in the 15th century to two brothers of Henry V — John, Duke of Bedford and Humphrey, Duke of Gloucester. It then passed to Humphrey Stafford, 1st Duke of Buckingham, but when he fell out of royal favour and was beheaded by Henry VIII in 1521, it passed to the crown. Edward VI gave it to Sir William Sidney. His grandson, Sir Philip Sidney, famed courtier and poet, was born at Penshurst and wrote much of his poetry there.

The house then passed through a succession of notable families, direct descendants of the Sidneys. The Shelleys became owners in the 18th century

The beautiful entrance front of Penshurst Place. The great hall and core of the older manor is in the centre of the picture, with one of the surviving towers of the curtain wall just right of centre.

The 19th century wing of Penshurst Place embodying older work of all periods.

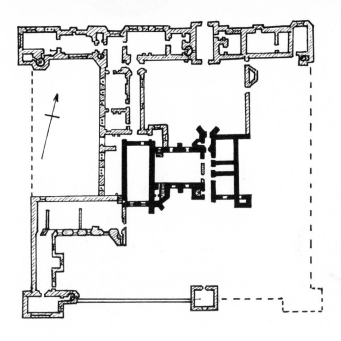

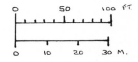

Ground plan of Penshurst Place. The thick black lines show the medieval core. The shaded areas are later additions and the dotted lines represent walls destroyed.

and in 1816, John Shelley began to restore Penshurst, which had been neglected for many years. John's elder son, Philip Charles, was created Lord De L'Isle and Dudley in 1835. Penshurst is still owned and lived in by the Sidneys (William Sidney, Viscount De L'Isle, and his family) who continue to bestow their care upon its fabric.

The hall-block at Penshurst is one of the finest medieval halls in Europe to survive the centuries, showing precisely the layout of the medieval domestic buildings and is in an excellent state of preservation. It shows also, high degrees of craftsmanship both in its stone and woodwork. Its beautifully timbered roof is original and is made of chestnut, instead of the more traditional oak. It did not have a fireplace but was heated by a central open hearth, the smoke from which escaped through a louvre in the ceiling.

Penshurst Place is built mostly from a beautiful pale cream coloured sandstone, flecked with bands of brownish/red stains of iron, but with some Tudor

Penshurst 'Castle' in 1812 from a drawing by Loch.   (Aylesford Galleries)

brick extensions. The stonework is generally in very good condition, clean and undamaged, and showing few signs of weathering. There is a great deal to see including, the great hall itself, its solar and attached apartments and most of the state rooms with their splendid furniture and paintings. The whole house carries with it a warm, bright and friendly atmosphere. A small armoury is housed within the solar undercroft and a toy museum in one of the buildings in the stable yard.

The grounds are partly formal and laid out in typical Tudor fashion, consisting of a series of walled gardens, and partly parkland. They are very extensive and quite delightful. A recent addition to the attractions at Penshurst is a venture playground — sufficiently removed from the house, however, so as not to detract from its atmosphere. The approach to the house through the village is enchanting, typical 'picture book' England.

Access: Open to the public April 14th to October 1st. Daily (except Mon. and Fri.) 2.00—6.00pm. Ample free parking. Excellent gift shop, refreshment and toilet facilities.
Map Ref. 528440.

QUEENBOROUGH CASTLE

Few people today are aware that Queenborough, on the Isle of Sheppey, once possessed a remarkable medieval castle. It stood in the field adjacent to the railway station, the only trace now being its large, circular mound and a few scraps of stone hidden amongst the hedges on its northern and eastern boundaries.

Part of the site has been sliced off by the nearby railway sidings yard and its north-west corner lies beneath a school playground, but otherwise the earthworks remain in good condition — if unspectacular. In dry weather, due to the hindrance of buried stone foundations to drainage and to crop and grass roots, the ground plan of the castle shows up in outline. This is particularly noticeable from the air and in aerial photographs.

The mound at Queenborough is almost certainly of prehistoric date, though not originally, I believe, of a defensive nature. The Saxons are thought to have had a settlement here also, but there is no substantiating proof — nor is there likely to be until the long overdue excavation of the site has been carried out. No castle, or manor house, however, stood on the site until the reign of Edward III. Most other castles occupy the sites of already existing manor houses. The design of the castle may have been dictated by the limitations of its site or the presence of the earlier earthworks, but there may also have been other influences, as we shall see.

Queenborough Castle represents something of a puzzle, no-one quite knowing why Edward chose to build it precisely where he did, why it should have taken such an unusual form and finally, why it should have been totally destroyed. Ironically, though little actual masonry survives, there is a wealth of documentation relating to the castle, largely because it remained, throughout its existence, a royal castle. It is fully documented in the various exchequer accounts and records, particularly the Calendar and Pipe Rolls.

In 1361, during a lull in the Hundred Years War, work on the castle commenced and by 1368 the central block — the keep, or rotunda — was complete. The rest of the castle and most of the interior decorations were largely complete by 1377. Edward visited the site himself in 1363 and from 1365 onwards the building accounts also include expenditure to the 'new' town at Queenborough.

Prior to Edward's interest in the area it was a tiny fishing hamlet known as Bynee, but he renamed it 'Queenborough' in honour of his queen — Phillipa of Hanuilt. He rebuilt the church there, adding a new chancel to the existing Norman tower. The town never grew, however, and after Edward III's death it soon fell into decline. It was never considered important enough to have its own town wall — somewhat strange considering that many other towns received defensive walls at this time.

In 1365 John de Foxley was appointed as the first Constable of the castle, before even the central rotunda was finished, and in 1368 the Wool Staple (a

Queenborough Castle as it probably appeared prior to its destruction, from a print by S. Hooper 1784. (C.F. Hansford)

port through which all wool exports had to pass) was moved to Queenborough from Sandwich. A sack of wool weighed about 300lb and it is possible that the winching gear installed to lift the stone and other building materials ashore from the cargo ships, may have been used to reload them with wool. The River Swale also once connected to the Wantsum Channel, which was then navigable, so perhaps this was the reason for Edward's hurried attempts at making Queenborough ready and endowing it with some importance. The castle was then much nearer to the sea and all the goods arriving or leaving by water were loaded at a small dock, under the watchful eye of the castle.

From a very early date Queenborough was provided with many features which would indicate that its occupants enjoyed a high standard of living. The castle is known to have had a garden and a fishpond, and in 1368 Fulk de Peyforer, then Clerk of Works, is recorded as having bought seeds to be sown there. Towards the end of the same year a clock was installed in one of the towers. It was a mechanical, weight-driven clock (one of the earliest known) and attached to it was a large bell. There was also a smaller clock in the castle chapel. The plumbing arrangements are believed to have been quite extensive too, for large amounts of lead conduit piping constantly appear in the castle records.

William of Wykeham, Edward III's renowned administrator, was Clerk of Works at Queenborough between 1361-62 and John Box was the Master Mason.

It would appear that, although often credited with its design, Henry Yevelle had nothing whatever to do with Queenborough, John Box being almost wholly responsible for its construction — until his death in 1376. That Queenborough was at least partly intended to repel a French attack, there can be little doubt, for in 1377 its year of completion, the castle was immediately put on a defensive footing. John de Foxley was commissioned to strongly arm the castle against a possible hostile invasion from the French — an invasion which fortunately, never materialised.

Queenborough became a great favourite of Edward III. He visited the castle on many occasions and issued numerous letters patent from within its walls, most of which are still in existence at the Public Record Office. In 1409 Thomas Arundel, Archbishop of Canterbury, was granted custody of the castle, though it remained a royal fortress, and for a while became one of his chain of palaces.

Henry VIII stayed there on occasions and modified its defences to the artillery of the day. It was again refortified by Elizabeth I. The existing plan of the castle dates from Tudor times, but it is not known how much of the castle, as then shown, was the result of Tudor alterations and how much of it was original medieval work.

Queenborough has found itself at the centre of a controversy in recent years. It is not known whether the castle was built for defence by the gun from the start, or if such defences were later additions. Perhaps inspired by the similarity in plan between Deal and Queenborough, some authorities suggest that this castle was the forerunner of the Henrician artillery forts constructed nearly 200 years after Queenborough. Personally, I believe Queenborough was designed primarily for defence by the bow but that its shape lent itself perfectly for easy, and early, adaption to defence by the gun. Queenborough is not as unique as is generally supposed, however. A similar structure was built in Majorca in 1310 and it also bears close resemblance to Castel del Monte in Italy.

Whatever the truth, the castle was certainly equipped with cannon at a very early date. In the Warderobe Account of 1365 there are references to nine hand guns and two larger guns being made at the Tower of London workshops for delivery to Queenborough.

Cannon, especially the early examples, did not become viable weapons in their own right until the late 15th and early 16th centuries, the traditional medieval siege engines being generally more powerful. Such early provision for guns in castles was usually for small hand guns set in suitably adapted, key-hole shaped loops in the walls, replacing the traditional arrow loops. If Queenborough was designed with guns in mind then it was probably these key-hole type gun loops that were provided, similar to the slightly later ones at Cooling and the West Gate, Canterbury.

Queenborough Castle represents the ultimate in concentricity, based entirely on a circular plan. Its central portion, the rotunda, was almost like a giant shell keep consisting of a central, circular courtyard surrounded by two concentric walls of great height. The space between these walls was divided by straight

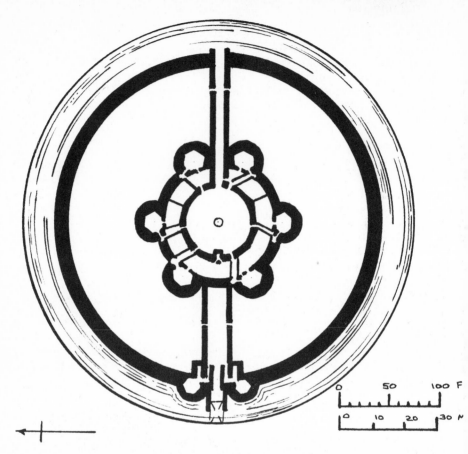

Ground plan of Queenborough Castle, representing the ultimate in concentric fortification.

'spokes' into a number of spacious – and by all accounts, sumptuously appointed – rooms. The outer one of these two walls was provisioned with six large, circular towers, four spaced equidistantly with the remaining two, on the east side, drawn together to form the inner gatehouse.

Completely surrounding the central block was another circular wall, creating an outer bailey. This wall was entirely plain, except for the interruption on its west side for the outer gatehouse. There was a well in the centre of the inner courtyard, which still survives though covered over, and a wet moat encircled the entire castle.

The most singularly outstanding feature of the castle was the entrance path, brilliantly contrived so as to leave an attacker exposed to fire throughout his approach. A glance at the plan will show that the outer gatehouse is situated on the opposite side of the castle to the inner gatehouse. Two sets of parallel walls — creating in effect, internal barbicans — ran from the outer gatehouse and the postern gate, on the east side of the outer curtain, to the rotunda.

An attacker seeking entry to the castle had to first pass through the outer gatehouse into the passageway on the western side. He was then forced to make a circuit of half the outer bailey to the passageway on the eastern side, which in turn gave access to the inner gatehouse and rotunda. Throughout his course of entry an attacker would be under fire from both the inner and outer curtain walls, the wall-walks of the two barbican passageways and also from the towers and two gatehouses — almost an impossible task, one would think.

The outer wall was much thicker than the inner one and also much lower. This meant that covering fire from both walls could be brought to bear at the same time, defenders on the inner wall firing over the heads of those on the outer wall. The six towers of the rotunda and the two of the outer gatehouse were all circular in exterior plan, but were provisioned with hexagonal shaped interior rooms. Each tower had a separate entrance passage directly accessible from the inner courtyard, as well as a door to the adjoining rooms of the rotunda.

It is a great pity that none of its structure has survived for it must have been a remarkable castle in its day. Aerial photographs reveal that the plan shown here is accurate. Queenborough Castle was built at a time when medieval castles were going into decline and represents the pinnacle of castle design — after which a new, less sophisticated era was entered.

The castle was held by the Royalists during the Civil War and in 1648 it was seized by Parliament. A survey of that year (still extant) recommended that the castle be pulled down. It was sold in 1650 to a Mr. John Wilkinson for £1792.12s.0½d. He pulled most of it down and sold off the materials. It was long thought that Parliament ordered the total destruction of the castle, but that was not so. It suffered the usual 'slighting' but most of the damage was caused by the local inhabitants and its later owners who, piece by piece, removed its fabric to sell or re-use in new buildings. Some of the castle timber was used to restore the belfry in the church tower.

Parts of the castle were still standing as late as 1807 for a Henry Seger purchased the barn, stable and coach house in that year. A pump house was installed over the well by the railway company but today, that too has disappeared. Considering its former magnificence, it is sad now to visit the insignificant mound that marks its site.

Ironically, seventeen years after the castle was demolished, it was badly missed when the Dutch fleet sailed up the River Medway and laid waste the English fleet anchored at Chatham. The Dutch landed at Queenborough en route and sacked the town.

Access: Freely accessible, immediately beside Queenborough Station.
         Map Ref. 913722.

RATS CASTLES

Scattered around the English countryside are various placenames called 'cold-harbours'. They take various forms, sometimes ancient earthworks, sometimes Roman ruins, while at other times no physical trace remains. The word is thought to be of Celtic origin and means 'a rough shelter', ie. a temporary, overnight shelter for travellers along a road or track.

The term 'Rats Castle' is thought to have a similar derivation referring, not to a castle in the usual sense of the word, but to a rough shelter along an ancient track. This further use of the word 'castle' has led to considerable confusion amongst historians, and as such, is further proof of the ancient origins of the term.

Rats Castles usually bear no traces of defensive earthworks. So far I have located three such sites in Kent, but there may well be others. While no earthworks remain — if indeed they ever existed — at each of the sites today, they all continue to bear the name, Rats Castle.

Access: In view of the above comments it was thought best not to list each Rats Castle separately, especially so since no visible or written evidence survives relating to any of them. The map references are given below, but the sites are extremely difficult to locate.
Map Refs. 627534 (near Mereworth), 612466 (near Tonbridge), 815417 (near Frittenden).

RECULVER ROMAN FORT

The famous ruins of Reculver Church stand as sentinels to shipping, perilously close to the cliff edge — a fate which has overtaken the neighbouring Roman fort, for about half of its structure has been claimed by the sea. Beside the church, which stands within the precincts of the fort, is a flat expanse of grass. This is what remains of the floor area within the fort.

No masonry exists at this level and to see the remains of the walls — of which considerable lengths still survive to a height of about 10ft — it is necessary to walk across to the nearby caravan park. From here a path skirts around the perimeter of the fort showing clearly the core of the foundations and lower levels of the walls. There are also some remains behind the public house which occupies the south-west corner of the fort near the sea-front.

Reculver Fort (or Regulbium to give its Roman name) was first built in the early years of the 3rd century and later remodelled and adapted in about 280 for use as a 'Fort of the Saxon Shore'. It was originally built to protect shipping at the western mouth of the Wantsum Channel — which was then a major shipping route and made the Isle of Thanet a true island.

174

The twin towers of Reculver Church standing within the Roman fort.

It was later used either to keep the early Saxon invaders at bay or to repel an attack on the rebellious Carausius from Rome itself — it is not known which. For further discussion on this point see the separate entry for Richborough Castle. For a while the fort was deserted but it was re-garrisoned between 340-370 during the renewed Saxon raids.

The fort dates from about the year 210 and is in fact older than the existing fort at Richborough, scene in AD43 of the landing of Aulus Plautius. It was roughly square with sides approximately 200 yards in length and was of very simple construction. It had no wall towers, the corners merely being rounded off, and no lacing courses of stone or brick in its flint rubble walls. The fort stood on the cliffs, at this point fairly low in profile, and was connected to a small harbour on the beach below, now alas, covered by the sea.

Excavations carried out by Roach Smith in the early 19th century revealed the walls at Reculver to be 10ft thick at the base rising in offsets to 8ft at the top. They were further protected by a defensive ditch and an earthen rampart. Parts of the east and south walls, and the corner that connects them, still survive and also a small length of the west wall. Much of its fabric has been pillaged through the centuries for building material.

Reculver Church was founded in about 669 by Egbert, King of Kent. It was largely rebuilt during the 12th century, however, when the twin towers were added to its west end. The ruins today are largely from this period. Cliff sub-sidence has caused severe damage to the church (and fort) and, coupled with

175

Part of the once massive walls of Reculver Roman fort.

other more suspicious reasons, caused it to be pulled down in 1809. The two towers, known as the Two Sisters, were preserved by Trinity House and have long been used as navigational landmarks by seamen.

A pitiful story has long been attached to Reculver fort that recent excavation has shown to have some basis in fact — but which makes it all the more uncanny. For many centuries there has been a local tradition at Reculver that the sound of babies' cries could be heard coming from the submerged part of the fort. Like most ghost stories it was dismissed as being mere folklore, but excavations uncovered the skeletons of a number of babies.

Human sacrifices are known to have been carried out at some other ancient sites for unknown ritual purposes, but history is silent about the circumstances surrounding these pitiful corpses. There may of course be quite a rational explanation — but that does not explain the cries long claimed to be heard by locals.

Reculver today is a small sea-side hamlet nestling peacefully between a fold in the cliffs which, a little further along the coast, are quite spectacular.

Access: Take signed road from A299 to Reculver. The fort and church ruins are maintained by the Department of the Environment. Open at all times.
Map Ref. 227694.

RICHBOROUGH CASTLE

The site of Richborough Castle is synonymous with the Roman invasion of Britain. Caesar's preliminary campaign of 55BC was followed by a lull of some 88 years before the invasion was begun in earnest. In AD43 Claudius sanctioned the official Roman invasion of Britain and sent four complete legions, with their auxiliaries, under Aulus Plautius. They landed at what is now Richborough, but then it looked very different. In Roman times the Isle of Thanet really was an island, separated from mainland Kent by the wide Wantsum Channel.

The Romans called the place Rutupiae and made a settlement there (though there is evidence of an Iron Age settlement of about 300BC) and it very soon developed into a supply depot and port. Richborough itself stood on a small island jutting out into the mouth of the Wantsum. A number of buildings were erected including a small civilian settlement, but at this time they were all constructed of timber. A main road was directed into the heart of the settlement, which later came to be known as Watling Street.

In about AD85 most of the timber buildings were swept away and a huge triumphal monument to commemorate the invasion of Britain was erected. It was encased in marble and furnished with fine bronze statuary. The foundations still survive, as do small traces of the marble and statuary, now on display in the museum on the site.

For a long time, however, Richborough was not a prime military base. It was not until the second half of the 3rd century that it received a fort. It was an earth and timber fort of considerable size and was provisioned with triple ditches — now excavated and exposed within the boundaries of the present fort.

Towards the end of the 3rd century the massive walls of the fort we now see were constructed, the earthworks of its predecessor being filled in. It is one of a chain of at least nine, possibly eleven forts stretching from Brancaster in Norfolk to Portchester in Hampshire, and known collectively as the 'Forts of the Saxon Shore'. Of these, no less than four are to be found in Kent, though in varying states of preservation. The other three were at Reculver (positioned at the western end of the Wantsum Channel), Stutfall and Dover.

Richborough, like most of the other forts, was built during the time of Carausius (AD287-293) who set himself up as Emperor of Britain. From that time until the Roman evacuation of Britain around AD410, the fort was used increasingly more by the military and as a port of arrival — perhaps also as the main port of embarkation when the Romans departed from these shores. Excavations made between 1922-30 by J.P. Bushe-Fox revealed intensive occupation during the late 4th and early 5th centuries.

There is now considerable dispute among historians as to why this chain of forts was erected. Officially they were built to repel Saxon invaders and were put in charge of a single official — the 'Count of the Saxon Shore'. In 1961,

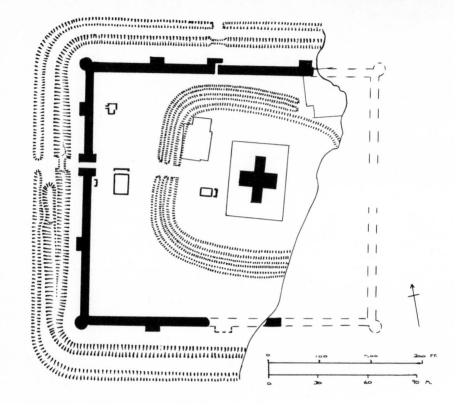

Ground plan of Richborough Castle, showing the earthworks of the present Roman fort and its predecessor.

however, an American scholar, Donald A. White, after years of patient research collecting evidence, suggested an alternative view.

It is now generally accepted that the Romans were as much influenced by the native British culture as the Britains were by that of the Romans. Indeed, in many respects, the Roman invasion was a retrograde step and not so influential as is often acclaimed. There is much evidence to suggest that the Romans within Britain tended to favour more the British way of life than the Roman. Unlike most other provinces of the Empire, Britain never did subject itself entirely to Roman rule. Carausius himself was of Belgic descent and therefore had closer ties with the Celts of Britain than with the Romans.

Carausius was placed in charge of Britain by Diocletian, to protect the seas from pirate attacks. In 286 Diocletian was forced to delegate his authority because the Empire had overstretched itself and he appointed Maximian, a soldier, to rule with him. At this time, the Roman historians tell us, Carausius mis-used his authority and set himself up as Emperor of Britain in defiance of Rome.

The official historians were very biased in their approach, however, and we can be sure that there was very much more involved than simply a mis-use of power. At any rate, Mr. White feels certain that Carausius, fearing a reprisal from Maximian and the Emperor, built the chain of 'Shore Forts' not to keep the Saxons out but to protect himself and his followers against a re-invasion from Rome itself.

Carausius was murdered by his Chief of Finance, Allectus, who then proclaimed himself Emperor in his place. In 293 Emperor Constantius Chlorus and Maximian skilfully launched an attack on Britain landing somewhere in Hampshire. Attacking from the landward side, the forts were more or less rendered ineffective since they had been designed specifically to defend the coast. Britain was thus again embraced by the Empire. After this the chain of forts were probably re-deployed to protect Britain's shores against the Saxons, whose attacks were now intensified.

A mere century and a quarter later, however, the Romans gave up this western outpost of their Empire to protect Rome itself from attack. Mr. White's theory is very convincing, particularly when it is realised that at the time of the forts' construction the Saxon raids were not of sufficient strength to warrant such defences. After the defeat of Allectus, Richborough became the most important

The walls of Richborough Castle still stand to a height of 25 ft in places. They consist of a flint rubble core with bonding courses of brick and chalk blocks, faced with ragstone.

fort in the chain and it is from there that most attacks against the Saxons were commanded in later years.

The fort today is extremely impressive covering an area of about five acres, its massive walls slumbering in the marshland near Sandwich. A little over half of the outer walls remain (the eastern and parts of the northern and southern walls having fallen) and still stand in places to 25ft, almost their full height.

They are massively constructed of a solid, flint rubble core with lacing courses of tiles at intervals. They were originally encased in blocks of squared, dressed stone, still evident in many places particularly on the outer face of the north wall. The use of these different materials creates many interesting patterns on the wall faces.

Like most other Roman forts, the walls contain no mural chambers, window openings or embrasures within their thickness (which varies between 12ft—13ft), all the buildings within the fort being free-standing and arranged in the usual grid pattern. In the north wall is a most interesting right-angled postern constructed in the thickness of one of the wall towers. The corner towers were round while those spaced along the walls were rectangular, with two guarding the main entrance on the west wall.

There are considerable remains at Richborough from all periods of its con-

Core of the Roman wall, Richborough Castle.

struction. Particularly impressive are the triple banks and ditches of the earlier fort and the double ramparts of the present fort. It is easy to underestimate the effectiveness of castle earthworks, particularly when looking at plans, but in fact they must have presented as daunting an obstacle to attackers as the walls themselves. One has to actually stand on the embankments to fully appreciate how powerful they really were. The visual impression of earthworks such as those at Richborough is most dramatic.

The approach to Richborough today from Sandwich is rather unglamorous. Firstly you cross marshland, then pass through a stretch of ugly industrial land, but then happily, revert back to marshland again. The massive cooling towers of the nearby power station loom up on the horizon, dwarfing the fort and somewhat distorting the perspective. Nevertheless, Richborough Castle is extremely impressive and will no doubt still be standing when the power station has long since fallen. About ½ mile south of the fort is an amphitheatre, open to view at all times.

Access: Department of the Environment. Open standard hours. Free car park.
Small museum on site.
Map Ref. 324603.

Part of the impressive ramparts and ditches of Richborough Castle.

ROCHESTER CASTLE

I must confess a certain bias towards Rochester Castle, it being responsible for first invoking my interest in the study of castles. Impressive from every approach, it possesses one of the finest original keeps in Europe. Such keeps as those at Dover and the Tower of London only have a better appearance today because of their long histories of careful maintenance and preservation. Its keep is also the tallest in England and only France has a comparable structure on the Continent.

The city of Rochester has a long history stretching back into prehistory. The Romans called it Durobrivae and the Saxons knew it as Hrofesceaster. The first castle built at Rochester was erected, not inside the protection of the Roman city walls, but on the prehistoric mound known as Boley Hill, immediately to the south. Evidence of the antiquity of this mound can still be seen today in the three large megalithic stones now resting on the lower slopes of the hill, but which in all probability were originally on top. This provides us with perhaps the most important piece of visible evidence to prove the prehistoric origins of most castle sites.

The Normans chose not to refortify the Roman walls of the city but instead erected a motte and bailey castle on the existing mound. They probably used it as a base from which to attack and subdue the city. Later, when time and a more settled environment allowed, they moved their castle to within the safety of the city walls, using the wall itself to form two sides of the bailey wall. The first castle had been built entirely from wood and was first mentioned in 1086 in the Domesday Book.

The growing strategic importance of Rochester, guarding the crossing of the London Road (Watling Street) over the River Medway, soon warranted the erection of a stronger stone castle. William II ordered a new castle to be built within the first year of his reign. Work probably commenced sometime in 1088 and Gundulph, Bishop of Rochester, was put in charge of its construction. He was also responsible for building St. Leonard's Tower at West Malling and the square, defensive tower attached to Rochester Cathedral.

Gundulph's castle was a simple, single enclosure which had a levelled courtyard and foundations of rammed gravel, with possibly one stone mural tower in the circuit of walls, for one of the 14th century towers opposite the Cathedral stands on similar foundations. Little of Gundulph's work remains today, but enough survives to show that the line of the present wall is the same as he originally built it. The broken end of the Esplanade wall, on the river side of the castle, also reveals signs of the original Roman city wall as well as the repairs and extensions of Saxon and Norman times. Another portion of Gundulph's curtain wall survives as the garden wall of houses on Castle Hill, now separated from the castle by a road. This wall is one of the earliest castle walls to be built in stone after the Norman Conquest.

183

Rochester Castle as it appeared in 1828 from a drawing by H. Gastineau.

(Aylesford Galleries)

The first of the major alterations and repairs to Gundulph's wall (excluding the building of the keep itself) came in the 13th century as a result of the damage caused in a siege of 1215 when a cylindrical, backless drum tower was inserted in the south-east corner of the curtain. This angle of the keep was also rebuilt on a half-cylindrical plan for the same reason.

All of the other towers in the curtain wall were begun, or rebuilt, sometime after 1360 during Edward III's reign, when almost every castle in the land was put in a defensible condition in response to the French threat. Two rectangular mural towers were built at this time on the town side of the castle. The southernmost one is minus its floors, roof and battlements. The other tower, however, is a fine specimen and is more-or-less intact. It still retains a beautiful vaulted ceiling of the 14th century (a rare survival in wall towers) and an original spiral staircase.

On the Esplanade wall of the castle, at the northern extremity, are the remains of what was once Edward III's Water Gate and postern. Practically none of its details have survived to the present day unfortunately, so its original appearance can only be surmised. It is generally thought to have been a low bastion protected by two cylindrical or rectangular towers with steps leading down to the river. In those times the river washed the walls of the castle and formed part of its defensive system, also feeding its moat. The mock-Norman archway and steps cut through the foundations were inserted during restoration work at the castle in the late 19th century.

The main entrance to the castle was a gatehouse at the end of Castle Street, but this was completely destroyed during the 18th and 19th centuries. It is now marked approximately by iron gates and was, by all accounts, a fine structure. A third gate may have existed in the south wall, probably a postern. A fourth tower may also have existed in the curtain wall between the gatehouse and the water gate, but no evidence, except in its presence on a model in Rochester Museum, exists today.

On the Esplanade wall ranging from the water gate to the crosswall of the bailey (erected in front of the keep in 1230-31 bisecting the bailey in two) was a fine array of domestic buildings. They were mostly of Henry III's time, but were improved during the 14th century. Traces of these grand apartments can still be seen where they adjoined the curtain wall from both within and without the castle. The wall top here, incidentally, is over 50ft to the road below. There were no towers along this stretch of wall. The ground level inside the castle is considerably higher than that outside so the roofs of the domestic range of buildings served as a fighting platform, the wall top rising above the general level elsewhere in the castle to accommodate them.

In a charter of Henry I's reign permission was granted for the building of a great tower. This was in 1127 (one of the few keeps to have a definite date fixed to it) and Archbishop William de Corbeil was placed in charge of its building. It was completed in or about the year 1139 and thereafter for some time became one of England's strongest and most important fortresses.

While the keep is the tallest in England, there is a slight discrepancy in its actual dimensions. It is frequently stated to be 125ft high to the copings of the battlements on the four corner turrets. From the tops of the turrets to ground level inside the keep, it is indeed 125ft, but the floor level here is not the original level and was excavated during the 19th century to find the depth of foundation. Not all of the earth removed was replaced so the ground level outside the keep is now considerably higher than that inside. The external height of the keep to the courtyard level is actually about 113ft.

I believe the discrepancy first arose when someone stated the height of the keep to be 113ft and then added on another 12ft to the tops of the turrets, when in fact it had already been included and represented the total height of the keep. The height to the copings of the battlements of the keep, excluding the turrets, is about 101ft.

Externally the keep measures 70ft square at the base, which is slightly battered and is therefore a little less at the top. The walls average between 11ft and 13ft thick. They are built of Kentish ragstone rubble with Caen stone dressings. About midway along each side are pilaster buttresses for added strength, and also at the corners where they are continued above the roof level to form the four turrets. It was one of the first keeps to be built with a forebuilding. It is a fine specimen about 28ft wide by 14ft deep and rises a full two-thirds of the height of the north wall of the keep.

Both the present and the original entrances to the keep are housed in this forebuilding, the modern doorway being hacked through during the 19th century restorations. Immediately inside is a wooden platform bridging the vaulted lower basement of the forebuilding. Formerly called a dungeon, it was probably a cess

185

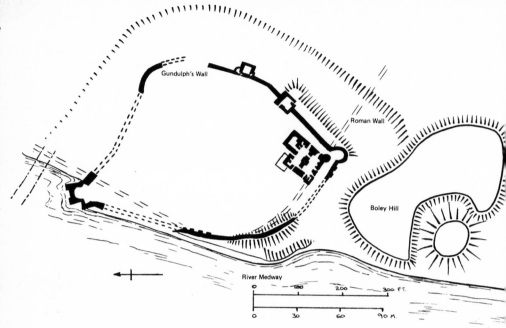

Ground plan of Rochester Castle showing the present castle and the site of the earlier motte and bailey on Boley Hill.

pit, for a latrine shaft from the upper storeys empties into it. It may have been used as a dungeon from time to time, but it is doubtful if it was designed as such. The floor above was probably a storeroom, while a chapel occupied the top level. The original entrance was on the first floor. A portcullis separated the keep itself from the forebuilding, its grooves still clearly visible inside the keep. Most of the entrance path, which was open to fire the whole time, still remains substantially intact.

Internally the keep is of four storeys and is divided into two nearly equal sections by a cross-wall, running east to west, and rising the full height of the tower. Through the centre of this cross-wall runs a tidal well which, unlike most of its kind, connects with every floor of the keep. The shaft links to an underground stream fed from the river.

At basement level of the keep a short flight of steps in the north wall descends to the lower basement of the forebuilding (the present entrance) and also at this level, a passageway gives access to the ground floor room of the forebuilding. A wooden platform bridges the basement of the keep itself, passing through a small, plain doorway in the cross-wall to the southern side of the tower. Although, sadly, it is roofless and without floors (though the joist holes for the floor timbers can be clearly seen at each level), the opportunity is provided to take in the entire interior of the keep at a single glance.

186

A spiral staircase in the north-east corner ascends from the basement, the full height of the keep. Another stair, now ruined, in the south-west corner starts from first floor level and also climbs to the battlements. The north-east stair is complete and provides a marvellous view of the interior arrangements. Especially fine are the Norman mouldings around the window, door and fireplace arches, principally of the chevron, zig-zag and roll and hollow orders. The lower windows are, for reasons of defence, small but deeply splayed internally.

The basement level of the keep was used mainly for storage and the first floor used by the domestic staff. A postern in the north-east corner connected, via a wooden bridge, directly to the wall walk of the curtain wall. There are no fireplaces at basement level but each of the three principal floors was provided with two — the first floor had an additional fireplace in the guardroom known as Gundulph's Chamber. Each fireplace was about 6ft wide and high with a rounded back, and connected to a flue which passed through the thickness of the wall to emerge at the pilaster buttresses mid-way along the south and north walls. The keep is exceptionally well provided with latrines, mural chambers, galleries and windows, all contained within the immense thickness of the walls.

The second floor of the keep contained the state apartments and was really two stages thrown into one for added light and spaciousness. The cross-wall is at all stages pierced by doorways, but here it is broken by four huge arches (about 18ft high and dressed in fine Caen stone) each arch of a different span and each column of a different size.

Rochester Castle keep from the bailey.

187

A barrel-vaulted gallery completely encircles this floor of the keep at the level of the upper windows, connecting with both staircases. It is not entirely certain what the original function of these galleries was. The windows opening from them certainly provided more light and they also provided an extra fighting platform. Domestic servants or retainers could also traverse the keep without disturbing those in the great hall below. The gallery at Rochester certainly provides the visitor with an added vantage point today.

The level of decoration is especially fine on this floor of the keep, except in the south-east corner where the repairs following the siege of 1215 were carried out. Although in harmony with the general Norman style, the repairs have been crudely executed with no real attempt at decoration. In the southern half of the keep on the third floor are two blocked arches — one originally a window of the upper chapel — and no attempt has been made to blend the repair work in, or for that matter, to entirely remove the damaged portions. It is curious to note also that, in the south-eastern corner of the third floor, no provision has been made for joist holes in the repaired wall to carry the floor.

From the battlements the disposition of the entire castle can be made out, as well as affording a magnificent view over the city and surrounding countryside. We are fortunate at Rochester also, in being able to see quite clearly the holes cut into the parapet wall to carry the joists for a timber hoarding.

Unlike most other castles, Rochester has been the scene of at least three memorable sieges. The first castle at Rochester, the motte and bailey on Boley

Rochester Castle bailey from top of keep. The windows and arches in curtain wall are of Henry III's range of buildings.

Hill, was part of Bishop Odo's Kentish estates. Odo, who had been banished from England in 1082, was later reinstated, and in 1087 when William Rufus came to the throne, Odo supported Robert, Duke of Normandy and William's elder brother. Events eventually led to the king laying siege to Rochester Castle in 1088, which surrendered without offering too much opposition. Afterwards Rufus, William II, ordered the building of a new stone castle, which was the one Gundulph began in 1088. Sometime between the building of the keep in 1127 and the second siege of the castle, Rochester reverted to crown ownership and was held for the king by a constable.

The second and most memorable siege of 1215 is now regarded as one of the most important feats in English military history. John's was a troubled reign and in 1215, the year before his death, many of his barons, still angered even after the signing of Magna Carta, rebelled against him. William de Albini is said to have been the leader of the rebels and with them he advanced to Rochester. Only three days after securing the castle the royalist army arrived and at once laid siege to it, leaving the rebels precious little time to obtain sufficient provisions. King John himself arrived on Monday 13th October.

John set his miners and sappers to work on the south-east angle of the curtain wall, then a weak spot in the defences. Using picks the sappers weakened the wall while simultaneously, a mine was set beneath the foundations. On setting fire to the timber supports, which were soaked in pigs fat, the foundations gave way bringing down part of the curtain. Once the breach had been made and with the help of siege engines, the entire bailey fell to John's men. The rebels were forced to retreat to the protection of the keep and were reduced to their last rations of food — after which they ate their horses. The mine which had brought down the curtain wall was further extended beneath the same angle of the great keep itself, and succeeded in making a breach in its mighty walls.

King John, seldom given due credit for his military ability, surely deserves some praise here. He succeeded in breaching the keep, causing considerable damage to the south and east walls, possibly bringing down the entire corner. The garrison withdrew behind the cross-wall but eventually surrendered on 30th November. One man only was executed, though John wanted to hang all the surviving rebels. He was persuaded, however, that such a deed would only further provoke his barons so they were sent to various royal prisons instead. Though mining operations and their consequences were well known to barons and castle engineers, the devastating results experienced at Rochester made many feel insecure in their castles for a long time after.

It is difficult to ascertain the extent of the damage caused by John's mine for while repair joins can be seen in the keep to almost half-way along each of the south and east walls, these repairs were not carried out for some time — between 1220 and 1260 in fact. We do not know exactly what happened and we cannot depend entirely upon contemporary chroniclers, but the fact remains that however light or extensive the damage, John did succeed in breaching the keep.

It was during Henry III's reign that the castle was repaired — somewhat clumsily — the breached angles of the keep and curtain wall being rebuilt in the stronger, half-cylindrical fashion. At this time also, the cross-wall in the bailey and the fine range of domestic buildings were built. It seems likely that these superseded the keep for residential purposes and that is the reason perhaps for the delay in repairing the keep.

The third siege at Rochester was in 1264 during the civil war between Henry III and his barons. This time the barons were led by Simon de Montfort, who laid siege to the castle. The attack came to an abrupt halt having lasted only nine days, however, when de Montfort withdrew on receiving news of the advancing royalist forces. The damage to the castle can only have been slight this time for repairs were not taken in hand until almost a century later. These were carried out, as has been noted, by Edward III. The castle was also attacked briefly, during Wat Tyler's Peasants' Revolt in 1381, suffering some damage as a result.

Rochester Castle never regained its importance after Edward III's reign and by Elizabeth I's time it was already in disrepair. Most of the remaining bailey buildings and a large section of the west curtain wall — and it is thought, the huge entrance door of the forebuilding — were then taken down and transported up river to Upnor. There the materials were used to help construct Upnor Castle, a blockhouse to defend the infant dockyard at Chatham. Rochester Castle then became a convenient quarry for building materials.

James I granted the castle to Sir Anthony Weldon in 1610. A descendant of his, Walker Weldon, tried unsuccessfully to sell the castle and instead decided to

Rochester Castle from the south-east. Note the rebuilt, half cylindrical corner turret of the keep and mural tower of curtain.

190

dismantle it, selling off all the materials of any value — facing stones, floor timbers, lead and the like. An attempt to pull the keep down completely was given up because of its immense strength and the high cost of demolition. Likewise, and fortunately for us today, a plan to convert it into a military barracks was also abandoned.

The castle was later acquired by the Earls of Jersey who sold it to Rochester Corporation in the late 19th century. The Corporation first leased the site and eventually bought it in 1884, having the foresight to see its recreational potential. The much needed repairs and restorations were made to the fabric by George Payne, and the bailey was converted into a public park. The old Rochester Corporation took good care of the castle throughout their long ownership and in 1964 they handed custody of it over to the Department of the Environment, who have continued to bestow their care and attention upon its preservation. Without doubt, Rochester is one of the most important and visually striking castles in England.

Charles Dickens greatly loved Rochester, his last wish being that when he died he be buried in the castle moat, then part of St. Nicholas churchyard. At the time of Dickens' death, however, the churchyard was closed to further burials. He was instead given a state funeral at Westminster Abbey, but his ghost is reputed to haunt the castle moat at Christmas time each year.

Access: Department of the Environment. Open standard hours. The castle stands in the city centre on the bank of the River Medway. Ample street parking also Council car park nearby. Toilets. Refreshments in summer months.
Map Ref. 742686.

ROMDEN CASTLE

The present building bearing the name Romden Castle, on the outskirts of Smarden, is a brick house built during the 18th century and modified in 1866. The house is similar in appearance to others of its time, such as Bleak House on the cliffs at Broadstairs. It consists of a large, central block with one end rounded into a bay, and a tall, four-storeyed central tower. Prior to 1866 there were two bay windows. It is not castellated in the usual sense, but does present some of the qualities of a sham castle — an impression largely given by the presence of the tower.

So far as I have been able to ascertain, no true castle has ever stood on the site known as Romden Castle. It has been suggested, however, that the word 'castle' may here have been derived from an ancient earthwork in the area, but I could find no evidence of such in the immediate vicinity, nor any documentary proof. It seems more likely to be a title merely added on as a suffix for prestigious reasons.

Access: Privately occupied. Not open to the public.
Map Ref. 895421.

SALTWOOD CASTLE

Saltwood Castle, standing on a steep hill above Hythe, is one of the most complete castles to survive the Middle Ages and in an excellent state of preservation. It is also, somewhat ironically, one of the least known.

The castle today stands well inland on a promontary between two streams but in Roman times, when much of Romney Marsh was under water, the sea washed the foot of this hill. Still a heavily wooded area, then it was virgin, primeval forest and the trees, as Alan Clark puts it, 'dipped their branches in the mingled waters of sea and stream' — hence the name, Salt-wood. The Romans are thought to have erected a watch tower here on the site still known as the Roman Tower — a medieval replacement. The massive stones used in the construction of its lowest courses would indicate that it stood at, or close to, the water's edge.

On top of the promontary in 488 Aesc, the son of Hengist, built a fortress, creating the level plateau and earthworks of what later became the inner bailey of the castle. The present walls revet this plateau in much the same way as they do at Eynsford Castle, so that the ground level inside is considerably higher than that outside. The earthworks were skilfully constructed to make the maximum use of the natural defensive qualities of the site. One of the streams was also cleverly diverted to feed the castle moat. A mound was added to the eastern end of the plateau, partly artificial and partly composed of a natural hillock. It was largely levelled to make way for the keep in the 12th century so it is not known for certain whether it was part of the Saxon fortress or if it was added by the Normans.

In 833 Saltwood is mentioned in a document of King Egbert and with few exceptions, all of its subsequent owners have been recorded in various manuscripts. In 1026 Canute and a number of bishops and nobles, including Earl Godwin of Kent, signed a deed which handed Saltwood over to the church — a simple act that was to have dire consequences nearly 150 years later. Church and State continually squabbled in the Middle Ages, particularly over property, and Saltwood soon found itself at the centre of the argument between Henry II and Thomas Becket, to be discussed later.

It has been suggested in 'The Victoria History of the County of Kent' that Saltwood received a stone curtain wall soon after the Conquest. The present wall of the inner bailey, however, was erected by Henry de Essex, Henry I's Standard Bearer. It is oval in shape and appears to follow the course of the Saxon defences. It was built with at least five towers in its circuit, two of which, the north and western ones, are flush with the outside wall, while the two to the south project outside the bailey but are flush with the inside wall. The fifth is really only a turret and contained two tiers of latrines.

The entrance was on the east side, as it is now, but this is also believed to be the site of the mound so its original details are unknown. A later owner, Sir

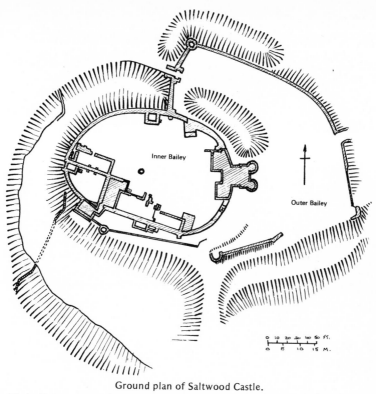

Inner Bailey

Outer Bailey

Ground plan of Saltwood Castle.

Ranulf de Broc, erected a tower-keep here in the late 12th century which was further modified in the 1380's into the fine gatehouse we see today.

The castle as built by Henry de Essex consisted of one ward only – the present inner bailey – the outer one being constructed in the late 14th century. When the outer bailey was added, the moat surrounding the inner bailey was maintained but further extended so as to enclose the entire castle. By the time of Stephen's reign, de Essex had risen to the rank of Warden of the Cinque Ports and Constable of England, his castle at Saltwood being regarded as one of the strongest in the south.

Essex ended his illustrious career, however, amid the most extraordinary circumstances in 1163, during Henry II's reign. He is supposed to have thrown the king's standard to the ground during an ambush in Wales and run away from the battle then in progress. He was accused of cowardice and treason by Robert de Montfort – coincidentally a descendant of the original Norman owners of Saltwood Castle – who challenged Essex to a duel. By that time, Essex was an old man and he lost the combat, Montfort leaving him for dead. A group of monks found him to be still alive, however, and nursed him back to health. He remained with the monks for the rest of his life, totally humiliated and relieved of all his wealth and estates.

193

Although Saltwood was officially the property of the Archbishop of Canterbury, for many years the king had taken over the responsibility of installing a castellan. When the position was vacated by Henry de Essex, however, Thomas Becket decided to intervene and requested Henry II to hand Saltwood back over to him to become the exclusive residence of the Archbishops.

The conflict between the king and the prelate was already advanced by this time and Henry decided that Saltwood was too important a castle to simply hand over to a potential enemy. Instead, he installed the disreputable Sir Ranulf de Broc, an arch enemy of the church, as castellan. Chroniclers of the time say that he 'turned Saltwood into a den of thieves'.

The story goes that on Christmas Day 1170, Henry II uttered his famous outburst against Becket which was overheard by four of his knights — William de Tracey, Reginald Fitzures, Hugh de Morville and Richard le Breton. They were supposedly colleagues of de Broc's and met at Saltwood Castle to plan Becket's assassination. De Broc was no doubt keen to remain in possession of Saltwood so in assisting with the plot he was able to secure his own position.

The four knights set off from Saltwood on the evening of 29th December with an armed escort from de Broc, and murdered Thomas Becket on the steps of his own Cathedral. Afterwards, the four met up again at Saltwood — to confirm to de Broc perhaps that Becket was dead — before fleeing to France. At least two of their number seem to have repented the foul deed for reputedly, William de Tracey's ghost haunts the road near Bridge and the ghost of one of the others (it is not known which) haunts Kemsing Church — neither of their spirits it seems, being able to rest.

As mentioned earlier, de Broc built a substantial tower-keep at Saltwood sometime during Henry II's reign and the castle thus fortified, remained largely unaltered until the works carried out by Archbishop William Courtenay in the 1380's. Despite Becket's murder — or maybe because of it — the castle remained in ecclesiastical hands until 1540, when Archbishop Cranmer handed it over to the crown at the Dissolution.

Saltwood Castle was a great favourite of Archbishop Courtenay's and he created a fine suite of apartments in the southern half of the inner bailey. He also constructed the outer bailey and transformed the old keep into a magnificent gatehouse. The gatehouse is strikingly similar to the West Gate at Canterbury (also erected by order of Courtenay) and was built, along with the other works carried out at the castle at this time, by Henry Yevelle. The clergy occupied the buildings in the bailey while the castellan and his retainers lived in the gatehouse. A fine suite of rooms was also provided in the gatehouse for the Archbishop, when he was in residence. Today, it forms the main residential block of the Clark family and clearly shows internally, the different phases in its construction.

Courtenay perhaps, had justification for strengthening Saltwood at that time for his predecessor, Archbishop Sudbury, had been murdered and the Lollards were harrassing the church and gentry. One prominent Lollard, William Thorpe,

194

Saltwood Castle in 1803 prior to its restoration, from a drawing by W.P. Sherlock
(Aylesford Galleries)

was imprisoned for sixteen years in the north tower at Saltwood for heresy. He escaped in 1380 following an earthquake that passed through southern England, causing considerable damage to the castle. It was largely as a result of this damage that Courtenay carried out his massive rebuilding programme.

After Saltwood had been conveyed back to the crown in 1540 it passed through a succession of hands including Thomas Cromwell and John Dudely, Earl of Warwick, and received a Tudor wing to the south side of the gatehouse. Unfortunately another earthquake in 1580 did considerable damage to the buildings in the inner bailey. Because of the high cost of repairs the castle was then rendered uninhabitable. Despite the damage and subsequent pilfering of the fabric for building materials — mostly confined to the outer bailey wall — and its partial use as a farm, the castle has survived in near perfect condition. When restoration work was carried out in recent times the fabric was found to be remarkably sound.

The Deedes family carried out some basic repairs to the castle but most of the restoration work was done in the last years of the 19th and the early years of this century. The castle was acquired by Lady Conway, of Allington Castle fame, and it is to her and the revivalist architect Sir Philip Tilden that we owe most of the restoration. A team of highly skilled masons was employed from 1934 to 1949, meticulously restoring the castle. The gatehouse was made habitable again and a new wing, in Gothic revivalist style and blending perfectly with the Tudor

195

wing, was added to its north side. The rest of the castle was consolidated and restoration on the outer barbican was begun, but the outbreak of war halted work.

When Lady Conway died, Sir Kenneth Clark (now Lord Clark) purchased the castle. He moved his immense library of books into the great hall and from a study in the castle he wrote most of his books, including the famous 'Civilisation' series. In 1970 Lord Clark moved out and his son, the Rt. Honourable Alan Clark M.P., moved in with his family.

The Clarks have greatly cared for Saltwood and further extended the restoration programme, which recently included the reflooding of part of the inner bailey water defences. They do so solely from their own resources and from public support, for at no time have they received any kind of grant to offset the costs. The future of this small, but important part our heritage is assured and in very capable hands.

The castle is immaculate, partly restored to a habitable residence, partly a romantic ruin — but all in splendid condition. The gatehouse is especially worthy of note. Its two lofty, half-cylindrical towers are placed fairly close together and between them, high up on the parapet, are four machicolations. The other defences of the gate can also be clearly seen, including a portcullis and the recess for a drawbridge — complete with two circular holes in the stonework through which its chains passed. The restored wings to the rear of the gatehouse have been perfectly blended with the old work. The repairs mostly took the form of consolidation only, and a great deal of original work still survives. Mrs. Clark informed me that during the drought of 1976, the foundations of other buildings in the bailey were clearly visible in the grass. As soon as funds permit, it is intended to excavate the entire inner bailey.

There is so much to see at Saltwood — more than at any other castle I have visited — that it is difficult to single out any one thing for attention. Perhaps the best feature, from a visitors point of view, is that access can be had to almost the entire battlement walk of the inner bailey. The best place to climb up to the wall-walk is near the ruined Knight's Hall (Saltwood had two halls in the inner bailey) a magnificent chamber with rows of large, traceried windows of the Decorated order. Corridors, passages and stairs seem to radiate in all directions and the wall-walk passes through all the towers in the circuit of walls. Steps also lead down to the fine range of buildings in the southern half of the bailey.

Still preserved there is Courtenay's Garden, more romantically known as the Secret Garden. Most castles were provided with such peaceful and domestic amenities, though this is often ignored by historians because few such gardens survive. This one at Saltwood still preserves statuary and ornately carved stone seats.

One of the first things to strike the visitor on this tour of the battlements and towers will be the high standard of living accommodation and comfort provided in even the meanest of the castle's apartments. Strategically placed windows admit a remarkable amount of light and there is generally a feeling that this

Saltwood Castle. Inner gatehouse seen from the bailey.

Saltwood Castle. Wall-walk and south tower, inner bailey.

castle, like most others but more apparent here, was first and foremost a home, not a fortress. Floors in the towers are covered by tiles and most of the windows were glazed at an early date — some windows still preserving their medieval glass.

There is much original timber in the castle too, the doors — quite a unique survival — showing clearly the way in which they were constructed. They fit snugly into the doorframes but have no framework as such themselves. They consist of two layers of boards, the outer one laid vertical and the inner one horizontal, to prevent warping and draughts. Immense and ornate hinges cover much of the surface area of the doors and serve also to hold them together, each pair of hinges being different. The locks consist of large wooden blocks, held to the doors by iron clasps.

Of the towers, two are especially interesting. The westernmost one contains a small chapel in its upper level complete with a rare, painted Saxon altar. Below is a dungeon which contains various implements of discipline, such as a set of 16th century stocks, manacles and chains. Thorpe's Tower, the northernmost tower of the inner bailey, is where William Thorpe was imprisoned for 16 years in the 14th century. A trap door in the floor of the upper level looks down into the dingy room in which he was confined — the trapdoor itself was where they lowered down his food.

The battlements are covered with an abundance of small rock plants, briar roses and other flowering plants, which in the summer are highly scented and a riot of colour. The larger types of plant are removed because of the damage they

Saltwood Castle. Exterior of the Knight's Hall, seen from the moat.

The imposing inner gatehouse
of Saltwood Castle.

might do to the solidity of the wall, but the smaller varieties actually consolidate the structure — as well as being enchantingly romantic. A great many species of bird nest quite happily in the nooks and crannies of the curtain wall. I observed swallows, wrens, robins, ravens, blue tits and even a woodpecker in a tree near the moat, while strutting around the inner bailey are a number of stately peacocks.

There is much more to see including a well in the centre of the inner bailey and the Roman Tower in the outer bailey. This tower has Roman foundations, a medieval upper stage and Tudor gun-ports inserted into the arrow loops. Of the outer bailey, less substantial remains are to be seen, though the course of the wall can be clearly followed and the earthworks and outer water defences are magnificent. Especially fine is the outer barbican and gate linked, by a stretch of curtain wall with a two-tier wall-walk, to a drum tower.

In most castles are to be seen a number of square, open holes in the external masonry, usually termed put-log holes, that is, the holes supposedly left behind when the scaffolding poles were removed during building and left open to facilitate future repairs. I have never been entirely satisfied with that explanation and here, at Saltwood, I have been able to investigate them properly for

199

the first time. They are found in great abundance at Saltwood, erratically spaced and at all different levels — in most cases too erratic to be of any use as scaffolding holes.

To begin with, they are not merely holes in the masonry, for their mouths are lined with dressed stone sides and lintels. They vary in depth from about 1ft to 18 inches on average but many are considerably deeper. Some even pass right through the wall and open as a similar hole on the inner surface — this applies not only to the curtain wall but also to the internal walls of some of the towers. Others connect to a vertical shaft in the thickness of the wall.

I believe that the holes were for various purposes and it is too simple and insufficient an explanation to merely dismiss them all as being scaffolding holes, though this may well have been a use for at least some of them. Those near to parapet level, I found to be a mixture — some were obviously intended to take a wooden hoarding, while others were for drainage from the wall-walks. Some holes closely resemble the compartments in medieval dovecotes and I found pigeons and other birds nesting quite happily in some of them. Perhaps a number of the holes then, were intended to encourage birds to nest — small birds and their eggs were considered a great delicacy in medieval times.

Certainly, some of the holes were drainage chutes from internal water systems, for traces of water-stained lead lining can still be seen within them, and their mouths have been chiselled into channels. These examples mostly correspond exactly to towers or internal rooms, which partly bears out this theory.

So far I have accounted for, or at least suggested possible alternative uses for, about half of the holes — but what of the others? It is possible that they could be some kind of internal drainage system for the wall itself, perhaps to keep it dry and free from damp. The large amount of mortar used in rubble walls would need a lot of drying out before becoming stable so the holes may have served to airate the core of the wall.

I offer these few suggestions merely as possible explanations. Certainly, these holes (found at most castles) are not all merely scaffolding holes, but seem to have been designed as part of the overall plan of the walls, for an as yet, unknown purpose. Whatever that purpose was, it was probably something quite fundamental. Much more research still needs to be done on the finer points of medieval life.

Saltwood Castle is an ideal place in which to study such details and for that reason alone, quite apart from its picturesque qualities for the casual visitor, deserves to be more widely recognised.

Access: Take signed road to castle from A20 near Hythe. Open to the public 2—5.30pm from May Spring Bank Holiday Sunday and Monday and any Sundays following. June and July open Sundays only. August open daily except Saturdays and Mondays — but open Bank Holiday Mondays. At other times by appointment. Free parking. Toilets. Refreshments. Map Ref. 162359.

SANDGATE CASTLE

Sandgate Castle is the fourth in a line of castles, or forts, erected along the east coast of Kent by Henry VIII during the invasion scare after 1538. The others were Deal, Walmer and Sandown castles — see separate entry under Deal Castle for a general background to the political events of the time.

Deal, Walmer and Sandown castles closely resembled one another, making great use of semi-circular bastions. At Sandgate the basic design was changed. The ground plan shows it to be roughly triangular but with eliptical rather than straight, angular sides. Originally it consisted of a central, round tower surrounded by two chemises. The outer chemise was lower in height than the inner one and at its three angles had wide, semi-circular lunettes. At the corresponding angles of the inner chemise were circular towers. A detached D-shaped tower served as the entrance on the north-west face of the outer chemise.

About half of the castle survives today though it was drastically altered in 1806, particularly on the seaward side, to convert it into a Martello Tower. All of the walls and towers were reduced in height and their battlements and embrasures removed. On the seaward side the outer bastions have been broken through and completely removed, so too has the south-eastern angle of the inner wall to reveal the exposed, central tower.

The broken outer bastion of Sandgate Castle, seen from the beach and revealing the central tower.

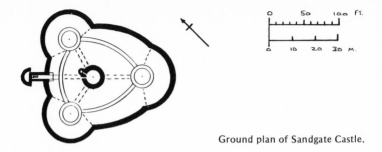

Ground plan of Sandgate Castle.

The tower, free-standing within a small courtyard, has also been suitably modified so that it conformed to the general design of a Martello Tower. None of these alterations have been carried out with much consideration for the fabric of the castle. On the seaward side the broken ends of the walls have been left jagged and irregular. The other towers and bastions have likewise been drastically altered and modified to house barrack-type accommodation.

The building accounts of Sandgate survive almost complete and from them we can learn a great deal about the building of Henry's forts. A German, Stephan Von Haschenperg, was the builder in charge. The accounts take the form mostly of inventories and the day-to-day administration of the construction work. Regrettably, they are far too detailed to relate here. Some interesting snippets of information emerge, however, such as a strike by the labourers at work on Deal Castle in June 1539 for more money. After the dispute was settled the instigators were promptly sent to prison, so vital was it to complete the fortifications in as short a time as possible.

Skilled masons, bricklayers and carpenters were hired from all over the country, some pressed into labour. The cost of this mammoth fortification exercise was met by the spoils taken from the recently dissolved monasteries — which also provided much of the building materials used. Various ecclesiastical features in the stonework can still be seen in all manner of odd places at some of the castles.

Few of the details of Henry VIII's castle at Sandgate survive in anything like the condition of Deal and Walmer castles, though there are still considerable remains. The castle can be viewed from both the road and the promenade, but it is best seen from the beach. Some reports of the castle state that it has been converted into a house, but this is not true. The castle is privately owned and used now mainly for storage, but the modern house built at the side stands outside the precincts of the walls, immediately adjacent to the north-eastern outer bastion.

Access: On private land. The castle stands on the seafront at Sandgate and can be easily seen from the beach.
Map Ref. 209352.

SANDOWN CASTLE

Sandown Castle was one of the chain of fortifications erected by Henry VIII between 1538 and 1540 in response to the threat of a combined French/German invasion. (See notes on Deal Castle for a fuller account of the political events which led up to this situation.)

In Tudor times the area of water between the east Kent coast and the Goodwin Sands was much favoured as a place of safe anchorage. It was known as the Downs and Henry protected it with three castles, the largest and strongest in his chain of coastal fortifications. They were Deal, Walmer and Sandown castles and became known as 'the Three Castles which keep the Downs'.

Deal was the largest of the three and occupied the central position, with the other two placed a mile along the coast to either side. Walmer and Sandown were almost identical to one another and consisted of a central, circular keep, surrounded by a strong concentric, circular wall. Attached to this were four massive semi-circular bastions. Sandown Castle, regrettably, has long since disappeared, but Deal and Walmer remain virtually intact. Because of their similarity, the separate entry in the Gazetteer for Walmer Castle will give the reader a good idea of the arrangements at Sandown.

Although Henry VIII's series of forts were essentially blockhouses on which heavy artillery were mounted, they still preserved something of the medieval castle in their overall design. While no element of feudalism can be found within them, their builders had not entirely divorced themselves from the principles of castle design. Perhaps they should no more be regarded as castles than the later fortifications of the 18th and 19th centuries, but there are enough similarities between them and medieval castles to warrant our attention here.

Happily, as it turned out, none of Henry VIII's fortifications were put to the test against a foreign invader, so most have very quiet histories. Virtually nothing is known of Sandown Castle, save that it put up a brief show of strength in the 17th century Civil War. It started out in the war, along with Deal and Walmer castles, on the side of Parliament, but then declared for the Royalists in an uprising of 1648. After a brief skirmish Colonel Rich successfully re-took each of the three castles, Sandown being the last to surrender. After the Restoration a captain and a small garrison was stationed at Sandown and residential buildings erected over part of the bastions.

Up until the late 19th century Sandown survived almost intact, as old photographs show, but changes in the position of the Goodwin Sands quite suddenly directed the full attention of the sea towards it. The sea first broke into the moat in 1785, but the castle was still defendable during the Napoleonic wars. An attempt was made to save it in 1856, but the sea and a fire rendered it uninhabitable. In a very short space of time the sea undermined much of the castle, which

Remains of the entrance bastion, Sandown Castle.

began to subside and fall down. The castle became dangerous so in 1894 the Royal Engineers were called in to blow it up. Some of the stone was later used for the extensions made at Walmer Castle.

All that remains today of the castle on this wind-swept corner of the coast is a small fragment of the inner wall of the west bastion, formerly the entrance. There is also a pile of stones on the beach, still relentlessly battered by the sea at high tide. At the time of writing, contractors on a new building site adjacent to the castle had unearthed a large quantity of castle stone, presumably dumped there by the Royal Engineers. The local council have erected an ornamental memorial on the roadside constructed of stones taken from the castle ruins, a fitting if somewhat sad tribute to a once great fortress.

Access: Follow the coast road at Deal to its northern limits. The castle, though scanty, is on the beach and is freely accessible.
Map Ref. 375544.

SANDWICH CASTLE

Sandwich is a delightful old town, claimed by many to be the most complete medieval town in Europe. Admittedly, at first glance it does not appear to deserve such an honour, but a closer inspection of its warren of tiny streets will be justification enough. Almost every street has a string of old buildings to offer the adventurous visitor. It has buildings from almost every period and of varying degrees of importance, from the grand Guildhall to the many small medieval cottages.

Despite its wealth of fine old buildings, Sandwich has lost two of its most distinguishing structures which, if still standing, would have completed this medieval picture. I speak of course of its castle and town walls.

Until the sea deserted Sandwich and silted up its harbour, it was a thriving, prosperous port — one of the five original Cinque Ports — so it is not surprising that in due course it came to be fortified. What is surprising perhaps, is that these defences have not survived when so much else in the town has.

Hasted recalls seeing the foundations of the castle in a field called 'Castle Mead', just outside the town walls, but sadly, they too have now disappeared. Another account, however, refers to the castle being inside the town walls in the south-west corner. Whichever is correct, a continuous wet moat fed by both the tide and the River Stour encircled them both — Sandown Gate connecting the two.

Sandwich, as a port, was a great favourite of Edward III and it is in his reign that we first hear mention of a castle there. It was supposedly a royal castle but whether or not it was actually built by the crown or simply acquired by it, is not known for certain. Its castellan was appointed by the Governor of Dover Castle.

Sandwich was sacked by the French in 1438 and in 1450 it received a town wall. Until then the town's defences are thought to have consisted of earthen ramparts and timber walls only. Five gates were built into the circuit of walls — of which one, Fisher Gate, survives — and a little later the bridge across the Stour was defended by a stone gate — Barbican Gate — which also survives.

Of the town walls only the earthen ramparts remain, though these form a continuous circuit and have been made into a promenade walk by the Council. They are similar to the earthen ramparts of Canterbury and it has been suggested that perhaps they never did carry a stone wall, the five gates perhaps being the only stone defences.

In 1451 the Great Bulwark was constructed, presumably to supplement the town walls. It consisted of two storeys and was well provisioned with cannons, but this did not prevent the French, under Pierre de Breze, from successfully taking it on 20th August 1457.

The Barbican Gate. One of two surviving gates in Sandwich's town defences.

A certain amount of confusion has arisen concerning this bulwark. Some historians believe it was constructed of stones taken from the castle, which then fell into disuse. Others believe that it was the castle itself, so altered as to suit the defensive requirements of the day.

It (or the castle) was held by the bastard Faucanberg — or Falconbridge — for the Earl of Warwick during the Wars of the Roses. He held it against the King but surrendered when Edward IV arrived in person to lay siege to it. Shortly after 1471 it was demolished.

Sandwich recovered from the silting up of its harbour by attracting Dutch and Flemish weavers to settle there. Today it still prospers and is a picturesque and highly fascinating town to explore on foot. Particularly fine are the two surviving gates. A walk around the ramparts is also a most rewarding experience.

Access: Castle site destroyed. Rampart walk of town walls freely accessible in town centre.
Map Ref. 330580.

206

SCOTNEY CASTLE

Famed today more for its splendid gardens than for any historical associations, Scotney Castle shows perfectly the changing roles of castles through the years. The history of the castle site is very ancient indeed, far preceding man's intervention upon the Earth, dating back to at least the Mesozoic Age. In the quarry at Scotney can be seen the fossilised footprints of Inguanadons made in the sand about 230 million years ago.

The boundary between Kent and Sussex used to follow the course of the River Bewl, but when this was diverted to feed the castle moat, the boundary became lost. Scotney was formerly in Sussex, but following boundary changes in 1897, it has since been in Kent.

The earliest recorded owner of the manor was a Lambert de Scoteni in 1137, which he held under the barony of Leeds Castle, but his manor house has entirely disappeared. In 1259 Walter de Scoteni is supposed to have been hanged at Winchester, under suspicious circumstances, accused of poisoning the brothers Gilbert and William de Clare. William died but Gilbert, who was Lord of Tonbridge Castle and opposed to Simon de Montfort, survived. After the barons' war that followed Scotney Castle reverted to crown ownership.

The next recorded owner of Scotney was John de Grofhurst of Horsmonden, in 1310. After his death, his wife married John de Ashburnham. Their son, Roger de Ashburnham, was a prominent local administrator and, with Sir John de Etchingham and Sir Edward Dallingrigge, became Conservator of the Peace in Kent and Sussex.

Between 1378-80 he built the present castle at Scotney in response to the French sackings of Rye, Winchelsea and Hastings in 1377. Ten years later, Dallingrigge built Bodiam Castle, in Sussex, which although much grander and stronger, used Scotney as its model. Scotney was rhombus shaped and originally had four corner towers (only one of which, the Ashburnham Tower, still remains) a central gatehouse on the south-west side and a hall range which bisected the internal court. Considerable portions of the hall range — remodelled in the 17th century — still survive, nestling alongside an Elizabethan house inserted on the south-east side. Old prints show the upper storeys of the domestic range to have been constructed from timber.

Stephen Lambhurst was the mason employed upon the castle's construction. He had spent the years 1373-78 working at Boxley Abbey. The main island on which the castle stands was revetted in stone and approached by another, smaller island, which acted as a kind of barbican, with drawbridges connecting the two together and to the mainland. Much of the stone curtain wall has been replaced by a brick, undefensive garden wall, but the revetment still remains showing clearly the castle's outline.

The moat was made to enclose both islands, forming a figure of eight, the same system used a few years later at Cooling Castle. It still survives in its entirety assuming, in parts, lake-like proportions. Although the defences of Scotney were comparatively slight, elements of its design — particularly the approach path — can be clearly seen at Bodiam.

Roger Ashburnham died in 1392. His son, William, died without issue and Scotney then passed to a John Hall, who sold it to the Chichele's in 1418. Henry Chichele, who was the then Archbishop of Canterbury, gave the estate to his niece. It then passed, by marriage, to the Darell family, remaining in their possession for some 360 years.

By the mid 16th century, the castle appears to have been indefensible — the will of Thomas Darell dated 1558, refers to only one tower still standing — and it then became entirely residential, the Elizabethan wing adjacent to the tower being built in about 1580. The then owner, Thomas Darell II had sympathies towards the Catholic cause and he constructed a number of hiding places within the walls. These were put to good use on various occasions in the 1590's when the Darell's hid the celebrated Jesuit, Father Richard Blount.

William Darell rebuilt much of the house in about 1630 but his death in 1639, the outbreak of Civil War and mounting family debts, prevented all of his plans for Scotney from being fully realised. His widow, Elizabeth Darell, insisted on keeping her children at home to educate them in the Catholic manner. She installed guns there to prevent her children being taken from her — one of the rare occasions when Scotney was actually put on a defensive footing.

Scotney Castle is believed to have been attacked only once, and that towards the end of the Darell occupation in the late 18th century. In addition to their sympathies towards the Catholics, the Darell's appear to have been involved in

Scotney Castle seen from across the lake.

smuggling, using Scotney Castle as a base. One night, it is not known when exactly, a party of revenue officers attacked the castle. In the ensuing struggle, one of the revenue men was killed and his body thrown into the moat. His ghost is still reputed to haunt the waters, seeking entry to the castle.

The affairs of the Darell's appear to have entered a complex round of law suits at this time. Squabbles amongst themselves inevitably left the family heavily in debt — to such an extent that their estates had to be sold off.

In 1778 Scotney Castle, then handsomely appointed (during the 1720's many Georgian style additions had been made and the conical roof and cupola also added to the tower) was sold to Edward Hussey. Between 1783 and 1792 the remainder of the Darell family estate was also purchased by him. The Hussey's had settled in Sussex from Staffordshire in about 1700, pursuing an interest in the growing iron industry of the south.

In 1836 a later descendant, another Edward Hussey, decided to rebuild Scotney. He designed both the new house and its extensive landscaped garden — some of his original sketch designs still survive. Work began in 1837 and continued until 1843. William Sawrey Gilpin gave artistic and landscaping advice, while Anthony Salvin was employed as the architect — a name we have already come across in the medieval revivalist trend, though at Scotney, the new house was more Tudor than medieval in style.

From the start, the gardens were designed to be unashamedly romantic. Georgian portions of the old castle were carefully taken down to reveal the romantic ruins of the Elizabethan and medieval sections — which are a careful blend of stone and brick — with the heavily machicolated tower forming the centre-piece.

The 'new' Scotney Castle, designed by Anthony Salvin.

209

The Ashburnham Tower and Elizabethan wing, Scotney Castle.

Scotney Castle. View from the inner courtyard showing hall range centre and Elizabethan wing, right.

The new 'castle' was built from stone quarried on site, the quarry afterwards being carefully landscaped to itself became an integral part of the gardens. An ornamental, ballustraded look-out point was also constructed, commanding an uninterrupted view of the old castle in the valley below. The stone is a mellow, honey colour with veins of iron ore, seen as rust coloured streaks, running through it. Large, natural outcrops of rock have also been made good use of throughout the garden, an effect later duplicated at Hever Castle. The gardens there have a similar, enchanting atmosphere.

The garden, as conceived by Edward Hussey, was allowed to slowly mature for over a hundred years before any significant changes were made. New plantings to enrich or replace old stock have greatly enhanced the overall picture. The word 'picture' is most appropriate here, for the careful and subtle blends of shrubs and flowers, evergreens and deciduous trees, are perhaps more akin to the strokes of an artist's hand than to the rambling beauty of nature alone.

There is something to see at Scotney in all seasons. In spring, the air is heavily scented by daffodils and magnolia, followed by the glorious displays of rhododendrons and azaleas. In summer, roses bloom in abundance, cascading over the castle ruins like a floral waterfall. In secluded corners, even palm trees flourish.

Perhaps the best time of year to visit Scotney, however, is in the fall, when the trees and shrubs don their gowns of autumn colouring and vie with one another in friendly rivalry, competing for the most spectacular displays. There is an abundance of bird and animal life in the gardens too, and wild flowers of many species grow almost as profusely as the cultivated varieties.

The approach to Scotney Castle is quite delightful, though care should be taken when entering or leaving the grounds. Passing through the village of Lamberhurst, on the A21 road to Hastings, a small sign ¾ mile down the road points to the concealed entrance, on the left. You then drive, for some distance, through a densely wooded valley, all part of the castle grounds, before finally emerging at a spacious car park, surrounded by trees.

Finally, not to be missed while touring the grounds is the Ice House, a conical pit surmounted by a tall, tent-shaped mound, thatched with heather. During the winter ice was cut from the moat and stored in the Ice House, where it remained frozen. In the days before electric refrigerators, food was kept fresh there throughout the summer.

Access: The new 'castle' is still privately owned and lived in by the Hussey family, but the old castle ruins and gardens, now in the care of the National Trust, are open to the public. Open 2—6pm daily, except Mondays and Tuesdays, from April to the end of October. (Open Bank Holiday Mondays but closed Good Friday). Regret, no dogs. There are toilets, free parking and gift shop facilities.
Map Ref. 689353.

SHOREHAM CASTLE

Shoreham Castle was also known, until 1738, as Lullingstone Castle, but when the then owner of Lullingstone Park, Percival Hart, transferred the title of 'castle' to his house, the original Lullingstone Castle subsequently became known as Castle Farm, Shoreham. All historical records prior to 1738 concerning Lullingstone Castle in fact refer to Shoreham. The history of what is now Lullingstone Castle is a quite separate story.

The castle was originally part of Bishop Odo's lands, the manor being held for him by three tenants. One of these was Osborne Peyforer, a member of a prominent Kentish family. In 1307 it is recorded as having passed to Hugo de Poyntz, who held it under the Archbishop of Canterbury.

Ownership of the castle then seems to have fallen into dispute, there following a law suit in Edward IV's reign to determine the rightful owner. Sir Roger de Chaundois later held it for one knight's fee and it subsequently came into the possession of the Newborough family. They held it, also by knight's service, from the crown, until the 16th century when it passed to the Polhill family. By the time of Henry VIII it was in ruins.

The Barrett family later bought the site and built a farmhouse from the castle ruins. Today, a few scraps of stone walling survive but so incorporated into modern farm buildings that they are hardly noticeable. The site has not been excavated, so the extent and layout of the original castle has never been determined.

The River Darenth was once part of the castle defences, but now it trickles peacefully by in front of the farm, quite oblivious to the changing fortunes of history.

Access: On private land. Not open to the public.
Map Ref. 524635.

SPIDERS CASTLE

This is another of those sites of probable ancient origin and unknown purpose, but which rather confusingly bears the name 'castle' (see notes against Rats Castles).

It is fruitless to speculate on the uses of such sites but the term appears time and again in folklore — though I can find no specific references to Kent. Perhaps then, it is within the complex pages of folklore that an answer is to be found, but which is regrettably beyond the scope of this book.

Access: On private land near Wye. There are no visible remains.
Map Ref. 047453.

SHURLAND CASTLE

Near Eastchurch, on the Isle of Sheppey, are the impressive, though sadly neglected remains of Shurland Hall. The present ruin dates to the early 16th century, but it stands on the site of a castle erected by Sir Geoffrey de Shurland, who was made Constable of Dover Castle in 1225. Prior to that, a manor house of the Shurland's is believed to have occupied the site.

Sir Geoffrey's son, Sir Robert de Shurland, played a prominent part in Edward I's siege of Caerlaverock Castle in 1300, and as a reward he was granted all the wreckage on the sea coasts of his estates. It was usually the king's privilege to claim any booty salvaged from wrecked ships as his own. Sir Robert is buried in Minster Abbey (Sheppey).

On his death, Sir Robert left no male heir and Shurland Castle passed, by the marriage of his only daughter, to William de Cheyney. A 16th century descendant of his, Sir Thomas Cheyney, was created Lord Warden of the Cinque Ports and Constable of Queenborough Castle. The Cheyney's, Sir Thomas in particular, had many honours bestowed upon them by the Tudor monarchs.

Sir Thomas Cheyney was also responsible for rebuilding Shurland. He demolished the old castle and replaced it with a large, Tudor-style courtyard house, which he renamed Shurland Hall. He re-used the stones from both Shurland Castle and Chilham Castle, another of the Cheyney properties, for its construction. Henry VIII stayed there with Anne Boleyn in the October of 1532 — a year before their marriage — on route to Calais to meet the French king.

By the end of the Tudor period, Shurland Hall had already fallen into disrepair. Sir Thomas's son, Sir Henry Cheyney, sold the property and it then passed through various hands before finally becoming a farmhouse. Now, even that minor distinction is denied it, for though it still stands on farmland, it is no longer lived in.

The remains today consist principally of the entrance range, which is brick built but with stone dressings and foundation courses. The entrance door looks to be original and the gatehouse still preserves certain defensive features — there are gunloops in the two octagonal turrets — but perhaps used here more for decorative purposes than for genuine reasons of defence.

Originally, the house and gardens were arranged around twelve separate quadrangles, considerable portions of which still remain including, the outer perimeter walls on the eastern side and some of the outbuildings. The perimeter wall is built of stone and heavily buttressed, but it is not defensible. It stands in front of a large pond, reputed to be haunted by an old woman on the evening of 23rd October each year.

The house sits on a low, wide mound looking thoroughly dejected, while trees growing inside the entrance block protrude their branches through the large, but broken windows with total disregard. Shurland Hall possesses none of the picturesque qualities of an overgrown ruin — more a feeling of sad dereliction.

Access: On private land. Not open to public but can be seen from A250 road to Leysdown.
Map Ref. 994716.

213

The imposing, if somewhat derelict entrance front of Shurland Hall.

STARBOROUGH CASTLE

Strictly speaking, Starborough Castle should not be included here for it lies just over the Kent border in Surrey. Some historians, however, refer to the castle as being in Kent and there have certainly been some boundary changes in this corner of the county, so perhaps Kent is its rightful home. I include it here, albeit briefly, because it once formed part of the Cobham estates.

Starborough was never as strongly fortified as that other Cobham property, Cooling Castle, being more of a fortified manor house. It was built in 1341 by Sir Reginald de Cobham — who fought at Crecy and Poitiers and who died of the Black Death — probably on the site of an earlier manor. One of his descendants, another Reginald, married the daughter of Lord Bardolf, a prestigious soldier who fought at Agincourt.

Little remains of the castle today unfortunately, except for a few scraps of curtain wall. It once consisted of a rectangular court with a round tower at each corner, but was destroyed by Parliament in 1648. The moat which formerly surrounded it, however, survives almost intact.

Access: Near the village of Lingfield. On private land. Not open to the public. Map Ref. 425441.

SISSINGHURST CASTLE

Sissinghurst Castle, like nearby Scotney, is famed more today for its gardens than for any historical associations. It is not really a castle at all, but a vast Elizabethan mansion. Between 1756 and 1763 French prisoners of war were detained there and it is they who gave it the suffix 'le chateau'. In France it is customary to call all such mansions chateaux and the title has clung to Sissinghurst ever since.

In the 12th century it was known as Saxingherste. The first recorded owners were the de Saxingherste's, taking their name from the site, and they built a large, moated manor house where the orchard now lies. Nothing of the house remains but two arms of the moat survive and a third arm, the Moat Walk, can still be traced. This original manor house, which was almost certainly unfortified, was added to over the years and by all accounts assumed grand proportions. In 1305 Edward I stayed there for four nights.

In 1490 the house was owned by the de Berham family, who sold it in that year to Thomas Baker of nearby Cranbrook. The Bakers completely demolished the medieval manor house and erected in its place a Tudor, red-brick mansion on the higher ground to the west. This too has now largely disappeared but the long entrance range with its central gateway, inserted by Sir John Baker in about 1535, still survives.

When Sir John Baker died in 1558 he left Sissinghurst to his son, Richard. Between 1560 and 1570 Sir Richard demolished most of his father's house and replaced it with an enormous Elizabethan mansion on a far larger scale. Elizabeth I stayed there for three days in 1573 shortly after its completion.

By the mid-18th century it was no longer habitable and was leased to the Government to house French prisoners of war. Sissinghurst earned a certain notoriety as a prison and in retaliation, the Frenchmen virtually demolished the interior of the house. It is hard to visualise today that this tranquil house and garden were once the scene of such deplorable conditions and depradation.

The house was still standing, though in a sad state of repair, in 1787 as is shown on engravings of the time, but by 1800 it was so ruinous that most of it was pulled down. The only portions to survive are the twin-turreted gate tower, a portion of the mansion known as the South Cottage and the Priest's House. The entrance range of Sir John Baker's house still survives also.

In 1930 V. Sackville-West, the famous writer and gardener and also a descendant of the Baker's, bought the property — mainly for its potential as a garden — and immediately set about the enormous task of restoration. Together with her husband, Sir Harold Nicolson, they designed the magnificent gardens we see today.

The gardens are extensive, though not over large, and can be comfortably walked round in an afternoon's visit. Their most striking feature perhaps, is the use of colour, different sections being planted with a predominance of one

The twin-turretted gatehouse of Sissinghurst Castle.

colour — such as the White Garden by the Priest's House. Soon after the end of World War II the gardens were first opened to the public and have been a popular centre of pilgrimage in the summer months ever since.

The approach to Sissinghurst is similar to that of Scotney Castle. A long, winding road leads across open fields and countryside to the castle. There is a large, tree-lined car park immediately in front of the entrance range, and though the castle remains are scanty they look extremely impressive on approach.

Access: National Trust Property. Open to the public every day from April 1st—October 15th. Mon.—Fri. 12 noon until 6.30pm. Sats., Suns, and Bank Holidays — 10.00am until 6.30pm. Excellent gift shop, farm produce shop, refreshment and toilet facilities. Free car park.
Map Ref. 808384.

STARKEY CASTLE

About three miles south-west of Rochester, on the Wouldham Marshes, stands Starkey Castle. Close to modern farm buildings, which occupy much of the castle site, are the considerable remains of a small fortified farmhouse built by Sir Humphrey Starkey, Recorder of London. Parts of the building date from the 14th century but it seems not to have earned the title 'castle' until about 1471.

The remains today consist of a rectangular, stone building (the original hall-block) with arched doorways and windows, and an external staircase. Attached to it is a well preserved garderobe wing and a later extension. There was once a chapel, built in the 15th century, but this has now been destroyed. The great hall with its fine oak roof still survives, though it has been divided into two floors at some time to provide flats for agricultural workers.

Very little is known of the castle, or its owners, but it closely resembles Lympne Castle, a similar though more extensively fortified structure. At the time of writing, the castle stands empty, though it is in excellent condition and is soon to be sold and made habitable again. In recent years the castle was used as a television film set.

Access: On private land, but can be clearly seen from the road.
Map Ref. 714656.

Front elevation of Starkey Castle. (Chatham News)

STOCKBURY CASTLE

The history of Stockbury Castle closely follows that of its near neighbours, Binbury and Thurnham. Like them, it formed part of Bishop Odo's Kentish lands during William I's reign, but on his exile in 1082 it passed to the Auberville family, who held it by knight service. In 1192, William de Auberville founded West Langdon Priory near Dover.

It later passed, through the female line, to Nicholas de Criol (or Kiriel) who was another of the Kentish nobles present at the siege of Caerlaverock Castle under Edward I. In 1300 he was created Knight Banneret for his services to the crown. Stockbury castle remained in the possession of his family until 1460, after which it appears to have been left to ruin. The Criol's main residence was at Westenhanger Castle and Stockbury may well have been deserted before this date.

The castle site almost certainly began as part of a prehistoric earthwork, the church now occupying the other portion. An ancient Downland track passes right by the two structures, leading to the village some ½ mile or so down the road. Evidence that the sites of the church and castle were originally one can be traced in the earthworks, for the church stands within what looks to be an attached, outer bailey. While church and castle are often found together, it would hardly be a convenient arrangement for the two to be contained within the one enclosure, as they are here.

The castle earthworks near the church are those of the inner bailey. They are crescent shaped and although relatively low, are well preserved, standing amid orchards with sheep grazing on the banks.

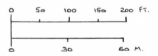

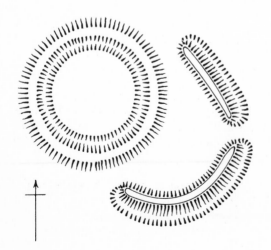

Ground plan of Stockbury Castle.

218

The overgrown but well preserved earthworks of Stockbury Castle.

Close to these ramparts are the remains of the motte with its adjoining ditch. The motte, again low in stature, was once about 200ft in diameter and was capable of supporting quite a large shell keep, but it has been considerably levelled and its ditch filled in to make way for the buildings of Church Farm. The earthworks at Stockbury are interesting because the mound and inner bailey fall just short of actually joining up and appear to have formed two separate enclosures.

Of the three castles built to protect this region of the Downs (Thurnham and Binbury being the other two) Stockbury preserves the best earthworks. They did not need to be substantially constructed because of their spectacular siting on the escarpment of a hill, but are nevertheless, very impressive. The castle did, and still does command an unrivalled view over the Downs.

In the grounds of the nearby farmhouse stands a small scrap of masonry from the castle, believed to be part of the keep. I had a chat to one of the farm labourers there. He told me that whilst digging in his cottage garden, adjacent to the farmhouse, he uncovered the foundations of some of the other castle buildings and a considerable stretch of wall.

Access: Situated on farmland but the earthworks can be clearly seen from the adjacent churchyard of St. Mary Magdalene's Church.
Map Ref. 846616.

219

STONE CASTLE

Stone Castle dates from the mid-12th century, it possibly being erected without licence during the troubled reign of King Stephen, but allowed to remain by Henry II on his accession to the throne. In Edward III's time, the castle was held from the Bishop of Rochester for half a knight's fee by Sir John de Northwood. It is not known, unfortunately, when the Northwood's first acquired it or for how long they held it, but it later passed to the Bonevant family. During the reign of Henry VIII, the castle was the property of Sir John Wyllshire, comptroller of the Town and Marches of Calais.

Eventually it passed back into the hands of the church, for in the 17th century it was owned by Dr. Thomas Plume, Archdeacon of Rochester. When he died in 1704 he bequeathed the castle to certain charitable organisations within the Rochester Diocese.

The sole remaining part of the medieval castle is a large, square tower about 40ft high and built almost entirely from flint. Even Hasted recalls seeing only the one tower still standing, though when Sir Richard Wiltshire had the adjoining house built onto this tower there were reputed to be considerable remains of the rest of the castle — including the Northwood Coat of Arms, sculptured into the stonework.

Stone Castle. The medieval tower on the left is all that remains of the original castle.

Henry Hakewill made alterations to the house in about 1830 and as it now stands, it is a fine example of a Gothicised mansion. It was built from flint, to blend with the 12th century tower, but with some brick and stone facings at the corners and around the windows and door arches.

Stone Castle today is owned by the Blue Circle Group cement company, and used by them as a research centre. While its interior may have been adapted for such use, the company is to be commended for preserving the castle in this highly industrialised area of the county.

Access: Strictly private property. Not open to the public.
Map Ref. 584741.

STOWTING CASTLE

A motte and bailey castle is clearly shown at Stowting on the O.S. map, but finding it today or trying to furnish documentary evidence for its existence, is indeed a difficult task.

The manor of Stowting was given in 1044 by Egelric Bigge to Christchurch, Canterbury. It became a limb of the manor of Aldington and was listed among the Archbishop's lands in the Domesday survey. In Henry II's reign the manor was held for the Archbishop by the Heringod family and it later passed, through his daughter, to William de Kirkby.

It then passed through the hands of a succession of prominent families until in Richard II's reign it became the property of Stephen de Valence. He did not consider it to be of much worth apparently, and he gave it to Sir Thomas Trivet. William Lambarde in his 'Perambulation' referred to a mansion and a park here in 1570 owned by Sir Thomas Kempe. Throughout all this time, however, there is no record of there ever having been a castle or fortified manor erected at Stowting.

It is difficult to say whether this manor is indeed the motte and bailey castle marked on the O.S. map. It is possible that the motte and bailey was occupied briefly, during the early years after the Conquest but that the site of the manor was later moved.

It is equally possible that the site marked as a motte and bailey never was a castle, but was perhaps another of the prehistoric mounds that were never later fortified and mistakenly labelled as a castle. The earthworks today are very scanty and consist principally of a low mound. If a castle ever did exist here, and it was not the site referred to above as Stowting manor, I would suggest that it never developed beyond its basic motte and bailey form and was deserted at an early date.

Access: Situated on farmland just north-west of Stowting Church. A footpath from near Stowting Court passes close to the castle site, but it lies about 80 yards east of the path itself.
Map Ref. 123419.

STUTFALL CASTLE

On the slopes below Lympne Castle lie the scattered remains of Stutfall Castle (Portus Lemanis). One of the Roman 'Forts of the Saxon Shore', it was built in about the year 280 on what was then, the coast. Whether, like the other forts in the series, this fort was built to protect the British from Saxon raiders or, as it is now widely believed, erected by the rebellious Carausius to keep his fellow Romans out, shall perhaps always remain open to question. For further discussion on this point see notes on Richborough Castle.

Not a great deal is known about the history of Stutfall. From a very early date land subsidence, caused by underground streams eroding the clay upon which the fort is built, has badly damaged its walls. Once covering some 10 acres in area, materials from its walls were also pillaged to build Lympne Church and Castle on the promontory above.

Attached to the fort, probably near to where the Royal Military Canal now runs, was a small harbour and on the hill above was once a watch tower, possibly now incorporated into Lympne Castle. It has been suggested that the Romans abandoned the fort on low ground at an early date (about 370) and built a new one on the higher ground occupied by the village and castle at Lympne. However, no substantiating evidence has yet been uncovered.

Excavations were carried out at Stutfall Castle in 1850 by Roach Smith, who had earlier excavated the Roman forts at Richborough and Reculver. His excavations were, for reasons of finance, only preliminary, but he uncovered many interesting finds. He was able to trace the original outline of the fort, the main gate and two substantial buildings erected within the precincts. He also discovered evidence of an earlier structure preceding the fort itself.

The fort was originally seven-sided in plan, with a straight south wall and two straight walls to the east and west. The north wall took the form of a four-sided bay. Semi-circular towers were provided at each angle of the bay, at the corners of the other walls and at intervals along each of the south, east and west walls. These towers took the form of bastions — mostly solid to the wall-walks though some have small chambers at ground floor level — on top of which siege engines, such as the ballista, were mounted on rotating platforms.

The walls were from 12ft to 14ft thick, from 20ft to 25ft high and built of flint and ragstone rubble with brick lacing courses, all solidly held together by the incredibly strong Roman cement. Overall, the fort was about 250 yards by 200 yards. It had a gateway in the east wall with an entrance passage about 12ft wide and was also provisioned with a number of posterns. Further excavations in 1904 by Sir Victor Horsley, south of the fort, revealed the foundations of a wall and steps that once led to the harbour.

The romantic ruins of the fort cling desperately to the hillside, the solid masses of masonry lying in tumbled heaps like giant, recumbent sheep. Despite

Stutfall Castle from a drawing of 1829 by G. Shepherd. The tumbled walls look much the same today.
(Aylesford Galleries)

the damage caused by repeated landslips and later pilfering of materials, some stretches of wall still stand to a height of about 23ft, though now partially buried. Once the walls stood on level ground at the water's edge (the sea has long since receded) but now they lie in ruins at all different levels, scattered down the hillside. It is a testament to the quality of the workmanship that huge chunks of wall have slid down the hill without breaking.

The site today is strangely haunting with the cliff face above now mellowed by grass and an abundance of wild flowers. The fort slumbers on, unrestored and romantic in its isolation, and is perhaps best seen from the ramparts of Lympne Castle.

Access: On private farmland but a public footpath running from near Lympne Castle to the Royal Military Canal, passes right by the ruins. Map Ref. 117343.

SUTTON VALENCE CASTLE

Sutton Valence is a charming village built on a number of converging hills. On the southern slopes of one of these hills stands Sutton Valence Castle, tucked away from the main road and half forgotten. Perched on top of the hill are the craggy remains of the castle keep, its southern wall partly revetting the hillside.

It is a comparatively small structure measuring only 38ft square externally with walls 8ft thick. The floor space inside the keep was thus only 22ft square. Built from Kentish ragstone it closely resembles a similar keep at Peveril in Derbyshire, and commanded a magnificent view over the beautiful Weald of Kent.

It stands now to a height of about 30ft but may once have been twice that height. It had surprisingly large windows in its upper storeys. At first floor level, in the south wall, is a tunnel-vaulted passageway and on the north side, in 1956, traces of a small forebuilding were discovered along with pottery dating from

The small, much ruined keep of Sutton Valence Castle.

about 1150. The keep is the sole remaining part of the castle, the rest having long since been demolished to make way for a hop garden. The surrounding ditch and earthworks have also been levelled. Until quite recently a mural tower and a short length of curtain wall could still be seen, but they too have now disappeared.

The castle today, however, is happily situated in the garden of one of the houses on the eastern extremity of the village. Surrounded by lawns and rose bushes, on my last visit a group of local enthusiasts were taking the site in hand, stripping off the undergrowth that had been allowed to smother it and restoring the stonework. Beneath the ivy and other choking vegetation the keep has been found to be in fairly good condition.

There is no record of a licence to crenellate but the castle is thought to date from Henry II's reign for the keep bears close resemblance to others erected at that time. It may have been built by William le Gros, Earl of Albemarle, towards the end of the 12th century. His daughter and sole heir to his estate married Baldwin de Bethune and, through their daughter, Sutton passed to the Mareschal family, Earls of Pembroke.

The estates of the Mareschal's then passed to Eleanor, King John's daughter, who married her father's (and brother's) arch enemy, Simon de Montfort. When his lands were forfeited following the fall of his rebellion the king repossessed all of his estates. Sutton was then granted by Henry III to William de Valence — the King's half brother — who supported him in putting down Montfort's rebellion. The castle subsequently became known by its double-barrelled name of Sutton Valence, which it still retains.

The castle had a very uneventful history and passed through a succession of owners including the Clifford, Hastings, Grey and Filmer families. By Henry IV's reign it is believed to have been in ruins and soon afterwards, like so many other castles, reverted to the humble role of a farm.

Access: On private land but can be clearly seen from the road. On A274 to Headcorn, turn left into Sutton Valence village pass straight through the village and take first right turn. This lane leads steeply back down to the village. At the bottom of the slope, the castle can be seen on the hill to the right.
Map Ref. 815493.

THURNHAM CASTLE

Thurnham Castle stands on the site of a Saxon fortress, long known as Godard's Castle, which may itself have been preceded by a Roman watchtower. Hasted tells us that many Roman finds have been made on the castle mound.

The history of Thurnham closely follows that of nearby Binbury and Stockbury castles. In early Norman times it formed part of Bishop Odo's estates and then passed through the Say and Turnham families before becoming part of the Northwood's Kentish holdings in 1270. By 1379 it had passed to Robert Corbye of Boughton Malherbe. It later passed to the Wottons.

The castle, of the motte and bailey type, sits on top of a natural chalk spur in the North Downs, here at a height of some 650ft above sea level. This spur forms the basis of the castle mound, which is partly artificial, but the impression of height is exaggerated by the road below which winds its way around the escarpment and cuts into the base of the mound. The earthworks are still considerable, though badly mutilated by chalk quarrying and farming, and still command an impressive view over the Downs — and also the main road from Sittingbourne to Maidstone and the much older Pilgrim's Way.

The outer baileys, as at Binbury, appear not to have been surrounded by substantial earthworks, though here great use has been made of the natural escarpment of the hillside. Again, as at Binbury and Stockbury, the castle was fortified in stone from a very early date, and although much overgrown, some traces of walling remain to be seen.

It is now very difficult to follow the exact outline of the castle, but it would seem to be considerably larger than Hasted's estimation of a mere ¼ acre in extent. A large outer bailey was attached to the southern slopes of the hill so as to partly enclose the chalk spur, or mound, and command the road leading down to Thurnham village. The mound and an inner bailey overlooked and protected the outer bailey, revealing an early application of a sophisticated form of defence, later fully developed in concentric castles.

Until the beginning of this century, considerable portions of the flint walls could be seen but now only scraps remain. They are also so heavily overgrown that they require a great deal of patient — and often painful — searching through thick bracken. The remains today are mostly from the inner bailey gatehouse and a small part of the shell keep that once crowned the motte. The motte itself is about 100ft high from the summit to the road below, and about 280ft in diameter at the base — 75ft at the top.

Most of the walls are now reduced to foundation courses only, but as late as 1907 Harold Sands in his 'Memorials of Old Kent' refers to two 25ft long walls, remains of the gatehouse passage, and a 90ft length of wall some 12ft high and 4ft thick. He also mentions a lengthy, 200ft stretch of wall on the southern side of the castle. Practically all of this has been either totally destroyed or reduced

The earthworks of Thurnham Castle command a spectacular view over the Downs.

to foundations only, so the visitor today searching the undergrowth for any considerable remains will be disappointed. The few surviving pieces are built of coursed rubble and flint, no dressing stones having endured the passage of time.

Lower down the hill, garden walls and the buildings of Thurnham Keep Farm are built from flint stones, possibly taken from the castle ruins. The earthworks, despite the mutilation of the rest of the castle, are still spectacular and quite exciting to explore. They should be negotiated with care, but the climb to the top is both rewarding and exhilarating.

About a mile south-east of Thurnham Castle is a moated mound believed to be 'Snakeshaw Castle'. It is situated away from the road near Snarkhurst Wood and can be approached only by a footpath which passes close to it. It appears never to have actually evolved into a castle proper, perhaps inheriting the name 'castle' from its pre-Norman origins, as indeed do many of the similar 'moat' sites marked on Ordnance Survey Maps.

Access: Take turning signed to Thurnham from A249. A public footpath at the bottom of the castle mound gives convenient access from the road to the castle earthworks. Difficult parking.
Map Refs. Thurnham Castle — 809581. Snakeshaw Castle — 819566.

TONBRIDGE CASTLE

Tonbridge Castle is quite unique, certainly among Kentish castles. Tonbridge and Malling District Council — who administer the site — have combined with the Kent Trust for Nature Conservation and created a nature trail in the castle grounds. It is a far-sighted venture by both parties concerned creating a unique and fascinating blend of political, social and natural history.

A large-format, well illustrated booklet is available at the castle, on the inside cover of which is a sketch plan of the castle with seven observation points marked. The booklet then conducts you round the grounds, pausing at each observation post and describing the plant, bird and animal life you can expect to see there. The Kent Trust for Nature Conservation recognise that ancient monuments, by the very nature of their surroundings, often attract wildlife to urban districts.

I shall mention one or two points of the nature trail to give the reader a flavour of what one might expect to find. For example, observation post No. 1 is the curtain wall connecting the gatehouse to the mound and shell keep. The nooks and crannies between the stones apparently harbour many species of spiders and insects — interesting in themselves — which in turn attract such birds as wrens, which feed on them.

Some of the larger crevices are also used as nesting places by the wrens or by house sparrows and pigeons. Where the curtain wall is shaded, moisture can be seen running down the stones which promotes the growth of ferns, mosses, lichens and liverworts. The booklet makes many fascinating observations, some particularly relevant to the study of history. For instance, lichens are so slow growing that it is possible to use them in dating ancient buildings.

Observation post No. 3 is the summit of the mound, the most ancient part of the castle site and of probable prehistoric origin. Originally, the mound was simply covered in grass but now a host of trees have taken root in its slopes. The booklet tells us which trees we are looking at — elm, sycamore and oak — and provides us with excellent illustrations.

And so the trail goes on, providing us with a whole new concept in looking at castles. An interesting side effect I noticed, on walking the trail, was that in searching for signs of the plant and wildlife noted in the booklet, my eyes became keener and I noticed one or two architectural points that I had missed on previous visits. All in all, I feel this to be an admirable combination for it promotes a cross-flow of interests and knowledge between historian and naturalist.

Tonbridge Castle is the finest example in Kent of a motte and bailey castle. All of its component parts, so to speak, and its later medieval developments can be clearly made out. The impressive mound is about 275 yards in circumference at the base, about 85 yards at the top and rises about 65ft above river level. It has been estimated to contain some 35,000 cubic yards of earth.

Tonbridge Castle gatehouse from a 19th century print.   (Aylesford Galleries)

The land on which the castle is built was granted by William the Conqueror to Richard de FitzGilbert — who is somewhat confusingly known in contemporary documents by the names of his various estates. Thus we find him referred to as de Clare (from his fief in Suffolk), de Bienfaite (from his fief in Normandy), de Tonbridge (from his fief in Kent) and lastly as de FitzGilbert, his proper name. He originally had a castle at Brionne in Normandy but exchanged it for the estate at Tonbridge just after the Conquest.

Soon after his arrival in Tonbridge he erected a timber motte and bailey castle, utilising the existing mound and attaching two baileys to it. When the castle was later refortified in stone, the outer bailey seems largely to have fallen into disuse.

The castle remained in the FitzGilbert (or Clare, to give the two most common names they used in England) family for about 250 years. They were a warlike family and feature prominently in the battles of the early Middle Ages. Richard himself was slain in 1091 at the siege of Courci in Normandy and his grandson, another Richard, was killed in Wales in 1136.

Tonbridge Castle passed in 1152 to Roger, Earl of Hertford and Clare. The castle then came under the See of Canterbury Cathedral but Roger de Clare refused to pay homage to Thomas Becket. De Clare was popular with the king and this event added yet more weight to the rift between Becket and Henry II.

On Roger's death in 1173, his son Richard — who became Duke of Gloucester — inherited the castle. His son, Gilbert, was one of the leading twenty five barons who forced John to sign the Magna Carta. John replied in 1215 by sieging — and taking — his castle at Tonbridge which was not returned to de Clare until after the king's death.

228

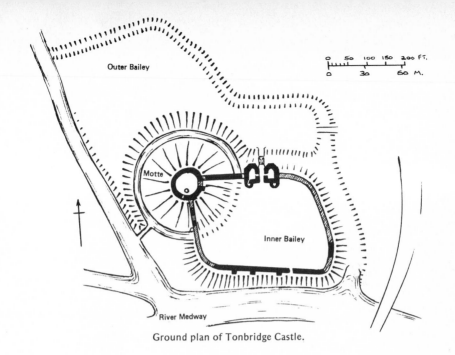

Ground plan of Tonbridge Castle.

It is not certain when exactly the keep on top of the motte was replaced in stone, but it is believed to have been carried out at quite an early date — sometime in the 11th century — for its entrance doors are known to have been of Norman design. It must have been slightly built, however, for it was refaced and strengthened in the 13th century. John had little trouble in taking the castle in 1215 so it may still have had some timber defences then. At the same time as the keep was built in stone, the powerful wing-walls up the side of the motte were constructed. The remainder of the curtain wall dates from about 1180.

Gilbert de Clare died in Britanny in 1230 and Henry III appointed Hugh de Burgh as custodian. This greatly incensed Archbishop Wethershed, who should have made the appointment, and he took his complaint to the Pope. De Burgh promptly married off his eight year old daughter to Richard de Clare, then only nine and still a minor. This action in turn angered the king who annulled the marriage and took over custodianship of the castle himself. Archbishop Wethershed, who had excommunicated everyone in the castle, received the Pope's blessing in the matter but unfortunately died on his return journey to England. Henry III then handed the castle back to its rightful heir, Richard de Clare, who was then of age.

A licence to build a town wall around Tonbridge, attached to the castle, was granted to Richard in 1259. It is not known whether or not it was built in stone for only parts of the earthworks remain today, but Tonbridge Castle itself was certainly strengthened at this time. By 1275 the great gatehouse had been built and may have served as the model for Edward I's later gatehouses at his castles

229

Tonbridge Castle. The gatehouse and Georgian mansion.

The wing-wall connecting the gatehouse at Tonbridge Castle to the shell keep on top of the mound.

in Wales. In that same year, Edward and his queen stayed at the castle briefly on their return to London from Europe, and were entertained in the upper hall of the gatehouse.

Gilbert de Clare, son of Richard, and known as the Red Earl because of his shock of red hair, had lost Tonbridge in an unsuccessful revolt against Henry III, but he was reinstated by Edward I. In 1290 Edward gave him the hand of his daughter, Princess Joan, and in 1297, en route to Flanders, Edward I again visited Tonbridge Castle and installed his son there.

Gilbert, the Red Earl, died in 1295 leaving a five year old son, also named Gilbert. He died at the young age of twenty four at the Battle of Bannockburn in 1314, and with him died out the de Clare family line. The castle then passed through the female line to his sister Eleanor and her husband, Hugh le Despencer. Hugh was later executed and the castle then passed to Eleanor's sister Margaret and her husband, Hugh de Audley. De Audley also unsuccessfully rebelled against the king and had to forfeit the castle in 1321. When Edward II died in 1327 however, de Audley received his estates back again. On his death in 1347 the castle passed to his daughter Margaret and her husband Ralph, Lord Stafford.

Following some three hundred years of political intrigue, Tonbridge Castle then settled down to a relatively peaceful existence remaining in the hands of the Stafford's until 1520. Their ownership did not end peacefully, however, in keeping with Tonbridge's turbulent history. The last two Stafford's, also Dukes of Buckingham, were executed for their political misdemeanors, the family line ending with Edmund Stafford's execution by Henry VIII. At this time, the castle was still in good repair and for a brief spell became crown property again.

At the time of the Civil War the castle was leased to Mr. Thomas Weller, who strongly supported Parliament. The castle was provisioned with a number of timber gun emplacements on the mound and cannon were mounted at every conceivable defence position. It successfully withstood a Royalist attack on 24th July 1643. Following the Civil War, however, Weller was instructed by Parliament to dismantle the castle. Although it was not slighted in the usual sense, from 1692 onwards when part of the south wall fell down, materials were pillaged from its structure by local builders.

In about 1739 stone is said to have been used to construct the locks on the River Medway. As a result of this destruction much of the curtain wall and keep, and most of the domestic apartments within the bailey, have disappeared.

Between 1790-92 Thomas Hooker, the then owner, began to build a mansion against the east wall of the gatehouse, incorporating part of the old chapel which till then had been used as a summer house. The mansion, though built in stone, is not a serious attempt at a Gothic revival castle being almost entirely Georgian in character.

The castle was later purchased by William Woodgate and in 1814 was sold to William Bailey. After his death in 1831 the castle was occupied by a succession of tenants. It was twice used as a school and in 1860 served as a military academy. In 1897 the Tonbridge Urban District Council decided to purchase the site in commemoration of Queen Victoria's Diamond Jubilee, but not without some opposition. In February 1900 the purchase was finally allowed to go through and the grounds were opened to the public on May 23rd of that year as a park. The Council, who now use the mansion as offices, have cared for the ancient castle ever since.

The castle stands on the banks of the River Medway and from the start, great use was made of water in its defences – the moat skirting the mound still survives, though now reduced to a mere stream. In addition to the keep and gatehouse there were once a number of wall towers and bastions, but there are few traces today. One of the towers, the Water Tower near to the river, was reported in the 17th century as being almost as grand as the gatehouse itself. Another of the towers on the south wall housed four latrines, the shafts from which can still be clearly seen from the riverside.

The shell keep on top of the mound was ovoid in plan but was not substantially built, its walls being only 4-5ft thick above the plynth. The walls partly revet the motte and stand to a height of about 8ft outside but only 4ft inside. In the centre of the keep is a hollow. An excavation carried out there revealed a central support for the timber buildings which were once ranged around the inner wall of the keep. There were two entrances to the keep, placed close to two substantial buttresses for extra protection, and a well housed within one of the timber buildings. The surviving wing-wall which climbs the mound is especially interesting, for at its intersection with the west wall of the gatehouse it is protected by a portcullis. This wall, and the remainder of the curtain wall, is some 9ft thick above its battered plynth.

The gatehouse is, in all respects, a remarkable structure and is still relatively complete, despite the loss of its upper floor and parapet. Every door in an exposed position is protected by its own portcullis, in addition to the normal defences of the gate passage. In the base of the westernmost, outer tower of the gatehouse is a small postern, giving access to the moat and once, also the outer bailey. The main hall on the third storey was sumptuously decorated and lit by a row of fine traceried windows. A fuller and more descriptive account of the gatehouse is contained within Part I of this book.

The castle grounds, which in the Middle Ages contained a vineyard, are beautifully kept by the Council as a public park and provide a delightful riverside setting, especially in the summer months. This, coupled with the nature trail and the castle's turbulent history, makes Tonbridge one of the most singularly important and visually attractive castles in Kent.

Access: Castle – Open to the public from May to Sept. Daily 10–1 and 2–5pm. Free parking. Small museum in gatehouse. Grounds – Open every day. Admission free.
Map Ref. 589466.

TONGE CASTLE

Tradition has it that in the year 450 Vortigern, King of Kent, offered Hengist as much land as he could cover with an ox hide. Hengist is supposed to have cut the hide into thongs and so enclosed a vast tract of land. The place became known as Tongas and he erected a castle on the site. It is an interesting story with little to substantiate it in fact, but there is certainly evidence of a Saxon or Danish earthwork preceding the present castle.

Its position close to a creek is in common with other similar earthworks, while just to the north and to the west, ancient trackways skirt around it. It is in keeping therefore, with other pre-Norman earthworks where ancient tracks pass close by and link several sites together. The track to the north — now marked partly by a modern road and upon which local inhabitants have discovered Roman and ancient British pottery — originally linked up with Bayford Castle, in Sittingbourne.

After the Norman Conquest Tonge became yet another of the properties of Bishop Odo. In 1087 it passed to Hugh de Port. Afterwards the manor passed to the St. Johns, but by 1306 it came into the possession of Ralph Fitzbernard. His daughter married into the Badlesmere family, one time castellans of Leeds Castle.

The manor then passed through successive families eventually becoming the property of Richard, Duke of York, whose son was later to become Edward IV. On his death the castle and its estates reverted to crown ownership. Edward VI granted it to Sir Ralph Fane in 1547 and it seems afterwards to have passed through a succession of undistinguished owners. By 1599 the nearby mill was already encroaching upon its site.

Following the ravages of the Black Death at the end of the 14th century, Tonge Castle seems to have been deserted. However, on a small island in the middle of the enlarged mill pond, a manor house is believed to have been built to replace the outdated castle, which had fallen into a sad state of repair. Later references to Tonge may refer to the manor house and not the castle. The fortunes of the house seem to have followed that of the castle though, for it too has disappeared.

The nearby mill pond was originally part of the castle moat and outer bailey. It was enlarged to its present, swollen size by the levelling of the bailey walls and earthworks and flooding the land with water from a tributary stream of Teynham Creek, which formerly fed the moat. A mill, though not the present one, seems always to have occupied this position, close to the castle walls.

Tonge Castle was of the motte and bailey type, its mound being nearly 80ft in circumference at the top. Although the outer bailey earthworks have been largely destroyed by farming and the flooding of the mill pond, the mound and parts of the inner bailey earthworks remain, though lessened in height and surrounded by a field and a small orchard.

The scanty remains of Tonge Castle earthworks.

A modern bungalow now sits on top of the mound, but while it was being built the opportunity was taken to excavate the site. Foundations of a rectangular stone building — probably a small keep — were discovered on top of the mound and some pottery dating from the 12th-14th centuries. A miller, digging in the late 18th century, also uncovered a brass helmet and some earthen urns.

Scattered all around the castle site and close to the mill are a number of megalithic stones, thought to have been contained originally within the earthworks, thus pointing once again to an ancient origin for the castle site.

Access: On the A2 between Sittingbourne and Teynham, take signed road to Tonge. Just south of railway, near the mill, stands the castle mound. On private property, not open to the public, but remains can be clearly seen from the road and footpaths which encircle it.
Map Ref. 933636.

234

UPNOR CASTLE

The history of Upnor Castle is synonymous with the history of Chatham Dockyard, or at least with its early years. Henry VIII had greatly expanded his navy as the threat of a combined French and German invasion grew. When the fear of invasion subsided the navy was maintained as an important part of national defence. As the fleet grew, so a place of safe anchorage became necessary in order to carry out repairs and refits, which on the timber ships of Henry's day would have been quite often.

The River Medway provided just such a safe haven. Its waters were slow running, it had a good rise and fall of tide, and it was sheltered by the surrounding hills. More important perhaps, its treacherous mud and sand banks made it difficult for navigation, except to those familiar with its waters. The reaches of the Medway below Gillingham Reach became used increasingly more by the fleet for anchorage. Gradually, throughout Henry's reign and that of his daughter, Elizabeth, land was acquired in Gillingham and buildings erected so that the ships could be repaired. The dockyard was thus born. It received its first dry-dock during the reign of James I and became also a major shipbuilding centre.

With the growing importance of the dockyard it was thought that some kind of protection should be supplied for the helpless fleet should an enterprising enemy decide to sail up the Medway. Ironically, these fears were realised about a hundred years later. When Elizabeth came to the throne in 1558, she immediately looked into the matter of defending the infant dockyard. She ordered that a blockhouse be constructed on the opposite bank of the river and in 1559, work started on the building of Upnor Castle.

The land, about six acres in extent, was bought from a Mr. Thomas Devinisshe of Frindsbury for the princely sum of £25. The foremost military engineer of the times, Sir Richard Lee, was instructed to design the castle. He drew up the plans and advised on the materials and labour force required and then returned to Berwick-Upon-Tweed, where he was designing a series of bulwarks to encircle that entire town.

Responsibility for the building then passed to his deputy, Humphrey Locke. Richard Watts, however, the famous Rochester Mayor and benefactor, was in charge of the day to day running of the works. By 1567 when building work was complete, Watts had acquired total control of the building operations. When one considers that Deal, Walmer and Sandown Castles were built simultaneously within 18 months, the building of this one small castle at Upnor took an extremely long time.

Some of the materials used on the castle's construction were pilfered from the destruction of existing buildings. While some of the stone was freshly quarried, a good deal of it came from the walls of Rochester Castle. Oak trees from the confiscated lands at Allington of Sir Thomas Wyatt were felled to provide the

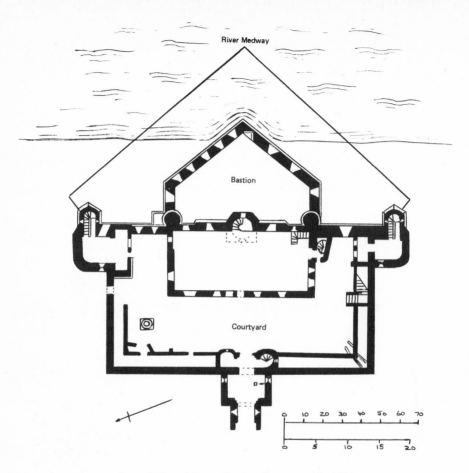

River Medway

Bastion

Courtyard

Ground plan of Upnor Castle as it appeared in 1601.

necessary timber. Most of the bricks used, which comprise the core of the castle, were newly fired.

The castle, or blockhouse as it should correctly be termed, as finished in 1567 consisted of the main rectangular building with its pointed bastion jutting out into the river and two small towers at either end of the riverside wall. Between 1599 and 1601 the castle was enlarged and strengthened. The bastion was raised and protected by a timber palisade in the water. The two towers were rebuilt to a much larger plan and a courtyard wall, complete with a gatehouse, was added beyond the main block. The great oak door in the entrance is believed to have come from Rochester Castle keep. An encircling ditch was then dug around the entire castle.

Certain other additions were made in succeeding centuries — notably the barrack blocks and other buildings of the 17th to 19th centuries — but these were mostly built away from the castle itself. Externally, the castle as it appeared in 1601 is largely as it looks today, though it was heightened in about 1668 when it was converted into a store and magazine. Internally, however, it has been much altered.

Other Tudor defences of the Medway included smaller blockhouses and bulwarks at Gravesend, Milton, Sheerness and Swaleness. A string of others were added in Stuart and later times, which included forts at Gillingham, Cookham Wood and Sheerness. A chain was strung across the river just below Upnor. When the Dutch sailed up the Medway in 1667 and laid waste about half the English fleet, Upnor failed the supreme test, the very reason for its existence. It was powerless to stop the advances of the Dutch warships. After that humiliating catastrophe, many of the Medway defences were repositioned in more strategic points. By 1668 Upnor Castle had passed out of service and had been relegated to use as a magazine and store.

It continued in this capacity until 1827 when it was converted into an Ordnance Laboratory. In 1891 the castle was transferred from the War Office to the Admiralty. It suffered some damage during World War II from two bombs dropped nearby. Following the subsequent repairs and restorations it was handed over to the then Ministry of Public Buildings and Works in 1961.

Front elevation of Upnor Castle, from the River Medway.   (Kent Messenger)

An attractive village has grown up around the castle. Unfortunately, entering the castle from the landward side, as one must, little of its imposing front elevation can be seen. To see it at its best the castle should be viewed from the river, but a fair impression can be had from the water bastion.

The castle is in splendid condition and despite alterations internally during subsequent centuries, it contains a great deal of original work. The ground floor of the main block is tiled with oak blocks. At this level are a collection of guns and archaelogical discoveries made during restorations. On the floor above is a fine visual display outlining the history of the castle and the Dutch raid. There are four port-hole type gun embrasures in the main room and one each in the two adjoining turrets at both ground and first floor levels. The ones on the first floor are certainly of later date for in Tudor times guns were mounted on the roof before the main block was heightened in the 17th century. A great deal of the original lead lining of the gun embrasures and windows still survives.

The gatehouse has a number of gun-ports but generally, the landward defences at Upnor were slight. It also had a serious weakness in its overall design. While the castle directly fronted the dockyard, only half of its guns could be brought to bear on an approaching enemy ship. The bastion was at one time roofed over, as flash marks on the stone from its lead roof bear witness. From the bastion two passageways, cut into the river bank (the main block revets the bank so that the bastion is below ground level) give access to more gun-ports and pass beneath the two towers. In the courtyard is a well and spaced at intervals around the castle is a collection of old guns, including some huge 19th century cannons.

Upnor, like so many of the best castles, is little known by the general public and is largely ignored by historians. This is a shame because it has so much to offer both visitor and historian alike.

Access: Department of the Environment. Open standard hours. Toilets. Large free car park (situated at top of village in woodland clearing). Map Ref. 758707.

A SOUTH-EAST VIEW OF UPNOR-CASTLE IN KENT

a. The Castle.
b. The South Tower, or Governor's Apartment.
c. The Store Keeper's House.
d. The Barracks.

River Medway.

A 19th century view of Upnor Castle from the River Medway. The view looks much the same today.

(Aylesford Galleries)

WALMER CASTLE

The history of Walmer Castle follows almost exactly that of Deal and Sandown. They are collectively known as 'the Three Castles which keep the Downs' — a safe anchorage point between the coast and the Goodwin Sands.

Built between 1538 and 1540 in response to the threat of invasion from the combined forces of France and Germany, Walmer Castle had an identical plan to the now vanished Sandown Castle. The sea, which has long-since claimed that castle, has fortunately been kept at bay at Walmer.

The castle saw virtually no action until the 17th century Civil War (see separate entry for Deal Castle). A garrison was maintained after the Restoration, under a captain, at each of the three castles of the Downs, but none of them again saw any action. All three had been placed under the overlordship of the Lord Warden of the Cinque Ports and gradually, as their military value declined, the castles came to be used more and more for residential purposes. In 1708 Walmer Castle was adapted for use as the official residence of the Lord Warden. In compliment to the various alterations made internally, a number of additional buildings were erected over the outer bastions and in the courtyard.

Unlike those at Deal, the buildings erected at Walmer were quite tasteful, and over the years the castle has developed into something of a miniature stately home. It is still the Lord Warden's official residence but is reserved for formal occasions these days. When the Warden is not in residence the castle is open to the public. Today it is purely a prestigious title, notable holders being William Pitt, the Duke of Wellington, Sir Winston Churchill, Sir Robert Menzies and in 1979, Her Royal Highness the Queen Mother.

The castle is basically similar to Deal but much smaller and simpler in design. Because also of its adaption as a residence, less of its original internal arrangements can be seen, though they still remain hidden beneath later work. The castle is quatrefoil in plan and consists of a central round tower, or keep, of two storeys, which is free-standing in the middle of a circular courtyard. Attached to the outer wall of the courtyard are four semi-circular bastions of one storey. A deep, dry moat follows the contours of the entire castle.

Sidney Toy in his book 'The Castles of Great Britain' suggests that the courtyard space, which is very narrow, was originally roofed over, level with the platform on top of the bastions. A spiral stairway in the centre of the tower rises through both storeys while another stair leads down to the basement giving access to a mural passage in the bastions. This passage is similar to the 'rounds' at Deal Castle and was provided with 56 gun-loops to sweep the moat. Again, as at Deal, larger cannon were mounted on the bastions and on the roof of the keep.

The castle today stands comfortably back from the sea approached by a stately, tree-lined drive. Its military starkness has been considerably mellowed by the residential additions and the pleasant, if unspectacular grounds in which it stands.

240

Walmer Castle. The entrance through one of the bastions.

Walmer Castle. The massive embrasures have been converted into modern windows. The door leads to the gardens.

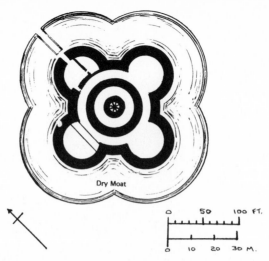

Dry Moat

0   50   100 FT.

0   10   20   30 M.

Ground plan of Walmer Castle.

Taken as a whole, the conversion from a fortress into a home has been extremely successful, the castle lending itself perfectly for such residential uses. The interior is magnificently furnished and decorated and the rooms are surprisingly large. Most of the embrasures have been adapted to take sash windows or, in some cases, modern picture windows, giving the rooms an unexpected lightness.

Many of the internal conversions and additional buildings were made during William Pitt's term of office (1792-1806) and most of the rest by Lord Granville (1865-1891) though all Lords Warden have usually left their mark in one way or another. A great deal of the fabric of the later buildings is of timber construction and these now fill almost half of the courtyard space. In 1874 Lord Granville increased the height of the entrance bastion to provide extra rooms and also added many of the mock medieval battlements. Despite all of these changes, however, much Tudor work remains to be seen, notably the timber, and a number of the embrasures have survived even if furnished now with window frames.

Unfortunately, while access can be made to the roofs of the basions, access cannot be made to their basements. The bastions are quite high and the moat appears to be deeper than that at Deal. The moat has been laid to lawn and skilfully planted out as an integral part of the garden forming a neat, picturesque frame to the castle. In Wellington's time the moat was used as a kitchen garden.

The gardens at Walmer are accessible from the south side of the castle by crossing a wooden bridge over the moat. William Pitt's niece, Lady Hester Stanhope, began laying out the gardens while staying at the castle and it is to her that we owe The Dell, an old quarry that she planted out with trees. Lord Granville greatly improved the grounds and planted the trees along the drive — and

Walmer Castle as it appeared in 1832 from a drawing by G. Shepherd. (Aylesford Galleries)

also those near the water-front which form a good wind-break. The gardens are mostly formal but very pleasant.

Not all of the Lords Warden have made their homes at Walmer — none of the more recent ones in fact — usually using it as an occasional summer residence only. Others, however, have spent many years there. The most notable of all the castle's permanent residents was the Duke of Wellington, who spent the latter part of his life there. The room in which he died on 14th September 1852 has been kept largely as he left it. The 'Duke of Wellington Room' and the room next to it, have been laid out as a museum of 'Wellingtonia' and include a pair of the famous boots.

Queen Victoria often visited the castle during Wellington's term of office. She always stayed in one particular room, which affords a fine view across the ramparts and out to the sea beyond. All of the Lords Warden have left some item of interest or piece of furniture behind as a kind of memento. A tour of the castle is quite a fascinating excursion into the more recent political past ensuring Walmer's continued presence in the annals of British history.

Adjoining the churchyard wall of the parish church, stand the ruined flint walls of a Norman, semi-fortified house known as Walmer Court. There are two square rooms with evidence of an upper storey, but nothing is known of it.

Access: Department of the Environment. Open standard hours — except when Lord Warden is in residence. Entrance to the castle is from the seafront 1 mile south of Deal.
Map Ref. 378501.

The romantic, overgrown ruins of Westenhanger Castle.

Westenhanger Castle. Remains of the gatehouse entrance passage.

WESTENHANGER CASTLE

Westenhanger Castle today is at once both sad and romantic. Sad, because it stands neglected between Folkestone Racecourse and a railway line, yet romantic because it is one of the few castles that still remains an overgrown ruin. Ivy climbs profusely over its walls and its towers shelter beneath mighty trees, while the grass of the once neat courtyard lawn now stands waist high. It is very picturesque and strangely haunting, but unless steps are taken soon to secure its fabric it may not be standing for very much longer.

Originally, the manor of Westenhanger was divided between two great families — Hugh de Montfort and William de Eddesham (or Addisham). By the early 13th century ownership had passed to the de Auberville's and soon after, by marriage, to the Kiriel (or Criol) family. No castle existed at that time but a licence to crenellate his manor was granted to John de Kiriel in 1344 during the French scare of Edward III's reign. He built a quadrangular, courtyard castle similar in design to Scotney and Cooling but much more closely resembling Bodiam in Sussex.

The Castle consisted of a rectangular court about 130ft by 90ft surrounded by domestic apartments and nine towers. It had round towers at each corner (except the south-east one which was square) and shallow, rectangular towers midway along three walls with a twin-towered gatehouse on the fourth. A 17th century plan shows it to be almost identical to Bodiam, though considerably weaker in overall strength.

The Kiriel's held possession of the castle until 1461 when it passed to Fogge of Ripton, near Ashford. By 1503 however, ownership had reverted to a descendant of the Kiriel's, Sir Edward Poyning, who made some notable Tudor additions. These have now mostly gone alas, except for a brick arched fireplace in the west wall near the gatehouse.

The castle then became crown property for a while until it was granted to Thomas Smythe in 1585. Like so many other castles, Westenhanger then passed through a long line of farming families, its buildings being taken down or converted for humbler uses.

In 1701 the castle was sold off and a great deal of its fabric used to build a nearby farmhouse. Poyning's Tudor house was demolished and a Queen Anne style house erected in its place in the north-east corner. This was again replaced by the present Georgian house later on in the 18th century. The tower in the north-east corner which adjoins it, also received a conical roof at this time and was partially converted into a dovecote. The tower remains in a fairly good state of preservation and the only one of the nine to survive in anything like its original condition. The house itself is in ruins now, though it still retains its roof and is relatively sound.

Of the original castle, a fraction only remains and what does survive is rapidly

Fair Rosamund's Tower, Westenhanger Castle.

falling into decay. The moat, which was once some 50ft across and fed by damming the River Stour and altering its course, is now dry. The north wall is substantially intact as is a long length of the east wall and about half of the western one. Apart from the north-east tower, there are remains also of the north and north-west towers.

The north-west one has associations with Rosamund Clifford, one of Henry II's mistresses, who was supposed to have lived there before her imprisonment at Woodstock. She may have stayed at Westenhanger in the manor house that previously stood there, but she certainly did not occupy this tower — Fair Rosamund's Tower — for it was not built until the mid-14th century.

On the west wall, traces of the gatehouse can still be seen, consisting mainly of the entrance passage walls. The portcullis grooves are still visible, so too are the shafts and corbels that once supported a stone vaulted roof, but the vaulting and the rest of the gatehouse have gone.

Despite its scanty and overgrown condition, Westenhanger Castle still preserves the enchantment and romantic flavour of an ivy clad ruin — a rarity indeed these days — an atmosphere sometimes lost in other, more immaculately preserved castles. It maintains that same air of excitement that must have befallen our Victorian ancestors when they chanced upon a ruined castle tucked away, like this one, in remote countryside. Unfortunately, it cannot remain so for very much longer for, as noted earlier, it is in dire need of repair.

Access: The remains are accessible from Folkestone Racecourse on the B2068 road, but permission must be obtained from the proprietors. Assuming permission has been granted, cross the winner's enclosure behind the main stadium and walk into the nearby wood, where the castle stands close to a farm entrance.
Map Ref. 121373.

WEST MALLING CASTLE

Considerable controversy surrounds this little castle at West Malling. Known as St. Leonard's Tower, it once stood beside a Norman church of the same name. It was built at the very early date of 1070 (1100 at the latest) making it one of the earliest surviving, pure Norman buildings in the country. Its position close to the church has led to the controversey, for while some authorities believe that it was a Norman castle keep, others argue that it was merely a large church tower.

Sidney Toy, the respected authority on castles, maintained that the tower was too slightly built to be defensible. He also stated that it contained no domestic amenities or outer defences and had too large window openings to be a keep, so dismissed it as being no more than an enlarged church tower. As much as I admire the work of Mr. Toy I find myself in disagreement with him on this matter.

Compared with such keeps as Rochester or Dover, St. Leonard's Tower is small, but it is nevertheless far greater in size than any church tower — especially one of Norman date. It was a common practice on the continent to erect single, unattached towers (or keeps) similar to the later tower houses of Northern England and Scotland. Some were built by minor landowners who could not afford to erect castles, some were temporary shelters on a baron's estates. Others, however, were built by the clergy near to their churches for their own protection, particularly in troubled areas.

As such, these towers were not attached to the churches in the usual sense, but neither were they castles complete with all the outer walls and defences normally associated with them. They were the simple defensive homes of the clergy, not designed to withstand an organised attack but to protect the priests from local skirmishes.

The Normans were not popular with the native Saxons in England and in the years immediately following the Conquest many went in fear of their lives. It is not surprising then, to find even the clergy building themselves castles or fortified homes. St. Leonard's Tower was built by Bishop Gundulph who erected a similar tower adjacent to his Cathedral at Rochester. Still known as Gundulph's Tower, the structure at Rochester is really a small, defensible keep and not merely a church tower. The tower at West Malling, I believe, is of the same type.

St. Leonard's Tower is well preserved and stands to almost its full height of about 60ft. It is very ornate, especially so when considering its early date, and stands on a sloping rock shelf. It is built mostly from Kentish ragstone but has Tuffa stone dressings — a hard but porous rock often favoured by the Romans for finishing off door and window arches.

It appears to have been of only two storeys above a basement that was only 5ft in height. The windows at the upper level are quite large, those in the east and south walls being set within blind arcades, and all the sills are deeply set into

St. Leonard's Tower, West Malling. One of the earliest Norman towers to be built in England.

the walls. The tower did not have corner turrets but was provided with a series of shallow, pillaster buttresses for added strength. The one at the north-west corner was slightly enlarged to contain a staircase.

The tower seems to have been in the possession of the church for most of its life and very little, unfortunately, is known about its early history and occupants. In the 17th century it belonged to the Rainey family and later to the Honeywoods. Afterwards it was used for a while as a gaol and finally as a hop store. It is now in the expert care of the Department of the Environment and stands almost opposite the delightful Manor Park country park at the southern extremity of West Malling village.

Access: At West Malling just off A20. Department of Environment. Open at all times. Admission free. Key at No. 115 St. Leonard's Street, opposite. Map Ref. 674570.

WHITSTABLE CASTLE

The structure known today as Whitstable Castle, although not a true medieval castle (yet neither is it entirely a 'mock gothic' castle) has a chequered past, intriniscally linked with the industrial history of the town in which it stands.

After the Norman Conquest, the manors of Whitstable, Seasalter and Swalecliffe were held by Bishop Odo, the Conqueror's half-brother. The manors were sub-leased, that of Whitstable being held for the Bishop by a man named Vitalis. Later, in the 13th century, it became the property of a certain knight, William de Tangreton.

During the French scare of Edward III's reign a coastal warning beacon was constructed at Whitstable, possibly on the site of the present castle and now perhaps incorporated into the older wing of the building. Part of this wing is believed to date from the 15th century.

Whitstable long depended upon the sea for its livelihood, but in the 16th century was added another important industry, the extraction of copperas from shallow mines. Copperas mines were first established at Whitstable by a Dutchman, Cornelius de Vos, who changed his name to Stevenson on settling in England. He died in 1594, after which many other local businessmen took over the industry. One of these, Nicholas Sympson, who in the 18th century owned Tankerton Manor, built a copperas works on a mound near the present castle.

By the late 18th century, however, the industry had gone into decline and in 1779 the then owner, Charles Pearson, demolished the works, using the materials to extend the manor house. He built the large, octagonal tower and it is from this point that the manor came to be known as Tankerton, and later Whitstable, Castle. His son, another Charles, further enlarged the house in about 1827, adding many of the castellated embellishments we see today in true, revivalist tradition.

The younger Charles also had connections with George Stephenson and the building of the first passenger steam train service in the world, opened in 1830 between Whitstable and Canterbury. Originally the railway was planned to terminate in the castle grounds, but was later diverted to the harbour.

One of the castle's more recent owners was a Mr. T.E. Adams, who added the billiard room. After his death his widow continued to live there until 1920. In 1921 it was purchased by Albert Mallandair as a summer residence.

In 1935, Whitstable Urban District Council bought the castle for £10,000. Some of the household staff were kept on for caretaking duties and in 1948 the grounds were opened as a public park. It later housed the council offices, but following local government re-organisation in 1972, was leased to the Whitstable Society and now fulfills the admirable function of community and amenity centre.

Whitstable Castle. A picturesque 'mock gothic' castle incorporating an older manor house.

For all its sham-like appearance, Whitstable Castle is an impressive structure, if not very military looking, complete with mock battlements, machicolations and arrow loops. It even has a few bartizan turrets perched at roof level in the manner of a Scottish tower house.

It is built partly from brick and partly from knapped flints with a dressed stone extension and stands, rather picturesquely, overlooking the sea. The park is well established and contains a number of exotic fan palms to complete the whole, imaginative picture. The castle interior provides us with a rare glimpse inside one of the many 'mock castles' built, but most of which are still privately lived in.

Access: The park is open most days until dusk and may be freely visited. Access to the castle interior may be had on application to the Secretary of the Castle Centre Association.
Map Ref. 113672.

MISCELLANEOUS EARTHWORKS

Moats, Mounds and Manor Houses

There are a vast number of earthworks in Kent of all manner, many of which do not fit neatly into any category. The moated homesteads (referred to on O.S. maps as moats and usually now the sites of farms) were constructed from ancient times — at least as long ago as the Celtic and Saxon periods — right up until the 16th and 17th centuries. Some expanded and grew into fortified manor houses, as at Hever, and some developed into mighty fortresses, as at Leeds, while others never rose above the rank of moated houses.

There are many examples of moated homesteads in Kent — far too many to include in this volume — most of which were never fortified. The moat usually provided the only form of defence — and this as much to protect the inhabitants from wild animals as from human energies. Wolves, bear and wild boar were still abundant in England at least until medieval times.

There is virtually no written record of the vast majority of moated homesteads. In many cases the original manor houses have disappeared and been replaced or incorporated into more modern buildings. I have given a list, far from complete, at the end of the gazetteer section with O.S. map references so that readers who are sufficiently interested can locate them. Below are a few details of some of · the more important examples.

BOUGHTON ALUPH. Boughton Court is a 19th century house built over a much older undercroft. Sir Thomas de Aldon was granted a licence to build a fortified house there in 1339 but it seems never to have developed beyond a manor house.

IGHTHAM MOTE. It is with some regret that I decided, after much deliberation, to exclude Ightham from the gazetteer section of this book. Although it is one of the most complete remaining examples of an ancient moated manor house, I felt I must exclude it. To have included it would have meant similar, separate entries for a great many other manor houses, for which there is no space.

The manor is quite delightful, sitting beautifully preserved behind its moat in the deeply wooded countryside near Sevenoaks. It is open to the public every Friday afternoon 2—5pm. (2—4pm between December—February) and a visit is strongly recommended.

In the woods to the north of the manor are the remains of earthworks from its Norman predecessor, possibly standing on the site of a prehistoric mound.

KENNARDINGTON. The slight earthwork remains here were claimed by G.T. Clark to be an early Norman motte and bailey castle, but there is no supportive evidence for this. [G.T. Clark also believed motte and baileys existed at Haydon

Mount and Newington — all supposedly with shell keeps. He may have confused Newington with nearby Tonge Castle, with Newnham near Doddington, or with Castle Toll at Newenden. Hayden Mount may also have been confused with Castle Toll for a nearby stream is called the Hayden Channel. None of these three 'castles' have yet been satisfactorily identified.]

MINSTER THANET — Cheeseman's Camp. There are remains here of earthworks and a moated manor house displaying slight traces of fortification, but nothing is known of it.

OLD SOAR MANOR — **Near Ightham.** The remains consist of the solar block of a late, unfortified knight's dwelling of the 13th century. The manor is under the joint protection of the National Trust and the Department of the Environment. It is well preserved and should be visited because of the similarity between it and the domestic buildings erected within castle baileys.

Open to the public April—September. Weekdays 9.30—7.00pm. Sundays 2—7pm.

SELLING — **Perry Wood.** There are remains here of a small mound, only 15ft high, believed by some authorities to be the site of a moat or a motte and bailey castle. There are no visible remains of any attached earthworks nor any written records. It has also been suggested that it was an adulterine castle erected in Stephen's reign, but only an excavation of the site will disclose its true origins.

THANINGTON — **Tonford Manor.** A licence to crenellate his house was granted to Sir Thomas Browne, Comptroller and Treasurer to Henry VI, in 1449. He built a semi-fortified manor house in flint within a square moat. It had a two storeyed gatehouse in one corner but virtually no other defences. It is a fine example of its type, the remains consisting of the gatehouse and a small length of wall, both now incorporated into an 18th century house.

WOULDHAM. In Shoulder of Mutton Wood stands a small mound. It has no attached earthworks but in this case, speculations on its origins casts an interesting light upon another possible use for some of the smaller earthworks. It is believed that the Normans surrounded their castles with a series of look-out towers, erected on top of mounds. If this is correct, then the mound at Wouldham may have been such a look-out for Rochester Castle, which is only three miles away.

There I must conclude this brief summary of moats, manors and other earthworks that do not qualify as castles. Ideally, such great houses as Knole and Boughton Monchelsea Place should have been included, but they fall rather beyond the scope of the present volume.

There are, in addition to those type of site already referred to, a vast number of smaller earthwork enclosures which, rightly or wrongly, have been attributed to the Romans, Saxons or Danes. Again, we are unlikely to know their original date or purpose, which may or may not have been of a defensive nature, since few are likely to be excavated.

It has been suggested that many were simply livestock compounds since seldom are any traces of habitation found within them. In addition to these, of course, are the countless numbers of prehistoric mounds of uncertain date and use which were never later adapted for any known purpose. The classification of earthworks is indeed a difficult task.

Hillforts

I have had to adopt the same approach to the many larger earthworks of Iron Age (or earlier) origins as I have with moats and mounds. As discussed in the Introduction and Part One of this book, many of those earthworks freely ascribed to be hillforts may never have been built for defence at all, but were perhaps simple enclosures of some sort, of an as yet unknown use.

Despite archaeological evidence, which serves only to date them in the main, there are few clues as to their original purpose. With the total lack of any written records we shall probably never know what that purpose was. Some of the larger examples, it seems, such as Oldbury near Sevenoaks and Bigbury near Canterbury, were built for defence, but I decline to speculate on them in very much detail. A great deal more research into their origins needs to be done before they can all be categorised as hillforts.

I have listed a number of them (again, far from exhaustive) at the end of the gazetteer section, and furnished them with O.S. map references. Seldom do such sites offer any interest, except to the academic or enthusiast, and most are relatively inaccessible — as well as being hard to find. None of the Kentish examples are in very good condition.

Because of the controversy that surrounds hillforts and because also of the lack of any historical information on them, I have decided to omit them from any specific entries in the gazetteer section. Virtually the only information available on them is in the form of archaeological reports following excavation of their sites.

I would direct interested readers to the accounts in the 'Victoria History of the County of Kent' and the various reports in 'Archaeologia Cantiana'. Accounts, usually in the form of inventories of the discoveries made, can be found there in much fuller detail than is possible for me to give.

List of 'Moat' Sites in Kent (O.S. 1:50 000 Series)

Name	Location	Map Ref.
Moat	Chiselhurst	459701
Moat, Filston Farm	½ mile S. Shoreham	516608
Moat	1 mile N. Crayford	528767
Moat	Isle of Harty, Sheppey	023663
Moat	1 mile S. Herne Bay	189661
Moat	2 miles S.E. Wingham	267557
Moat, Henden Manor	1 mile S.W. Ide Hill	483505
Moat, Broxham Manor	½ mile W. Four Elms	457484
Moat, Filston Hall	¾ mile S. Shoreham	516607
Moat	Leigh	555466
Moat, St. Julian's Farm	2½ miles W. Shipbourne	553518
Moat	¾ mile N.W. Hadlow	626506
Moat	½ mile S.E. Yalding	704498
Moat	¾ mile S.E. Chainhurst	737467
Moat	2 miles S. Sutton Valence	818464
Moat, Groombridge Place	½ mile N. Groombridge	534375
Owls Castle Farm	1½ miles W. Scotney Castle	663348
Moats (concentric) Share Farm	1 mile S.E. Horsmonden	715393
Moat	2 miles S.E. Goudhurst	738348
Moat	1 mile S.W. Staplehurst	775424
Ightham Mote	2½ miles S.W. Ightham	584535
Old Soar Manor	2 miles S.E. Ightham	619541
Moat	1¼ miles S.W. Staplehurst	775414
Moat	2 miles W. Sandhurst	764280
Moat	1 mile S. Frittenden	816391
Moat	1½ miles S.W. Wye	031464
Moat	1 mile S.E. Hinxhill	059411
Moat	1 mile S.W. Mersham	039393
Moat	Bilsington	041343
Moat	Hatch Park	059411
Moat	1½ miles S.S.W. Wye	031464
Moat	½ mile S.W. Mersham	038394
Moat	½ mile W. Sevington	030407
Moat	½ mile N.E. Kingsnorth	012395
Moat	¾ mile S. Ashford	994396
Moat	¾ mile S.W. Ashford	988416
Moat	½ mile S.W. Great Chart	974414
Moat, Wootton Manor	1 mile S.E. Charing	963479
Moat	1½ miles N.W. Little Chart	922465

Moat (Coldbridge Farm)	1 mile S. Boughton Malherbe	885479
Moats	Old Romney	035255
Moat	1 mile N.W. Ivychurch	022288
Moat	1½ mile N.W. Wittersham	882284
Moat	¾ mile N. Castle Toll	854295

List of Hillforts and other Earthworks in Kent (O.S. 1:50 000 Series)

Name	Location	Map Ref.
Caesar's Camp, hillfort	Holwood, 1 mile S.S.E. Keston	423638
Hillfort	1½ miles S.E. Keston	432640
Earthwork	1 mile N.W. Farningham	534674
Caesar's Camp, hillfort	1½ miles S.W. Farnborough	424636/8
Earthworks	Cobham	685694
Mounds (numerous)	Isle of Harty, Sheppey	
Keycol Hill, hillfort	Newington, nr. Sittingbourne	869649
Bigbury, hillfort	1 mile S.W. Harbledown	117577
Camp	Shepherdswell	274472/8
Earthwork	1 mile S. Selling	042554
Earthworks	1 mile N.W. Chilham	060549
The Mount	1 mile S.W. Knockholt	466584
Earthwork, Hogtrough Hill	1 mile N.W. Brasted	459569
Earthwork	2 miles W. Otford	499591
Mound	1½ miles N.W. Wrotham	589602
Earthwork	1¼ miles N.W. Wrotham	593598
Oldbury, hillfort	¾ mile W. Ightham	582556/69
Earthwork	¾ mile S. Trottiscliffe	635592
Earthwork	½ mile S.W. Barming Station	722564
Earthwork	1½ miles S.E. Farleigh	734508
Mound	2½ miles S.W. Bredhurst	768613
Earthworks (Series)	Boughton Monchelsea area	From 764515
		To 785505
High Rocks, hillfort	Tunbridge Wells	564382
Castle Hill, hillfort	1½ miles N.E. Southborough	607437
Earthwork	1½ miles S. Staplehurst	784407
Enclosure	Kenardington Church	975324
Tolsford Hill, Camp	1 mile S.E. Postling	155382
Earthwork	1½ miles S.W. Chilham	091529
Earthwork	¼ mile N. Hastingleigh	091454
Earthwork	1½ miles S.E. Chilham	091528
Earthworks	1 mile N.W. Chilham	060549
Earthwork	½ mile N. Lenham	902529

SELECT BIBLIOGRAPHY

'The Castles of Great Britain' — Sidney Toy (Heinemann) (1953).
'Castles' — B.H. St. J. O'Neil (HMSO) (1954).
'Norman Castles in Britain' — Derek Renn (John Baker) (1968).
'Castles in England and Wales' — W. Douglas Simpson (Batsford) (1969).
Department of the Environment and private guide books.
'The Buildings of England' (Kent 2 vols.) Ed. N. Pevsner (Penguin).
'The History of the King's Works' (Vols. I-III) General Editor H.M. Colvin (HMSO) (1963-70).
'The Castles of England' — Frederick Wilkinson (George Philip) (1973).
'The Observers Book of Castles' — Brian K. Davison (Warne) (1979).
'The Medieval Economy and Society' — M.M. Postan (Penguin) (1972).
'The Anglo Saxon Chronicle' (translation) — G.N. Garmonsway (Dent) (1953).
'English Society in the Early Middle Ages' — Doris Mary Stenton (Penguin) (1951).
'The National Trust Book· of British Castles' — Paul Johnson (Weidenfeld and Nicolson) (1978).
'English Castles' — R. Allen Brown (Batsford) (2nd ed. 1976).
'Castles of Britain' — Christina and Bamber Gascoigne (Thames and Hudson) (1975).
'Life in the Castle in Medieval England' — John Burke (Batsford) (1978).
'Life in a Medieval Castle' — J. and F. Gies (Abelard-Schuman) (1975).
'The Pattern of English Building' — Alec Clifton-Taylor (Faber) (1972).
'Castles of the Western World' — Armin Tuulse (Thames and Hudson) (1958).
'The Master Builders' — John Harvey (Thames and Hudson) (1971).
'Strongholds of the Realm' — Charles Kightly and Peter Cheze-Brown (Thames and Hudson) (1979).
'Memorials of Old Kent' — Harold Sands (1907).
'Early Norman Castles of the British Isles' — E.S. Armitage (John Murray) (1912).
'Victoria History of the County of Kent' — Ed. William Page (Constable) (1908).
'History of the County of Kent' — Hasted.
'Perambulation of Kent' — William Lambard.
'Archaeologia Cantiana' (numerous volumes, see collective indexes).

INDEX

Albini, William de   124,189
Alfred, King   18,19,85,94
Allington Castle   34,44,47,51,54,68,73
   78-84,105,137,165,195,235
Anglo Saxon Chronicle   18,19,85,115
Arois, William de   130
Arsick, Sir William de   151
Arundel, Archbishop Thomas   145,171
Ashburnham, Roger de   63,207,208
Astley, Sir John   81
Aubervilles, (family)   218,245
Audley, Hugh de   231

Badlesmere, Bartholomew de   101,145
Baddlesmere, (family)   233
Baker, (family)   215
Baliol, Alexander de   100
Banquel, Sir John de   88
Barbicans   84,121,173,199,207
Bath Houses   55,145
Bayford Castle   85-86,94,233
Becket, Thomas (Archbishop)   123,192,
   194,228
Bethune, Baldwin de   224
Bigbury Hillfort   253
Binbury Castle   21,87, 218,219,225
Black Death   61,141,165,214,233
Bodiam Castle   49,51,63,64,79,107,132,
   207,208,245
Boleyn (or Bullen), Anne   80,136,137,
   138,213
Bonbury Castle   87
Box, John   61,171
Bréant, Foulke de (Also Brent Fulk de)
   100,141
Brenchley Castle   87-88
Breton, Richard le   194
Broc, Sir Ranulf de   193,194
Bromley Castle   88
Brooke, Elizabeth   80
Brooke, George   105
Burgh, Hubert de   90,117,119,121
Burgh, Hugh de   229
Burghs   18
Burh-bol   19,26

Caerlaverock, Siege of   103,151,213,218
Caesar's Camp   24,130
Canterbury Castle   89-93
Canterbury, City Walls   62,69,89,91,92,
   205

Canterbury, West Gate   47,91,171,194
Carausius   17,175,177,178,179,222
Castle Rough   85,94-95
Castle Service   19,26,35
Castle Toll   96,252
Chapels   51,83,109,120,145,154,170,186,
   188,198,217
Cheyney (family)   85,213
Cheyney, Humphrey   85
Cheyney, Sir Thomas   101,213
Cheyney, Sir William   213
Chichelle, Archbishop Henry   208
Chiddingstone Castle   97-98
Chilham Castle   33,74,99-102,213
Chilham, Richard de   100
Civil War   68,71-73,92,111,147,173,203,
   208,231
Clare, (family)   88,164,207,228,229,231
Clare, Gilbert de   207,228,229,231
Clare, Richard de   88,228,229,231
Clare, Roger de   228
Clare, William de   207
Clocks   170
Cobham, (family)   79,80,104,105,106,
   136,214
Cobham, Sir John de   63,104,105,106,136
Cobham, Sir Reginald   136,214
Coldbridge Castle   103
Concentric Castles   33,34,57,59,60,61,
   117,145,171,203,225
Cooling Castle   34,40,41,43,47,61,63,
   79,104-109,132,136,171,208,214,245
Corbeil, Archbishop William de   29,185
Corbye Robert   103,225
Courteney, Archbishop William   91,194,
   195,196
Cranmer, Archbishop Thomas   96,153,
   194
Crevecoeur, Hamo de   143
Crevecoeur, Hamon de   143,164
Crevecoeur, Robert de   143
Criol (or Kiriel), family   124,125,218,
   245
Criol (or Kiriel), Nicholas de   218
Culpepper, (family)   146
Dalyngrigge, Sir Edward   63,207
Darell, (family)   208,209
Deal Castle   68,69,70,71,110-114,171,
   201,202,203,235,240,242

Dent-de-Lion Castle (also Daundelyon) 65,**132-134**
Dent-de-Lion, John   132
Deptford Castle   **114**
Despencer, Hugh le   231
Devereux, Sir John   165
Digges, Sir Dudley   101
Dover Castle   19,28,29,33,34,35,39,40, 44,47,55,56,57,61,68,71,72,79,84,90, 93,99,100,**115-122**,183,247
Dover, de (family)   100
Dover Roman Fort   18,115,177
Drains   40,55,200
Drawbridges   37,44,45,47,83,88,91, 106,108,113,120,140,196,207

Eddesham (or Addisham), William de 245
Edward I, King   35,57,58,60,79,85,96, 103,136,143,145,151,215,218,229,231
Edward II, King   34,145,231
Edward III, King   61,62,66,145,153,169, 170,171,190,205
Edward IV, King   206,233
Edward VI, King   80,233
Edward The Confessor   85
Egbert, King of Kent   175,192
Elizabeth I, Queen   70,71,81,171,235
Essex, Henry de   192,193,194
Etchingham, Sir John de   207
Eustace, Earl of Boulogne   115
Eynsford Castle   29,49,52,54,**123-129**, 192
Eynsford, (family)   123,124

Fairseat Castle   **129**
Fireplaces   53,84,93,114,126,128,167, 187
FitzAucher, (family)   96
FitzGilbert, Richard de   228
Fitzurse, Reginald   194
Folkestone Castle   21,24,**130-132**
Forebuildings   83,93,100,119,120,128, 185,186,223
Foxley, John de   169,171
Gardens   60,143,170,196,213
Garlinge Castle   65,**132-134**
Ghosts   138,176,191,194,209,213
Godard's Castle   225
Godwin, Earl   85,192
Gravel Castle   **134**
Grofhurst, John de   207
Gros, William le   224
Gundulph, Bishop   29,123,183,184,189, 247

Hadlow Castle   75,135
Haesten   85,94
Harold, King   115
Haydon Mount   251,252
Hengist   192,233
Henry I, King   185
Henry II, King   31,32,33,34,36,56,57, 79,115,117,123,193,194,228,246
Henry III, King   34,54,55,74,90,117, 118,151,185,189,229
Henry IV, King   66,105,145
Henry V, King   119,145
Henry VI, King   65
Henry VII, King   69,79
Henry VIII, King   61,69,70,71,80,110, 112,113,114,117,119,136,138,145,153, 156,171,201,202,203,235
Herland, Hugh   66
Hever Castle   41,44,45,62,68,73,88,**136-140**,211,251
Hever, William de   136
Hillforts   15,16,18,57,115,253,255
Hoardings (or Hoardes)   37,41,42,128, 188,200
Hussey, (family)   209,211
Iaernside, Bjorn   85
Ightham Mote   125,251
James of St George   58,59
John, King   100,117,118,124,189,228, 229

Kemsing Castle   **141**
Kennardington Castle   **251-252**
Kingsgate Castle   75,132,**141-142**
Kiriel (or Criol), family   124,125,218, 245
Kirkby, William de   221
Knowle Castle   **87**
Knox Bridge Castle   **142**

Lambhurst, Stephen   207
Lanfranc, Archbishop   123,159
Latrines   55,119,127,186,187,192,232
Lee, Sir Richard   235
Leeds Castle   29,34,35,41,44,55,59,61, 63,68,73,84,101,**143-150**, 164,207, 233,251
Leybourne Castle   25,43,76,**151-155**
Leybourne, (family)   85,103,151,153, 154
Leybourne, Juliana de   103,153
Leybourne, Sir Roger de   143,151
Leybourne, William de   103,143,151
Lollards   91,194
Longchamp, Osbert de   79

260

Lovelace, (family)   85
Lucy, de (family)   99,100
Lullingstone Castle   126,**156-158**, 212
Lympne Castle   18,52,66,**159-163**, 217, 222,223

Machicolations   41,42,43,83,91,104, 108,140,143,155,196,209,
Magminot, Gilbert de   87,114
Mareschal's, Earls of Pembroke   224
Maurice the Engineer   32
May, Walter Barton   75,135
Mereworth Castle   75,**164**
Meutrierrés   42,113
Mining operations   34,**38-39**,118,121,189
Minster (Thanet), Cheeseman's Camp   252
Montfort, Hugh   245
Montfort, Robert de   193
Montfort, Simon de   190,207,224
Morville, Hugh de   194
Motte and bailey castles   21,23,24,25,27, 29,31,72,79,87,88,89,96,99,129,131, 142,151,163,183,188,219,221,225, 227,228,229,233,251,252

Napoleonic wars   29,117,122,203
Newenden   96,252
Newington Castle   252
Newnham Castle   **163**,252
Northwood (or Northwode), family   87, 220,225
Nottingham, Robert de   85

Odo, Bishop of Bayeux, (Earl of Kent) 79,87,99,119,123,135,143,151,189, 212,218,225,233,249
Oldbury Hill   15,253
Old Soar Manor   252
Oldcastle, Sir John   105
Otford   66

Peche, John   156
Penchester, Stephen de   79,119,165
Penshurst Place   52,53,63,68,162,**165-168**
Peyforer, Fulk de   103,170
Peyforer, Osborne   212
Portcullis   45,47,109,113,133,140,155, 186,196,232,246
Poyning, Sir Edward   242
Poyntz, Hugo de   212
Pulteney, Sir John de   63,165
Putlog holes   155,199-200

Queenborough Castle   26,30,60,61, 68,70,71,110,**169-173**,213

Rats Castles   174,212
Reculver Roman Fort   16,18,**174-176**, 177,222
Rich, Colonel Nathaniel   111,203
Richard I, King   117,151
Richborough Castle   16,17,18,175,**177-181**,222
Rochester Castle   21,24,28,29,31,38,41, 49,52,53,54,55,61,62,68,71,73,84,90, 92,93,100,123,124,**182-191**,235,236, 247,252
Rochester City Walls   62
Rokesle, John de   156
Romden Castle   **191**

St. Ledger, Sir Thomas   145
Saltwood Castle   40,44,47,49,55,60,66, 73,79,91,126,155,159,**192-200**
Salvin, Anthony   75,76,209
Sandgate Castle   69,70,110,**201-202**
Sandown Castle   70,71,110,111,201,**203-204**,235,240
Sandwich Castle   62,63,**205-206**
Sandwich, town walls   71,132,205
Saxingherste, de (family)   215
Saxon Shore Forts   17,18,110,115,159, 174,**177-179**,222
Scoteni, Lambert de   207
Scoteni, Walter de   207
Scotney Castle   34,41,63,64,76,107, 132,136,**207-211**,215,216,245
Selling Castle   252
Seyntleger, Ralph de   96
Shell keeps   27,28,61,143,171,219,225, 227,229,232,252
Shoreham Castle   156,**212**
Shurland Castle (or Hall)   101,**213-214**
Shurland, Sir Geoffrey de   213
Shurland, Sir Robert de   213
Sieges   31,36-47,66-67,105-106,117, 118,121,188-190
Simpson's Moat   88
Sissinghurst Castle   76,136,**215-216**
Slighting   73,111,147,173
Snakeshaw Castle   226
Spiders Castle   212
Stafford, (family)   231
Starborough Castle   **214**
Starkey Castle   52,62,**217**
Starkey, Sir Humphrey   217
Stephen, King   31,32,34,79,123
Stockbury Castle   21,25,30,155,**218-219**, 225
Stockings Wood Castle   87

Upnor Castle   68,69,70,190,**235-239**
Valence, Stephen de   221
Valence, William de   224
Vortigern   233

Walmer Castle   68,69,71,110,111,113,
    201,202,203,204,**240-243**
Walmer Court   243
Warenne, William de   24,79
Weldon, Sir Anthony   91,190
Weldon, Walker   92,190
Westenhanger Castle   64,76,218,**244-246**
West Malling Castle, (St. Leonard's Tower)
    183,**247-248**
Wethershed, Archbishop   229
White, Donald A.   178,179
Whitstable Castle   75,**249-250**
William I, King   19,20,21,99,114,143,
    151,228
William II, King   183,189
Wiltshire, Sir Richard   220
Windows   48,54-55, 84,93,124,128,
    196,242,247
Wouldham   252
Wyatt, (family)   79,80,81
Wyatt, Sir Henry   79,80,84
Wyatt, Sir Thomas   80,83,84,105,106,
    137,235

Wykeham, William of   61,170
Wyllshire, Sir John   220

Yetts   47
Yevelle, Henry   66,106,145,171,194
Stone Castle   75,**220-221**
Stowting Castle   **221**
Streatfield, Henry   97
Stutfall Castle   163,177,**222-223**
Sudbury, Archbishop   194
Sutton Valence Castle   **223-224**
Swift, Richard   66

Tangreton, William de   249
Tankerton Castle   249
Thanington Castle, (Tonford Manor)   252
Thorpe, William   194,198
Thurnham Castle   21,87,218,219,**225-226**
Tonbridge Castle   21,24,27,42,43,47,
    55,59,72,75,88,**227-232**
Tonge Castle   21,85,**233-234**, 252
Town walls   32,62,69,71,89,91,92,169,
    183,205,206,229,235
Tracey, William de   194
Tunnels   100,117,118,121,1221,55
Turnham, (family)   225
Tyler, Wat   190

Meresborough Books

PUBLISHERS AND WHOLESALERS OF BOOKS ON KENT
7 STATION ROAD, RAINHAM, GILLINGHAM, KENT. ME8 7RS
Telephone Medway (0634) 371591

We are publishers specializing in books on Kent. Below is a list of titles available at the time of going to press. They are available from most bookshops throughout Kent, including The Rainham Bookshop, 7 Station Road, Rainham, Kent.

BYGONE KENT
A monthly journal on all aspects of Kent History. 95p per month. Annual Subscription £10.50.

KENT CASTLES by John Guy
The first comprehensive guide to all the castles and castle sites in Kent. The first part outlines the history of castles and castle building. The second part gives the history of over 60 castles in Kent with a guide for the modern visitor. 264 pages. Over 150 illustrations. Hardback. To be published late May at £7.50 (£7.95 post free).

THE CANTERBURY AND WHITSTABLE RAILWAY 1830-1980: A PICTORIAL SURVEY
(Published with the Locomotive Club of Great Britain.) 28 pages. Over 30 pictures and maps. 75p (95p post free).

THE HOME GUARD IN KENT by Keith Gulvin
(Published with North Kent Books.) 96 pages, hardback. Well illustrated. An important book for the historian as well as being of great interest to all those who took part. £3.75 (£4.20 post free).

MEDWAY MEMORIES by Norman Clout
A series of talks first broadcast on Radio Medway, Summer 1980. £1.50 (£1.80 post free).

ROCHESTER'S HERITAGE TRAIL
(Published for The City of Rochester Society). A useful guide for the visitor to most places of interest in Rochester. 95p (£1.15 post free).

OLD MAIDSTONE by Kay Baldock and Irene Hales
Over 100 old postcards from the early years of this century. 52 large format pages. £1.95 (£2.25 post free).

WATERMILLS & WINDMILLS OF KENT by William Coles Finch.
The classic book on all Kent mills reprinted at £10.00, now available at £4.95 (£5.95 post free).

JUST OFF THE SWALE by Don Sattin.
The story of the barge building village of Conyer. £3.95 (£4.35 post free).

STROOD A PICTORIAL HISTORY by Avril Bloomfield
Over 100 fascinating old photographs. £2.95 (£3.35 post free).

PUBLISHED BY NORTH KENT BOOKS

A BRIEF HISTORY OF ROCHESTER AIRPORT by Medway Branch of the Royal Aeronautical Society £1.50 (£1.70 post free)

A SHORT HISTORY by J.M. Preston
Short Brothers aviation activities in Kent, 1908-1964. £1.20 (£1.40 post free)

INDUSTRIAL MEDWAY by J.M. Preston
An historical survey of the numerous industries based on the Medway Estuary. Was £4.95 Now £3.75 (£4.35 post free)

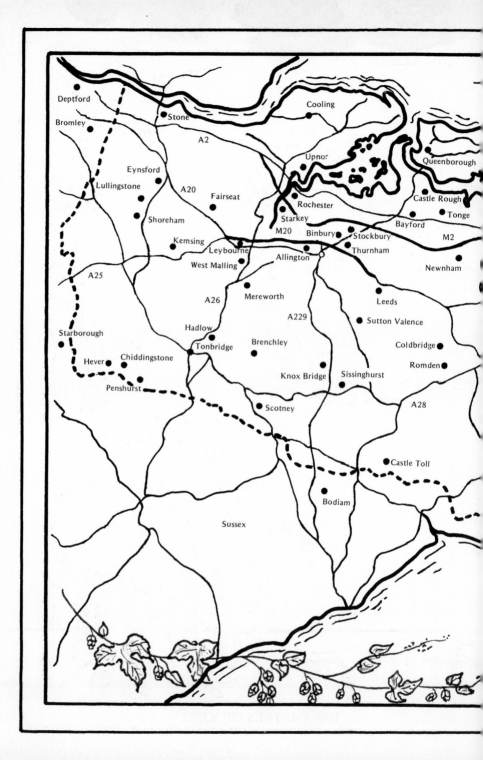